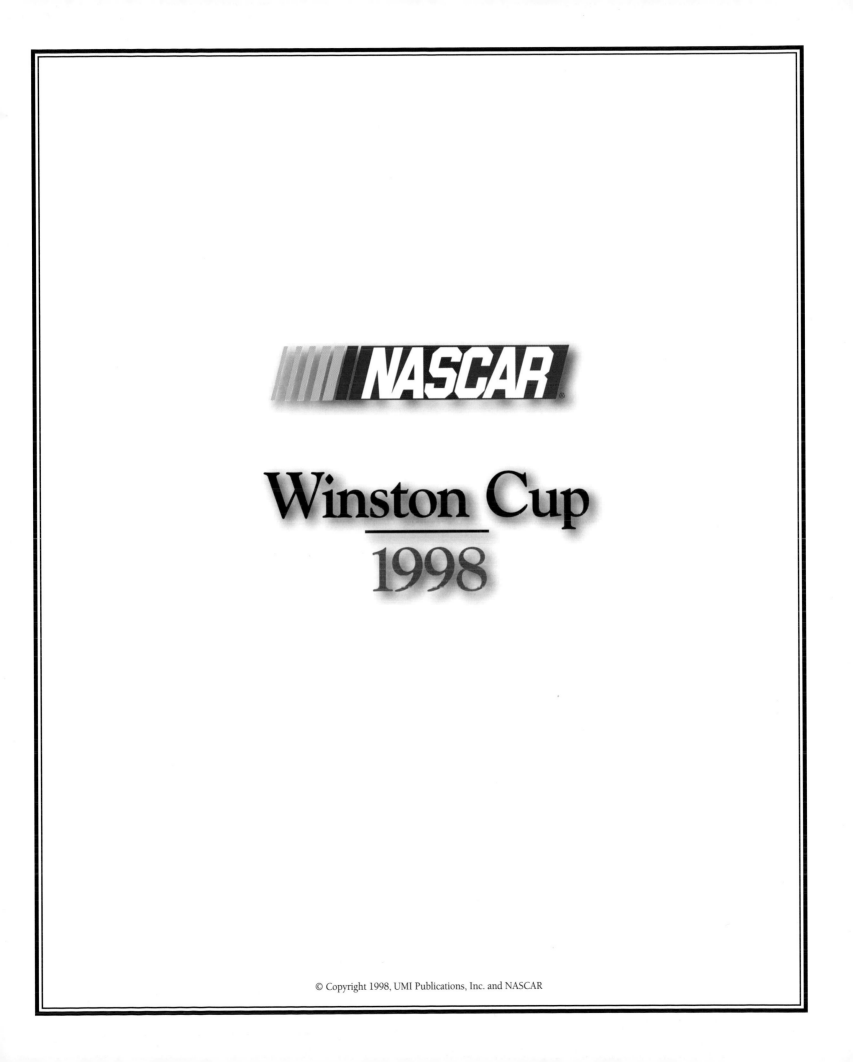

In Memory Of...

T. Wayne Robertson

To most fans, T. Wayne Robertson was the person who appeared on the stage at the Waldorf-Astoria Hotel each December to present the NASCAR Winston Cup point fund bonus checks to the top 10 drivers. To competitors, track owners, NASCAR officials and media members, and to thousands who met him at one time or another during his career at Winston, Wayne was counselor, advisor, decision maker, listener and, most of all, friend.

"T. Wayne" continued Winston's legacy begun by friend and predecessor Ralph Seagraves, but forged his own identity as one of the most influential men in the sports world. That he did it behind the scenes, for the most part, was his choice, but few decisions were made without consulting him.

His intention was for the sport to grow and prosper, and for Winston to receive its due as part of that growth. He was instrumental in creating The Winston, promoting growth of the point fund, creating the Winston Million and the Winston No Bull 5 bonus programs, and in starting the NASCAR Winston Cup Preview held in Winston-Salem each January. Most of all, he helped company after company become involved in NASCAR racing, always delighted to talk with corporate executives and encourage them to participate in the sport.

His death, one month before the start of the season, saddened everyone involved with the sport. T. Wayne Robertson was a friend to all — from corporate executives to volunteer crew members. His passing created a huge void in our sport, and he will be deeply missed.

Ralph Seagraves

NASCAR Winston Cup racing lost one of its pioneers when Ralph Seagraves died in 1998. Many of the new generations of fans didn't know Ralph or his contributions to the sport because he retired as the head of R.J. Reynolds' Special Events Operations in 1985. But during the 13 years he was at the helm after Winston became involved in NASCAR Winston Cup racing, Ralph was one of the leaders in helping the sport grow.

Under his direction Winston spent millions in newspaper advertising to help track owners sell tickets, and other millions were spent building and painting various structures at tracks, including scoring stands, press boxes and infield media centers. He also helped Winston move into a sponsorship relationship with the National Hot Rod Association, and throughout his reign as the head of RJR's sports involvement, he worked to help other companies become involved with NASCAR and NHRA racing.

His wide smile and back-patting informality were the perfect ingredients at a time when the sport needed someone to welcome other companies with open arms. Ralph was a friend to all, and his contributions to the sport were recognized when he was elected to the National Motorsports Press Association's Hall of Fame in 1992 and to the International Drag Racing Hall of Fame in 1993.

Acknowledgments

It is with great pleasure that UMI Publications, Inc. presents NASCAR Winston Cup 1998, a chronicle of NASCAR's 50th anniversary season. And what a season it was. It seems fitting that in NASCAR's 50th year, so many milestones were accomplished, and so many records broken.

The year began in grand style with seven-time NASCAR Winston Cup Champion Dale Earnhardt winning the Daytona 500 in his 20th try, laying claim to one of the very few trophies he had yet to add to his astounding collection. Perennial contender Mark Martin and his Valvoline team put together a career year, taking seven trips to the winner's circle plus a win in the sport's all-star event, The Winston. Jeremy Mayfield had a break-out season, leading the points in the first half of the year, scoring his first career win at Pocono in June and finishing with the right to walk on stage at the Waldorf-Astoria as a top-10 finisher in the point standings. And rising star Kenny Irwin put a lock on the Raybestos Rookie of the Year title by winning his first career pole in the season finale at Atlanta.

But the year belonged to Jeff Gordon. The 27-year-old champion had an incredible season, tying Richard Petty's modern-era record of 13 wins in a single season to capture his third NASCAR Winston Cup championship in the last four years. His accomplishments during the season are far too many to list here, but each is recorded on the pages that follow for you to recall each time you read this book.

In all, the 1998 season certainly will be remembered as one of the most significant in the history of the sport, and it's all here for you to relive again and again.

We would like to express our special thanks and appreciation to our friends at NASCAR, without whom this book would not be possible. Mr. Bill France, Mr. Jim France, Mr. Brian France, Mr. Paul Brooks, Mr. George Pyne, Mr. John Griffin, Ms. Kelly Crouch and Mr. Paul Schaefer are all deserving of our thanks for their help and guidance.

Special thanks also to the members of the NASCAR Winston Cup team at the R.J. Reynolds Tobacco Company for their assistance and support. Mr. Cliff Pennell, Mr. Greg Littell, Mr. John Powell, Mr. Nat Walker, Mr. Larry Prillaman, Mr. Curtis Gray, Mr. Steve Tucker, Mr. Chris Powell, Mr. Dennis Dawson, Mr. Mitch Cox, Ms. Mary Casey, Mr. Mark Rutledge and Mr. Chad Willis are all deserving of our deep appreciation.

Once again, Mr. Bob Kelly applied his wisdom and expertise to mold the events of the 1998 season into an informative and entertaining story for us to enjoy for years to come. We owe our gratitude to Mr. Kelly for his fine efforts throughout the year. Of course, our story would not be complete without a fine collection of images captured during the season-long campaign both on and off the track. Special thanks go to Mr. David Chobat, Mr. Don Grassman and Mr. Ernest Masche, who followed the grueling 10-month tour to bring us some of the best photography available anywhere in the sport.

Most of all, we thank you, the fans of NASCAR Winston Cup racing. It is you who make the sport possible, and who are responsible for its continued growth and success. This book is for you, with our appreciation.

Please enjoy.

Publisher
Ivan Mothershead

Associate Publisher
Charlie Keiger

Vice President
Rick Peters

Controller
Lewis Patton

National Advertising Manager
Mark Cantey

National Advertising Sales
Paul Kaperonis

Managing Editor
Ward Woodbury

Art Director
Brett Shippy

Senior Designers
Michael McBride
Paul Bond

Manager of Information Systems
Chris Devera

Administrative Staff
Mary Flowe
Dorothy Gates
Carla Greene
Heather Guy
Jim Peterson
Joanie Tarbert
Linda Yagos

Foreword by Bill France

Thank you for being an important part of NASCAR's 50th Anniversary.

Our year-long celebration was all-inclusive. The NASCAR stars of the past, present and future stepped into our huge anniversary spotlight. We celebrated our heritage, our work, our fans, and built for the future.

The NASCAR family — everyone from our enthusiastic fans to the teams at every level of NASCAR racing — experienced our story. From our humble beginning and our colorful pioneers, NASCAR has become America's premier form of motorsports.

Today, many young people go to sleep at night and dream of having a career in NASCAR. I know, because I get some pretty neat letters from young NASCAR fans, just as many of our drivers do.

When I was a kid, I didn't have much time to dream about the future. I was too busy worrying about our next race. My dad and mom were the dreamers. They had a vision of NASCAR that would benefit our drivers, teams, tracks, and, of course, our fans. I'm sure they would be pleased with what we have continued to build, based on their unique ability to see the benefits of hard work.

We haven't always had a smooth road during our first 50 years, but together, we've used those opportunities to build character. We've never stopped moving ahead.

Perseverance is a key trait of any NASCAR race team member. Our participants bring a lot of strength to the table. In what other league could a man keep coming back to the same premier event for 20 years before achieving an ultimate goal? Ask 1998 Daytona 500 winner Dale Earnhardt. Where else can an entire league of athletes be offered million-dollar bonuses in five events over a single season, and cash in three times? Ask two-time Winston No Bull 5 winner Jeff Gordon, or his million-dollar "No Bull" peer, Dale Jarrett. Thanks to series sponsor, Winston, and our entire family of sponsors, the brightest stars in American motorsports also achieve the greatest rewards.

Our stars were many throughout our 50th Anniversary season. Jeff Gordon and Mark Martin provided a classic duel for the 1998 NASCAR Winston Cup Series championship for much of the season. These two individuals achieved career high seasons through their single-minded focus on winning.

Other established stars had bright seasons as well. Both Rusty Wallace and Ricky Rudd extended seasonal race win streaks. Bright young stars also showed their future potential as Jeremy Mayfield, Bobby Labonte and Jeff Burton made it to victory lane.

Our track operators who host our competitors and fans are also the best in motorsports. They continually expand their facilities and services for both competitors and fans. No other group of privately held professional sports stadium operators provide their league with so many amenities for participants and fans alike.

I journeyed into a part of history myself during the summer of 1998. Betty Jane and I went "home" to Bowman Gray Stadium in Winston-Salem, N.C. It's a quarter-mile track that my Dad and Alvin Hawkins started promoting in 1948, NASCAR's founding year. It's also where Betty Jane and I met for the first time. The NASCAR Winston Cup Series raced at Bowman Gray 29 times between 1958 and 1971. I remember Richard Petty scoring his 100th career win there in 1969. As I recall it, he was driving a Ford that day. Our Bowman Gray visit this summer was a pleasant way to personally pay tribute to NASCAR's early years. Today there's still nothing like seeing NASCAR Modifieds on a Saturday night at the Stadium, just like there's nothing like seeing a NASCAR Winston Cup race anyplace in the country on Sunday.

Our 50th Anniversary celebration is history, and it enriched us all by telling our story, from the beginning. Our next chapter, the 1999 NASCAR Winston Cup Series season, is upon us. Those exciting new chapters will be written week by week, just as they have for 50 years.

We hope you enjoy this volume of work that captures the color and spirit of the 1998 NASCAR Winston Cup Series campaign. You are part of the excitement and history of NASCAR's 50th Anniversary.

Sincerely,

Bill France
NASCAR

Table of Contents

Preface

If ever there were question marks and topics of discussion around a warm stove during the wintertime, the months between the conclusion of the 1997 season at Atlanta and the opening race of the 1998 season in February at Daytona provided plenty of grist for NASCAR Winston Cup fans.

It seemed in the closing weeks of the 1997 campaign, every day brought headlines that would have great effect on the coming season, and even after the competition on the track was completed and the awards were given out in New York City, the headlines just kept coming.

The 1998 season would mark the 50th anniversary of NASCAR, and the sanctioning body, with the assistance of its marketing partners, put together a plan that would stretch throughout the entire year to share its legacy with the world. Series sponsor Winston and R.J. Reynolds also announced the introduction of the No Bull 5. The program offered drivers finishing in the top five of specific races the opportunity to win a $1-million bonus in the next race included on the Winston No Bull 5 schedule. The top

(Right) *Penske Racing and driver Rusty Wallace did a significant portion of the development work on Ford's new Taurus during 1997. Despite extensive off-season testing, Ford teams would start the 1998 season only with clues about how the new car would actually perform in NASCAR Winston Cup competition.*

(Below) *The Rookie Class of 1998 poses for a class picture as they prepare for a much-anticipated battle for freshman honors. Jerry Nadeau (left) would take the wheel for a new team fielded by Bill Elliott and Dan Marino. Kenny Irwin (center) dons the vaunted Texaco colors for the powerful Robert Yates team. And Steve Park (right) prepares to take the wheel for Dale and Teresa Earnhardt in that team's first full season on the tour.*

five finishers in that race would then be eligible for another $1-million bonus if one of them were to win the next race in the program.

The program began with the top five finishers of the 1997 DieHard 500 at Talladega being offered the chance to win $1 million if any of them could win the Daytona 500. The other events in the program for 1998 were the Coca-Cola 600 at Charlotte, the Brickyard 400 at Indianapolis, the Pepsi Southern 500 at Darlington and the Winston 500 at Talladega, which would switch dates with the DieHard race in 1998 at the mammoth superspeedway.

With as much as $5 million available in bonus money in those five races, there were even more reasons to prepare for the season-opener at Daytona.

There was little doubt who would enter the 1998 season as the favorite to win the NASCAR Winston Cup title. Jeff Gordon had run the table in 1997, opening the year with victories in the Busch Clash and then the Daytona 500. He added wins in the Coca-Cola 600 and the Mountain Dew Southern 500 to become only the second driver in history to win the Winston Million, joining the elite club that had previously included only Bill Elliott, who claimed the $1-million prize from Winston in 1985, the first year it was offered.

Gordon went on to score victories in 10 races plus The Winston, the sport's all-star race, and then held on by his fingernails in the final events of the season to claim his second NASCAR Winston Cup championship in the last three years. Jeff's winnings at the end of the season set a new mark in excess of $6 million, and also set some lofty goals for the DuPont team as it took aim at its third title in four years.

One of the reasons Gordon and the Rainbow Warriors ranked so high among those who chose them to repeat as champions was the question mark that hung over all the Ford teams. With Ford ending production of the Thunderbirds, the Blue Oval teams would be fielding an all-new Ford Taurus in competition in 1998, and no one knew what to expect. The final templates for the cars were not approved until January, giving the Ford teams very little time to test the cars in their final configuration. Whether the cars would come off the trailers at Daytona and be competitive, or whether it would take months to work them into manageable challengers, was a huge question facing every Ford team.

Mark Martin had been in the hunt for his first NASCAR Winston Cup title until the closing race of the 1997 season, and some thought Mark would pick up that challenge, Taurus or no Taurus. Martin, however, was working with essentially a new group of people after moving his Valvoline-sponsored team from Jack Roush's Liberty, N.C., enclave to the

(Right) *As the new season begins to unfold, NASCAR Winston Cup Champion Jeff Gordon ponders his quest to defend his title and capture a third championship over four successive seasons.*

Charlotte area during the winter. Following the example of Roush teammate Jeff Burton, whose Exide Ford team had run from the Charlotte area since it was formed, Roush opened his second Charlotte-based shop. The Michigan businessman needed the shop space Martin's team had occupied at Liberty for another effort, anyway. He had put Steve Hmiel in charge of a new effort with Cheerios as the sponsor and Johnny Benson as the driver. With PRIMESTAR now the primary sponsor of Ted Musgrave's Fords, and with Chad Little's John Deere team now under the Roush umbrella, Jack found himself with five NASCAR Winston Cup teams to field for 1998.

Benson's move from Bahari Racing to the Roush stable opened the door for Derrike Cope to join the Bahari effort after the Skittles team decided to cast its lot with Ernie Irvan. Irvan's contract with Robert Yates Racing had not been renewed, and the Californian signed on with the Skittles team, making Cope a free agent.

Taking Irvan's place in the Texaco/Havoline Fords from the Yates shop was Kenny Irwin, who had cut a swath through the NASCAR Craftsman Truck Series in 1997. Irwin would be one of several talented rookies who were expected to battle for the Raybestos Rookie of the Year award in 1998. Others included Steve Park and Jerry Nadeau, and many felt the battle for the rookie title would be one of the finest in years.

Park, who instantly became competitive in the NASCAR Busch Series, would step up to the NASCAR Winston Cup level in Chevrolets fielded by Dale and Teresa Earnhardt. Pennzoil left Bahari to put its yellow paint on the new Earnhardt/Park effort, and Earnhardt worked a deal with Richard Jackson to swap numbers. Park would now drive the No. 1 cars. Nadeau was selected to drive for a new team co-owned by Bill Elliott and Miami Dolphins quarterback Dan Marino, with

During the winter months, Roush Racing moved to the forefront of multi-car teams, assembling an impressive array of talent and sponsorships. In addition to the well-established teams of Jeff Burton and Mark Martin, Ted Musgrave's cars were repainted, with PRIMESTAR stepping up as the primary sponsor on the "16" cars (top). Johnny Benson was teamed with Steve Hmiel and sponsor Cheerios to form the newest Roush team (center). Chad Little (left) moved his John Deere colors from Pontiacs to Fords after coming under the mighty Roush umbrella before the end of the 1997 season.

9

ample backing from FirstPlus Financial. The new team would be No. 13, the same number that Marino made famous on his teal football jerseys.

Enough, you say?

Nope.

Roger Penske bought Carl Haas' share of the Kranefuss-Haas team and paired young Jeremy Mayfield with veteran Rusty Wallace in a team effort, believing that the two teams would help each other become even more competitive. Mobil 1 stepped up as the primary sponsor of Mayfield's car, the number was changed to "12" and the cars were painted in matching colors.

Sterling Marlin made the decision to leave Morgan-McClure where he had found huge success with the Kodak Chevrolets and moved to Felix Sabates' stable to drive the Coors-sponsored Monte Carlos. That left the Kodak car open for Bobby Hamilton, who stepped from Richard Petty's STP Pontiacs, after having been a major part of helping Petty Enterprises return to the front of the field on a race-to-race basis. Petty wasted no time in hiring John Andretti as the shoe for the red-and-blue Pontiacs.

Andretti's departure from Cale Yarborough's team left Cale floundering for a little while. In a matter of days, Cale had lost his driver, his crew chief and his sponsor, but within weeks,

Ernie Irvan surveys the competition, wearing his new colors for the 1998 season. Irvan took the wheel in the Skittles Pontiacs for the MB2 team after '97 driver Derrike Cope moved to Bahari Racing, taking the seat left vacant when Benson took the job with Roush.

As NASCAR's 50th season prepares to get underway, seven-time champion and established driving legend Dale Earnhardt pulls alongside two-time champion and, most assuredly, legend-to-be Jeff Gordon, on Daytona's high banks.

Yarborough rebounded by hiring Andy Hillman as the team's crew chief, Greg Sacks as the driver and then signed Thorn Apple Valley as the team's sponsor for the 1998 season.

There was more.

The Cartoon Network left Diamond Ridge Motorsports and signed on with Harry Melling's team to sponsor Lake Speed. Bill Ingle was named team manager at Stavola Brothers Racing, with the team switching to Chevrolets and a new paint scheme for sponsor Circuit City and driver Hut Stricklin. Todd Bodine became the driver for a new team fielding Pontiacs and carrying Tabasco as the primary sponsor.

Little changed to the two teams many felt would be the most serious challengers to Gordon as he sought to repeat his 1997 NASCAR Winston Cup championship. Dale Jarrett, who fought for the championship until the final race at Atlanta in the fall of 1997, was expected to be one of Gordon's biggest challengers if the Taurus turned out to be a competitive race car.

And then there was the "other" Dale.

Dale Earnhardt had closed the 1997 season with a rush, and Richard Childress' team clearly had returned to the competitive stance that propelled Earnhardt to six of his seven

NASCAR Winston Cup titles. Earnhardt and the team worked incredibly hard throughout 1997 without a victory to show for their efforts. Dale's 15-year string of winning at least one race each season had come to an end, but no one doubted that Earnhardt still had the fire and desire to win, and that the team was on the threshold of returning to the forefront of competition on a weekly basis.

When picking the favorites to win the 1998 championship, Earnhardt may not have been at the top of every ballot, but there was no mistaking the fact that the team was back. Few imagined they would be denied a trip to victory lane for a second straight year.

Bobby Hamilton (left), who moved to the Kodak team from Richard Petty's STP Pontiacs after the 1997 season, consults with his new owner and team manager, Larry McClure (center), and co-owner Ed McClure (right) atop the team's transporter. The team was hoping that Hamilton, a proven winner on the intermediate tracks, could expand on the success they had experienced on superspeedways in the past.

NASCAR Winston Cup Champion
Jeff Gordon

At the end of last season, after we had won the NASCAR Winston Cup championship, all of us at Hendrick Motorsports and the DuPont team knew we would have our work cut out for us if we wanted to go back to New York as the champions in NASCAR's 50th anniversary season.

Obviously, it wasn't going to be an easy task — for several reasons. No driver had been able to successfully defend his championship since Dale Earnhardt did it in 1994. The level of competition within the sport had increased dramatically in the five years since Dale was able to do it, and there was a great unknown out there, too.

Ford was coming with its Taurus, and even though everyone was talking about how it wouldn't turn out to be a good race car, all of us knew better. We knew that one way or another, that thing with the Blue Oval on it would end up being a good race car.

(Right) *Jeff Gordon proclaims he is Champion, three times over. At age 27, Gordon joins a select club with members Petty, Yarborough, Waltrip and Earnhardt, as the only drivers to have captured three championships in their careers.*

(Below) *Gordon crests the hill at Sears Point on the way to his fourth win of the year, taking the victory from the pole, his first at the track closest to his birthplace, nearby Vallejo, California.*

1998 NASCAR Winston Cup Champion

When we started the season at Daytona last February, we knew that we had a good car and our crew was right on the money. We ran at the front of the pack throughout the day until we lost a cylinder late in the race and eventually finished 16th. Well, we thought, we were competitive and what happened couldn't have been avoided.

At Rockingham, we struggled with a chassis that didn't seem to want to handle, and at one point, we were running in 31st. But Ray and the crew kept making changes and adjustments and, at the end, we beat Rusty by over a second and scored our first victory of the season. At Las Vegas, we felt we were in real trouble. Fords took 13 of the first 14 positions, and we were 17th. Neither Ray nor I could figure out how to make our car handle during the weekend out there in Vegas.

At Atlanta, we finished 19th and we were pitiful again. The Fords had quickly become very good on the tracks, and when NASCAR took cars to the wind tunnel after the race, we hoped we would get some kind of rule change or something that would allow us to be more competitive with them.

By the time we got to Darlington, NASCAR had announced a rule change, and although we didn't win at Darlington, I was able to chase down Dale Jarrett at the end of the race and I felt that we were competitive again. At Bristol, we beat Terry and DJ at the end, mostly because of a great pit stop by the Rainbow Warriors that put me in the lead in the late going.

We went to Texas and were involved in a second-lap crash that collected a bunch of cars. It was just one of those things where I didn't qualify very well and then got in the middle of the mess. At Martinsville, Bobby Hamilton laid it on all of us, and we finished eighth, and at Talladega, we finished fifth in the freight-train draft at the finish. We went to California, and I knew that, although we didn't have a great car, we could get a good finish. Mark went on to win that race, and we used a late-race pit stop to climb from ninth to fourth.

The weekends at Charlotte really turned out to be a wake-up call for our team — and for me. We had The Winston almost in our pocket, and then, unbelievably, ran out of fuel on the final lap and Mark went on to win. We won the pole for the Coca-Cola 600, and then I slept through my alarm clock and missed the first practice. I arrived at the track to see Terry Labonte in my car, and my crew looking at me with a "what's going on here" stare. Man, we needed to get things turned

The biggest question we all had was how long it would take for it to become competitive.

The folks at Chevrolet had been developing the Monte Carlo for a long time, and just about every single thing had been tweaked out of that car. We have a new one under development, and it will be coming in 1999, but for 1998, we would have to do battle with the tried and true model. We did have a new engine package, though, with the SB2, and we hoped that what we had would be more than sufficient to counteract whatever the Ford and Pontiac forces would throw at us.

Winning our second championship in three years and the third straight for Hendrick Motorsports, counting Terry Labonte's title in 1996, was a special thrill for us in 1997. We held on and came out of Atlanta as the champions, and we had a great time in New York. We wanted to go back this year the same way. We have been there as the champions, and have been there as the non-champions. Believe me, it's a lot more fun when we have won the title and are sitting at the head table.

around! I can't begin to tell you how embarrassing it is to try to tell your crew chief and your crew members that you overslept.

On the final pit stop at Charlotte, Ray made the call to go for four tires while some of the other cars came back out in front of us after taking just two. Ray's call was the right one, and we were able to use those four tires and post the victory. It put us into the point lead for the first time in the season and sent us to Dover looking for a win for the DuPont folks at their "home" track. In the end at Dover we had to either gamble by staying on the track and try to make it to the finish on fuel, or come in and get a splash and know that we had enough. Ray was thinking of the championship then, and we came in, went back out and finished third, despite dominating the race.

Then came Richmond. Rusty and I were racing for the lead with about 30 laps left in the race, and I ended up in the wall. We lost the race car and the point lead by finishing 37th because of the wreck. But looking back, it might have been the most important race of the season in some ways. There was a new determination and focus within our team following that race.

At Michigan, only a piece of roll-bar padding that brought out the final yellow kept us from winning. We were third, and then we finished second at Pocono when Jeremy Mayfield won his first race. Then we went to the newly configured Sears Point, where I really have wanted to win because it is so close to where I was born. This year we were able to do that. It was very special — and it put us back in the point lead, as well.

Jeff Burton was outstanding at New Hampshire where we finished third before heading back to Pocono. It was a great weekend for us there, leading the most laps and winning, and then we went to The Brickyard. Winning at Indy is extra special, and when we were able to do it, we also won the $1-million bonus from the Winston No Bull 5 program, which made it even sweeter for the team. At The Glen, we won our third straight road-course race, and then went back to Michigan.

A late caution flag and two tires on pit road put us third for the final restart and helped us move to the victory, giving us four straight wins. At Bristol, Mark beat us while we struggled to fifth place, ending that winning streak, but at New

Hampshire, we went back to victory lane with another great two-tire stop late in the race. That was the race that prompted a lot of outcry, and the next thing we knew, our tires were being tested every which way. While all the charges were flying around, we went to Darlington, and although Jeff Burton was really strong, in the end, we had the opportunity to win our fourth straight Pepsi Southern 500, and we accomplished it.

(Above Right) *Constant companion and soul-mate, wife Brooke is an essential part of Jeff's life, on and off the track.*

(Right) *Jeff celebrates win No. 12 — and the championship — with John Hendrick, brother of team owner Rick Hendrick, who stepped in as head of Hendrick Motorsports in 1998 in Rick's absence and led the group to a record-setting season.*

That win gave us our second Winston No Bull 5 million-dollar bonus, but more important to the team and to me was the fact that we had won four straight Pepsi Southern 500s at Darlington — something no one in history had done before. It also was our 10th win of the season, making us the first team to win at least 10 races in three consecutive seasons. Mark blew up that weekend and, although we didn't know it at the time, the Pepsi Southern 500 was one of the biggest turning points of the season. We came out of Darlington with a 199-point lead over Mark.

Jeff Burton and I had a real thriller of a race in the closing laps at Richmond with him winning, and at Dover, Mark dominated the race and beat us. But that second place, and another the following weekend at Martinsville, just kept the pressure on the other teams. Mark won handily at Charlotte and we finished fifth, and we went to Talladega. Mark was in a multi-car accident, and we finished second to Dale Jarrett and, in many ways, Mark was out of the point race.

(Above) *Quiet and pensive in the garage at Rockingham, Gordon contemplates the setup on his Chevrolet, ready to provide his input as the crew prepares for the race.*

(Above Right) *With a win in the Pepsi Southern 500 at Darlington, his 10th win of the year, Jeff won his second $1-million bonus in Winston's No Bull 5 program and, at the same time, became the first driver in history to win the Labor Day classic four consecutive years.*

At Daytona, we ran the Pepsi 400 under the lights for the first time and man, let me tell you, it was special. First of all, I never would have believed that you could light a superspeedway like that and have it be as good as it is. That it was a Pepsi-sponsored race was even better, and the fact that we had

scored our 11th victory of the season was pretty unbelievable. It put us more than 350 points ahead with just three races left on the schedule and really put us in the driver's seat for the championship.

At Phoenix, we struggled and finished seventh, ending a string of 17 consecutive top-five finishes, but we went to Rockingham knowing that we would clinch the title there. We did it early in the race, and at the end, had a chance to fight from behind and take the lead with less than 10 laps left in the race. We had never won a race in October or November, and to clinch the championship and win the race while doing it was a wonderful feeling.

It made going to Atlanta a pleasure, because the championship fight was over and we could go the track and race for fun instead of having the pressure of the point battle on us. That whole day at Atlanta was pretty unbelievable. To go all day waiting for the race to really get going, to have the rain delays, and then to finish the race under the lights was great. But to have the track come to us, and to be able to come from behind after the final pit stop and win our 13th race of the season, then celebrate winning the championship, was simply spectacular. Cinching the Manufacturer's Championship with that victory was icing on the cake for all of us.

Everyone asks how it feels to have won the championship. I can only say that it is an unbelievable feeling. You start at the beginning of the year and you have your ups and downs, just like every other team. But this group of people who are the Rainbow Warriors and the whole Hendrick Motorsports team is simply special. There is more focus, more determination every year. You might think that after you win the championship, things could be on "cruise control" a little bit. But that doesn't happen with this team. There is so much pride, so much determination to continue to prove they are the best, it makes a driver much better. As a driver, you don't want to let all those guys down. They work hard every day — not just the guys who are at the track, working on the cars in the garage area, or those who come on race weekends to work on pit road. It goes all the way back to the research and development guys, to the guys who build the chassis, to the guys who fabricate the bodies on the cars. I mean, you really don't understand the dedication, the craftsmanship, the precision, the focus, until you are in the middle of it the way I have been fortunate enough to be.

It was special to have been part of all the things we accomplished this season. Winning the championship. Winning 13 races to tie Richard Petty's record for victories in a single season. Having 17 straight top-five finishes. Winning two rounds of the Winston No Bull 5 bonus program. Winning at The Brickyard for a second time. Winning a fourth consecutive Pepsi Southern 500. Winning the first race under the lights at Daytona, the Pepsi 400.

All those things were awesome. But the most important thing, and perhaps the most overlooked thing, was the fact that Hendrick Motorsports became the first team to ever win four straight championships. It is a tribute to Rick Hendrick, who was unable to be with us all year, to his brother, John, who stepped in and guided things this season, and to every member of the entire organization. Having a group of people behind you who were able to win four straight championships is something that few drivers ever have in their career.

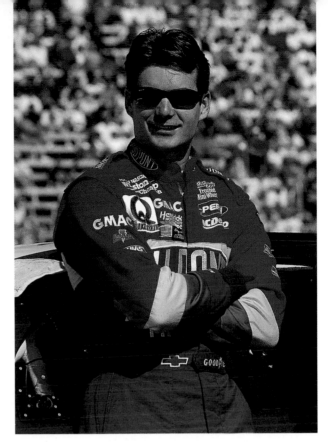

(Above) *Jeff Gordon is relaxed and confident at Rockingham in November, awaiting the start of the ACDelco 400, the penultimate event of the 1998 season. Needing only to claim a 40th-place finish in the race to ice the championship, Jeff knows Cup No. 3 is in the bag.*

(Left) *Awaiting him in victory lane is the ACDelco 400 race-winner's trophy, Jeff's 12th of the season, and the champion's champagne.*

I'd like to say a special thanks to every member of the Rainbow Warriors, and to Ray. Without the hard work and dedication throughout the year, we wouldn't have won the championship. And I would also like to thank my wife, Brooke, who makes every day a special one for me.

It was a wonderful year, and I hope it was also a special one for the fans. NASCAR's 50th anniversary season was a great one, with a lot of opportunities for fans and sponsors to share in the excitement. I know it was a wonderful season for all of us competitors, and I hope that you, the fans, also had a great time.

In closing, I would like to thank all of you for your support of our sport, and for helping it continue to grow. All of the Rainbow Warriors, and myself, thank you for your devotion and for your ongoing support.

I hope to see you at the tracks during the 1999 season.

Jeff Gordon

Jeff Gordon
1998 NASCAR Winston Cup Champion

Daytona 500

The atmosphere of drama, always thick at the season-opener, permeated the air at the 2.5-mile Daytona International Speedway when the teams assembled to contest the first event of the year.

The biggest question mark hanging over the teams was whether the new Ford Taurus would be a good race car from the start of the season. Most believed it would be a great car for the Blue Oval teams on all but the biggest tracks, and the Ford development folks had been willing to give up a little in the four events at Daytona and Talladega in order to keep the car's promise intact for all the other events on the schedule.

There had been plenty of other developments since the last race of 1997 at Atlanta, and many drivers were trying to work their way into a comfortable position with their new teams. The Hendrick Motorsports efforts of defending champion Jeff Gordon, Ricky Craven and Terry Labonte were still missing their car owner, Rick Hendrick, who continued his battle against leukemia. Hendrick had not been to any events in 1997,

(Right) *Hoisting the Daytona 500 winner's trophy in victory lane, Dale Earnhardt was both elated and relieved, having finally reached one of the few milestones that had eluded him throughout his career.*

(Below) *Dale Earnhardt accepts handshakes and congratulations from fans and team members along pit road after posting the Daytona 500 win. His victory, which ended a 59-race winless streak for the seven-time champion, was hugely popular and seemed like a fitting way to kick off NASCAR's 50th Anniversary season.*

Speedweeks at Daytona not only marks the opening of another NASCAR season, it also is a reunion for drivers and their families, team members, industry representatives and, of course, the fans. (Top) Chad Little happily signs a sweatshirt for an enthusiastic admirer. (Above) David Green is all smiles in the Daytona garage, accompaied by his daughter, Kaylie. (Right) Ward Burton gives his son, Jeb, a lift on his way to compete in Bill Davis' Pontiacs for the third full season.

and would remain at home throughout 1998 while fighting the disease.

There had been a myriad of changes in team personnel throughout the winter months, and several of the teams turned up with new crew chiefs, including Darrell Waltrip, who had dismissed Jeff Hammond and named Dave McCarty as the new head wrench for his effort. Lee Leslie was ramrodding Dave Marcis' effort, while Mike Beam had been promoted to Chief Operating Officer of Bill Elliott Racing, replaced by Joe Garone as the crew chief for the McDonald's Ford.

In the Sabco camp, Sterling Marlin found himself working with Buddy Barnes, Gary Grossenbacher was named the crew chief for Wally Dallenbach and Scott Eggleston was the new crew chief for Joe Nemechek.

Waltrip had found a new sponsor, with SpeedBlock and Builder's Square taking up the slack for the departed Western Auto. Brett and Geoff Bodine had also found sponsors for their teams, with Brett painting Paychex on his white Fords, and Geoff unveiling sponsorship from Philips electronics.

One team that had expected to attend was missing from the garage area. Bud Moore, who had planned to run three-time ARCA champion Tim Steele for the entire season, had seen his plans unravel after Daytona testing. Steele, suffering the lingering after-effects of an accident while testing at Atlanta in November, was unable to race, and Moore's team was not at Daytona.

With NASCAR beginning its 50th Anniversary celebration, it was impossible to walk through the garage area and not feel the absence of Winston's T. Wayne Robertson. Wayne had been part of the sport since Winston began its association with NASCAR in 1971, and had become one of the most influential men in racing. To him, everyone was important, whether it was a car owner, corporate executive, floor sweeper, weekend warrior, media member or security guard.

The fact that he was not at Daytona, and would not be again, was not missed by a single person in the garage area. His absence was a difficult way for everyone to begin the season.

(Right) *An obvious absence at Daytona was that of T. Wayne Robertson, one of the most visible, influential and likable personalities in the sport for more than two decades. The message on Jimmy Spencer's car reflects the sentiments of everyone who knew him.*

(Below) *The Gatorade Twin 125s were not without incident as competitors were vying for starting spots in the coveted Daytona 500. Rookie contender Steve Park (1), veteran Darrell Waltrip (17) and newcomer Mark Gibson (59) were among the victims after completing just eight laps of the second qualifying race. Park was able to make it into the field on Sunday based on his qualifying speed and Waltrip took the former champion's provisional. Gibson's attempt to make the big race ended right here.*

With more than $7 million at stake — more than $1 million of which would be pocketed by the winner of the Daytona 500 — and with the Winston No Bull 5 program prepared to pay an additional $1 million bonus if either Terry or Bobby Labonte, Ken Schrader, Ernie Irvan or John Andretti won the race, there was great inspiration for every team to perform well during qualifying. Some 56 teams were vying for the 43 available spots in the field, and qualifying sessions were extremely critical to many. NASCAR had changed the provisional system during the winter, increasing the number of provisionals for every race to seven instead of a maximum of five, and decreasing the number of qualifying positions by two. That made qualifying and the results of the Gatorade Twin 125s even more important, especially to new teams like those of Todd Bodine, Johnny Benson, Jerry Nadeau and Steve Park. None of those drivers had car owner points from 1997 to fall back on, and they would have to qualify for the Daytona 500, or watch from the sidelines when the race took the green flag.

Both Bobby and Terry Labonte stamped themselves as serious contenders for the No Bull 5 bonus from Winston

(Right) *Bobby Hamilton (4) finds himself in the unenviable position of being caught between drafting columns, as Kenny Irwin (28) and Ricky Rudd (10) take the low line, while Mark Martin (6) and John Andretti (43) blow by on the high side.*

(Below) *The Interstate Batteries Pontiac leads the pack through the tri-oval during the early laps of the race. Bobby Labonte started on the pole and led the first 14 circuits before giving way to Sterling Marlin.*

when they locked up the front-row positions during pole qualifying, with Bobby just acing his older brother to claim the Bud pole. Rusty Wallace took his Miller Ford to victory in the Bud Shootout, giving the Taurus a victory in it's initial outing, and Sterling Marlin rocketed to victory in the first Gatorade Twin 125.

Guess who won the other one? To no one's surprise, Dale Earnhardt, for the ninth consecutive year, won his Gatorade Twin, and made his own statement that, yes, this just might be the year when he ended his career-long search for a Daytona 500 victory.

Earnhardt came to Daytona totally focused, and Richard Childress' Goodwrench team had purposefully worked its way through Speedweeks, with driver and crew determined to end the 59-race winless streak they were mired in. Dale's string of 15 consecutive seasons with at least one NASCAR Winston Cup victory had ended in 1997, and some garage observers felt that he no longer had what it took to win on the tour.

When the green flag dropped on the field, Earnhardt wasted no time working his way to the point, and led more than half of the race. With 26 laps remaining in the event, the second caution flag of the afternoon waved and the field headed for pit road for what most expected to be the final time. The determination of driver and crew showed once again, with Earnhardt taking a pair of right-side tires and fuel, and exiting pit road ahead of the field for the final green-flag restart.

Teammate Mike Skinner was behind him for the green, with Jeremy Mayfield, Rusty Wallace and Jeff Gordon lined up behind the Lowe's Chevrolet. On the break, Dale got some help from Skinner as the two Monte Carlos tried to make a run

from the Fords, but new teammates Mayfield, carrying primary sponsorship from Mobil 1, and Wallace were not about to let Earnhardt get away. Gordon was also determined to start his season with a victory, as was Bobby Labonte, who made his moves toward the front.

Earnhardt watched in his mirror as the interlopers attempted to make their runs at him. One by one, they made a mistake here or there — sliding high in one of the turns, being passed in another — and with just three laps left in the race, Gordon lost a cylinder and fell off the pace. Labonte, Wallace and Mayfield gathered it up for one last run at Earnhardt, but on lap 199 with just a single lap left, their efforts came up short. John Andretti, Jimmy Spencer and Lake Speed were involved in a scuffle on the backstretch, bringing the white and yellow flags out at the flagstand to greet the leaders when they flashed to the line. Whoever got to the flags first would win the Daytona 500, and Earnhardt was determined it would be the black Chevrolet.

The seven-time champion used Rick Mast's Ford as a pick,

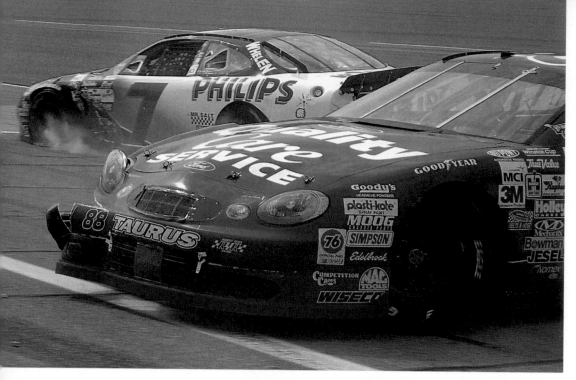

Charlotte would be a great place for him to score that bonus, but in some ways the Daytona victory was much more important to him.

Earnhardt's victory brought closure to his dream of winning the Daytona 500, and the triumph was one that was appreciated throughout the garage area. Crew members from every team in the field lined pit road to salute his victory, and Earnhardt found himself wet-eyed as he headed for victory lane and embraces from wife Teresa, car owner Childress, crew chief Larry McReynolds and the rest of his team members.

Relaxed and joking after the victory, Dale made his first visit to the Houston Lawing Press Box after the event, taking his seat at the front of the assembled media members and cracking the wide grin that had been absent for some time. Referring to the many times he appeared to have had the Daytona 500 won, but then lost in the closing laps due to almost every imaginable thing that could happen to his Chevrolets, he tossed a stuffed monkey across the room at the media members, and cracked, "The monkey is finally off my back."

and watched in the mirror as Labonte and Mayfield failed in their efforts to beat him to the flag. When Earnhardt crossed the line, he had claimed the victory that had eluded him throughout his illustrious career and had snapped the long winless string for both himself and Childress' team.

Ken Schrader, racing with a fractured sternum, was a very gutsy fourth, with Rusty fifth ahead of Irvan and Chad Little, while Skinner finished eighth ahead of Michael Waltrip and Elliott.

Earnhardt's winnings totaled more than $1 million, and with the victory, he became eligible for the next phase of the Winston No Bull 5, to be held at Charlotte in May. Never one to overlook potential bonuses, Dale acknowledged that

Dale Earnhardt gets some help from teammate Mike Skinner (31) on the last restart, helping both of them scoot past the lapped car of Sterling Marlin.

24

With Earnhardt holding a slight lead and within sight of the yellow and white flags, the Goodwrench crew erupts in jubilation knowing that, finally, their driver had kicked the monkey off his back.

Daytona 500

[Race #1 • Daytona International Speedway • February 15, 1998]

Fin. Pos.	Start Pos.	Car #	Driver	Team	Fin. Pos.	Start Pos.	Car #	Driver	Team
1	4	3	Dale Earnhardt	GM Goodwrench Service Plus Chevrolet	23	23	73	Mike Wallace	X-1R Chevrolet
2	1	18	Bobby Labonte	Interstate Batteries Pontiac	24	42	11	Brett Bodine	Paychex Ford
3	13	12	Jeremy Mayfield	Mobil 1 Ford	25	9	22	Ward Burton	MBNA America Pontiac
4	31	33	Ken Schrader	Skoal Bandit Chevrolet	26	28	42	Joe Nemechek	BellSouth Chevrolet
5	12	2	Rusty Wallace	Miller Lite Ford	27	34	90	Dick Trickle	Heilig-Meyers/Simmons Ford
6	10	36	Ernie Irvan	Skittles Pontiac	28	41	41	Steve Grissom	Kodiak Chevrolet
7	21	97	Chad Little	John Deere Ford	29	18	95	Andy Hillenburg	Shoney's Inn Chevrolet
8	8	31	Mike Skinner	Lowe's Chevrolet	30	27	75	Rick Mast	Remington Arms Ford
9	6	21	Michael Waltrip	CITGO Ford	31	25	7	Geoff Bodine	Phillips Consumer Comm. Ford
10	19	94	Bill Elliott	McDonald's Ford	32	30	77	Robert Pressley	Jasper Engines Ford
11	39	44	Kyle Petty	Hot Wheels Pontiac	33	43	17	Darrell Waltrip	Speedblock/Builder's Square Chevrolet
12	22	4	Bobby Hamilton	Kodak MAX Film Chevrolet	34	5	88	Dale Jarrett	Quality Care/Ford Credit Ford
13	2	5	Terry Labonte	Kellogg's Corn Flakes Chevrolet	35	36	47	Billy Standridge	Team Fans Can Race Ford
14	32	50	Ricky Craven	Budweiser Chevrolet	36	35	71	Dave Marcis	Realtree Camouflage Chevrolet
15	29	24	Jeff Gordon	DuPont Refinishes Chevrolet	37	11	30	Derrike Cope	Gumout Pontiac
16	7	23	Jimmy Spencer	Winston/No Bull Ford	38	15	6	Mark Martin	Valvoline Ford
17	16	9	Lake Speed	Cartoon Network Ford	39	24	98	Greg Sacks	Thorn Apple Valley Ford
18	17	43	John Andretti	STP Pontiac	40	14	99	Jeff Burton	Exide Batteries Ford
19	38	28	Kenny Irwin	Texaco Havoline Ford	41	33	1	Steve Park	Pennzoil Chevrolet
20	37	16	Ted Musgrave	PRIMESTAR Ford	42	40	10	Ricky Rudd	Tide Ford
21	26	13	Jerry Nadeau	FirstPlus Financial Ford	43	20	91	Kevin Lepage	Little Joe's Auto Chevrolet
22	3	40	Sterling Marlin	Coors Light Chevrolet					

GM Goodwrench Service Plus 400

In his storied career, media members could count on two fingers the number of times they had seen a crack in Dale Earnhardt's veneer. He has proudly carried the monikers of "One Tough Customer" and "The Intimidator" that have been hung on him in the past, and had backed up those catch-phrases with performances on tracks across the country that had earned some 70 victories and seven NASCAR Winston Cup titles.

He seldom lets the public see the true Earnhardt, but media members remembered an emotional Dale after he won his first NASCAR Winston Cup championship in 1980 at Ontario, Calif. When his dad, the late Ralph Earnhardt, was inducted into the National Motorsports Press Association Hall of Fame in 1989, Dale again let media members see how touched he was with the honor for his father, and his family.

At Daytona, after the Hollywood script was completed and Earnhardt rolled to his first Daytona 500 victory after two decades of trying to win the race, it was a misty-eyed Dale in victory lane, puckering up to give the black Goodwrench Service Plus Monte Carlo a kiss. That the victory came in the kick-off of NASCAR's 50th Anniversary celebration while the sanctioning body was honoring the legends of its history, made the victory even more emotional for Earnhardt.

(Right) *Jeff Gordon (24) is able to hold the outside line in heavy traffic after spending the first half of the event fighting an ill-handling race car. At one point, Gordon fell all the way to 31st place, forcing him to work his way through the field on the way to his initial win of the season.*

(Below) *Rusty Wallace brings his Miller Lite Taurus to a stop on pit road for tires and fuel under green. On the strength of his fifth place at Daytona and a second-place finish here at Rockingham, Rusty jumped to an early-season lead in the point standings.*

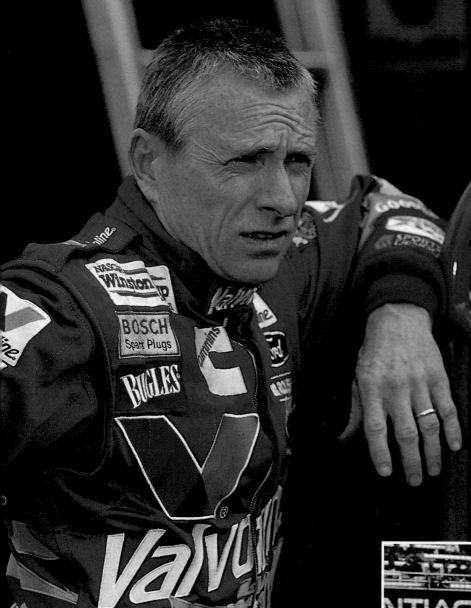

Mark Martin contemplates his challenge at Rockingham, having started his season with a disappointing 38th-place finish in the Daytona 500. Martin rebounded well in the race, leading the most laps and finishing third with his Valvoline Ford.

While Earnhardt had the visitors holding their stomachs with his rendition of the evening, speedway officials were making their announcement that the name of the track had been changed to the North Carolina Speedway, bringing it into line with other tracks in Roger Penske's speedway empire. A new logo was also unveiled for the track, and it was announced that improvements and changes would take place, beginning with grandstands along the backstretch.

The Speedway was not the only thing that had changed since the previous weekend at Daytona. NASCAR mandated that Fords and Chevrolets would see spoiler and nose clearance changes, moving to five-inch-high rear spoilers and five inches of clearance at the front of the cars, putting the "Five and Five" rule into effect at all but the restrictor-plate tracks of Daytona and Talladega. The first race for the "Five and Five" rule would be this weekend in the GM Goodwrench Service Plus 400.

A week later, the teams were assembled at Rockingham and Earnhardt's victory brought visitor after visitor to his team's transporter and garage stall, offering congratulations to the driver who has been the epitome of NASCAR Winston Cup racing for the last two decades. It didn't matter if the visitor was a longtime Earnhardt supporter, or one who had been displeased every time Dale won a race. The Daytona 500 victory transcended all. Everyone had a laugh when Earnhardt talked of his walk-on performance last Monday evening to do the "Top 10 Reasons It Took Me 20 Years to Win the Daytona 500" on the "The David Letterman Show."

Jimmy Spencer waits patiently to climb behind the wheel and begin racing from the 28th starting spot. His look of confidence turned out to be well founded; Spencer climbed through the field and took a fourth-place finish, boosting him to sixth in the points at the end of the day.

An unexpected trio consisting of David Green driving the CAT Chevrolet, Kenny Wallace (81) and pole-winner Rick Mast lead the field into the first turn at the drop of the green flag on the GM Goodwrench Service Plus 400.

Hut Stricklin's failure to qualify the Stavola Brothers' Circuit City Chevrolet for the Daytona 500 sent Bill Ingle packing from the Harrisburg, N.C., shop, and within 24 hours, Ricky Rudd announced that Ingle would return to the Tide Ford team as team manager. Ingle and Rudd had been highly successful before Ingle left at the end of 1994 after the team had won once and finished fifth in the standings in its first season with Rudd as the team's owner and driver.

As with the Circuit City team, failing to make the Daytona 500 had been a burr under the saddle for some teams during the week between races. There was no mistaking the fire in the eyes of several crews as they went about making preparations for Bud Pole qualifying on the 1.017-mile oval. And when the first session was completed, several of the teams felt vindicated with their Rockingham starting positions.

Kenny Wallace was on the outside of the front row, and David Green had his Caterpillar Chevrolet on the inside of the second row. Johnny Benson was eighth fastest, while Stricklin whipped the red-and-white Monte Carlo to the final position in the top 10. Jeff Gordon, who had struggled in the final laps at Daytona, was fourth fastest, and Jeremy Mayfield continued his strong performances with a lap good for the inside of the third row, just a tick faster than Mark Martin and Rusty Wallace. John Andretti had the STP Pontiac cranked, and took the ninth starting spot.

Who was on the Bud Pole? None other than Rick Mast, who had notched just three career NASCAR Winston Cup poles prior to his visit to The Rock. It came with a Remington Taurus that Mast said had seen bodies put on and cut off as many as a half-dozen times before it arrived at the track. It was the first pole for car owner Butch Mock's team since Morgan Shepherd sat on the pole at Watkins Glen in 1989.

With many of the sport's biggest names missing the top 25, Dale Jarrett was the fastest second-round qualifier, and found himself 32nd on the grid for the start of the race. Provisionals went to Earnhardt, Bobby Labonte, Greg Sacks, Ernie Irvan, Lake Speed, Chad Little and Darrell Waltrip, while those who failed to make the field were Todd Bodine, Kevin Lepage, Wally Dallenbach, Shepherd, Dave Marcis and Gary Bradberry.

For the first half of the race, it was a Taurus parade at the front of the field. Mast led for the first 52 laps before Benson, Martin and Elliott took their turns at the point. Jarrett surfaced as a contender at quarter-distance, and then Martin returned to the point before yielding it to Rusty Wallace. Gordon, who many in the

crowd expected to be able to battle on equal terms with the Fords, found his DuPont Monte Carlo drifting backward in the field, handling poorly. At one point, the defending NASCAR Winston Cup champion found himself running an unfamiliar 31st. His crew worked on the Chevrolet during every opportunity and, by the middle of the race, began to turn the handling of the rainbow-hued machine around for its driver.

Jeff began to run in a contending position, but it still appeared that a Taurus would score its first points victory of the season although no one knew which one of several contenders would notch the initial win for the marque. It turned out that none of them would.

Gordon moved back to the point on lap 327, and remained at the front of the lead-lap pack when it lined up for a green-flag restart following the fifth caution of the afternoon. When the green fell on lap 362, Wallace immediately pushed his Miller Ford past the Chevrolet, but Gordon fought his way back to the lead on lap 363. Jeff remained at the point after a seven-car wreck triggered by Steve Park and Ernie Irvan set the stage for a final 21-lap shootout.

Gordon eased away to a one-second lead over Rusty when the green fell on the field for the final time, and there was nothing the Miller driver could do to cut into Jeff's margin. The handling on Rusty's Taurus had gone away, and he was forced to settle for second place.

The victory was the 30th of Gordon's NASCAR Winston Cup career, and he was surprised to have won, having started the race with a car he felt was incapable of running at the front of the pack. His crew had performed well, making change after change on the car until the Chevrolet handled at its peak just when it was needed.

Wallace's second place moved him to the lead in the point standings, while Mark Martin finished third in the race, ahead of Jimmy Spencer. Geoff Bodine had a solid run to fifth in his second race for Philips, and Elliott came home sixth, ahead of Jarrett. Terry Labonte, Bobby Hamilton and Ricky Craven claimed the final positions in the top 10, with 13 cars finishing on the lead lap.

The Kellogg's crew goes to work on pit road to give driver Terry Labonte fresh rubber for his charge through the field. After starting 21st, the two-time champion managed to reach the top 10 and was able to secure an eighth-place finish.

Protecting his late-race lead over Rusty Wallace (2), Jeff Gordon scoots to the inside of Derrike Cope (30), forcing Rusty to set up for Rockingham's fist turn on the outside.

GM Goodwrench Service Plus 400

[RACE #2 • NORTH CAROLINA SPEEDWAY • FEBRUARY 22, 1998]

Fin. Pos.	Start Pos.	Car #	Driver	Team	Fin. Pos.	Start Pos.	Car #	Driver	Team
1	4	24	Jeff Gordon	DuPont Refinishes Chevrolet	23	31	33	Ken Schrader	Skoal Bandit Chevrolet
2	7	2	Rusty Wallace	Miller Lite Ford	24	25	44	Kyle Petty	Hot Wheels Pontiac
3	6	6	Mark Martin	Valvoline/Cummins Ford	25	27	40	Sterling Marlin	Coors Light Chevrolet
4	28	23	Jimmy Spencer	Winston/No Bull Ford	26	29	28	Kenny Irwin	Texaco Havoline Ford
5	20	7	Geoff Bodine	Philips Consumer Comm. Ford	27	41	9	Lake Speed	Cartoon Network Ford
6	16	94	Bill Elliott	McDonald's Ford	28	34	13	Jerry Nadeau	FirstPlus Financial Ford
7	32	88	Dale Jarrett	Quality Care/Ford Credit Ford	29	10	8	Hut Stricklin	Circuit City Chevrolet
8	21	5	Terry Labonte	Kellogg's Corn Flakes Chevrolet	30	8	26	Johnny Benson	Cheerios Ford
9	33	4	Bobby Hamilton	Kodak MAX Film Chevrolet	31	19	1	Steve Park	Pennzoil Chevrolet
10	22	50	Ricky Craven	Budweiser Chevrolet	32	18	31	Mike Skinner	Lowe's Chevrolet
11	14	22	Ward Burton	MBNA America Pontiac	33	38	18	Bobby Labonte	Interstate Batteries Pontiac
12	1	75	Rick Mast	Remington Arms Ford	34	13	21	Michael Waltrip	CITGO Ford
13	9	43	John Andretti	STP Pontiac	35	11	16	Ted Musgrave	PRIMESTAR Ford
14	5	12	Jeremy Mayfield	Mobil 1 Ford	36	39	98	Greg Sacks	Thorn Apple Valley Ford
15	35	30	Derrike Cope	Gumout Pontiac	37	15	90	Dick Trickle	Heilig-Meyers/Simmons Ford
16	24	11	Brett Bodine	Paychex Ford	38	2	81	Kenny Wallace	Square D Ford
17	37	3	Dale Earnhardt	GM Goodwrench Service Plus Chevrolet	39	17	42	Joe Nemechek	BellSouth Chevrolet
18	12	99	Jeff Burton	Exide Batteries Ford	40	26	77	Robert Pressley	Jasper Engines Ford
19	40	36	Ernie Irvan	Skittles Pontiac	41	43	17	Darrell Waltrip	SpeedBlock/Builders Square Chevrolet
20	23	41	Steve Grissom	Kodiak Chevrolet	42	3	96	David Green	Caterpillar Chevrolet
21	42	97	Chad Little	John Deere Ford	43	30	10	Ricky Rudd	Tide Ford
22	36	29	Jeff Green	Team Monte Carlo Chevrolet					

Las Vegas 400

During the first weekend of March last year, teams were in the Capital of the Confederacy, struggling through a rainy Richmond Friday that wiped qualifying from the books and forced the race lineup to be determined by car owner points, postmarks on entry blanks, provisionals and the order in which some teams signed in at the track.

What a difference a year makes!

This year, the third event of the season offered the opportunity for the NASCAR Winston Cup tour to visit famed Las Vegas, Nevada, for the inaugural Cup outing on the 1.5-mile oval carved out of the desert just a few miles from the glittering city.

A look at the top of the NASCAR Winston Cup point standings after the first two races of the year was enough to cause many fans to do a double take. There was no way around it.

On top, with the best start to a season in his career, was none other than Rusty Wallace, who is better known for having to pull himself from the depths of the point standings after disappointing Daytona 500s. This year, however, Rusty had finished fifth at The Beach, and then had threatened to win at Rockingham before being forced to settle for the bridesmaid's position. The combined finishes put him 33 points in front of Daytona 500 winner Dale Earnhardt after the first two races, and it marked the first time Wallace had fronted the standings since May 1993.

(Right) *Definitely one to embrace the "show biz" atmosphere of Las Vegas, Darrell Waltrip dons a very snazzy pair of sunglasses and a wry smile that hints of his wit and humor amidst the cameras and media types present for this highly-visible event.*

(Below) *Safety workers give the traditional Western send-off from pit road as pole-winner Dale Jarrett and outside front-row starter Geoff Bodine prepare the field for the start of the inaugural Las Vegas 400.*

Rusty Wallace's Taurus and driver's suit carry an Elvis theme, complete with piano keys and gold-colored guitars. Although Wallace worked his way to the lead on three occasions during the race, Elvis' magic was no match for the power of Martin's Roush Ford.

Gordon's Rockingham win had vaulted him to third place in points, while Jeremy Mayfield's surprising performances at Daytona and Rockingham had him fourth, just nine points behind Gordon and two ahead of Bill Elliott, who had turned in solid runs in the first two events of the season. Terry Labonte found himself seventh in points ahead of Bobby Hamilton, while Ricky Craven and Ernie Irvan completed the top 10, with Irvan two points ahead of Ken Schrader, still feeling the effects of the fractured sternum he suffered at Daytona.

Many pooh-poohed Richie Clyne's dream of a superspeedway and motorsports complex some 17 miles out in the wasteland when he brought the concept to other investors. But Clyne's dream became a 107,000-seat, 100-corporate-suite reality, and with the outstanding facility came the first visit of the Cuppers in competition. What greeted them was a sold-out crowd, a week of entertainment and civic activities that rivaled few in recent memory, and opportunities for team sponsors to wine, dine, entertain customers and enjoy a weekend that perhaps has been unparalleled in the sport's history. Where else, for example, would you find the likes of Willie Nelson, Chicago, George Carlin and David Cassidy booked into hotels at a race venue, the same weekend as the event?

And where else would you find Elvis on the hood of a race car, or a car's color scheme changed in front of your eyes by an illusionist?

As part of a special promotion, Rusty's Miller Ford wore the likeness of a leather-clad Elvis on the hood, as well as a gold guitar on the flanks, and the response from fans meant an enormous sale of

(Above) *Bobby Labonte (18) and rookie contender Kenny Irwin (28) take advantage of the roomy racing surface on the spectacular 1.5-mile oval to race side by side through the tri-oval. Hounding Labonte from behind is Dick Trickle followed by Bobby's brother, Terry.*

(Left) *Ernie Irvan prepares for his 400-mile run in a freshly-painted Pontiac carrying M&Ms in place of the usual Skittles brand of candy.*

The pole went to Dale Jarrett, who clicked off a late-session run to bump Geoff Bodine from the pole. Still, it was an outstanding lap for Bodine, who had high hopes that the Philips sponsorship would help turn his Mattei Motorsports team around and return him to victory lane.

diecast collectibles donning the special paint scheme. Ernie Irvan's Skittles Pontiac became a yellow M&Ms Grand Prix, and Ernie went for a prone levitation ride during the festivities prior to the race.

Only in Las Vegas!

As teams prepared to qualify for the Bud Pole, Sterling Marlin and Chad Little found themselves working with different crew chiefs. Buddy Barnes had been released from his duties at Sabco as Sterling Marlin's crew chief, and Tony Glover had assumed that role for the Vegas race. At Little's John Deere-sponsored effort, Jeff Hammond was on board after being dismissed by Darrell Waltrip in December. Both drivers made the field in first-day qualifying, with Sterling taking the 21st spot and Little listed in 17th.

Ward Burton and Bill Elliott made up the second row, while Jeff Gordon and Rockingham pole-sitter Rick Mast were fifth and sixth fastest. Mark Martin and Joe Nemechek made up the fourth row ahead of Derrike Cope and Wallace's Elvismobile. Jimmy Spencer was the fastest driver in the second round of qualifying, while Ken Schrader, Kenny Irwin, Ricky Craven, Steve Grissom, Bobby Hamilton, Hut Stricklin and Lake Speed were forced to use provisionals. Those missing the race included Tony Raines, Gary Bradberry, Todd Bodine, Dave Marcis, Larry Gunselman, Butch Gilliland and rookie-of-the-year contenders Jerry Nadeau and Steve Park.

For those who wondered if the Ford dominance at

Crew chief Joe Garone, among the more intense competitors along pit road each week, hustles around the front of the McDonald's Ford on a four-tire stop. Driver Bill Elliott was able to collect a top-10 finish in the race, solidifying his fifth place in the point standings.

Rockingham had been a fluke, the answer came during the inaugural running of the Las Vegas 400. It was a Taurus parade.

The drum major at the front was Martin, who decided to put his Valvoline Ford at the point for his own personal reasons. Early in the race, he felt a vibration in the transmission that he was sure would be terminal. "I decided that if I was going to fall out of the race, then, I would be leading when I did," Mark said after the event. "There were sparks flying and smoke coming out of the gearshift boot after every pit stop, but somehow the thing held together, although I'm sure it wouldn't have if we had been racing 500 miles today instead of 400."

It held together well enough for Martin to lead the most laps in

the race for the second straight event, and when the Las Vegas 400 was over, Martin had beaten Roush Racing teammate Jeff Burton by just over 1.6 seconds. The win was the 23rd of Martin's NASCAR Winston Cup career, and it vindicated his decision to move his team from Jack Roush's flagship headquarters in Liberty, N.C., to the Charlotte area during the winter months. Martin had felt that in some ways, he was stymied with the Liberty operation, and wanted to move the Valvoline effort so he could work more closely with Burton and team manager Buddy Parrott. Roush gave his blessing and Mark headed the project, which included new blood at nearly every position within the team in the new location.

It was a major risk, he knew, and to have victory come to him

and the team in just their third outing together, after leading the most laps at Rockingham, was a tribute to the new crew's dedication and work ethic, he was justly proud to point out after the win.

Wallace fought to third place, while Johnny Benson was fourth in the Cheerios Ford ahead of another solid performance from Mayfield and the Mobil 1 Taurus. Ted Musgrave finished sixth ahead of Jimmy Spencer, who had a great run to victory in Saturday's NASCAR Busch Series race to begin his wonderful weekend. Earnhardt came home eighth, Elliott was ninth and Little finished 10th in his first race with new crew chief Hammond.

The howling began.

Roush's five teams had all finished in the top 10, an outstanding performance by each of the groups, and the Tauruses took the first seven positions and 13 of the first 14 spots in the inaugural running of the race. Worse, from the General Motors' perspective, was the fact that the Fords had led all but 14 of the 267 laps. With the upcoming Atlanta track expected to be another "downforce" race, the GM competitors could be heard from Vegas to Daytona, with little need for telephone wires.

Topping off a day of domination, Mark Martin displays his first trophy of the year accompanied by some not-so-typical victory lane assistants. Only in Las Vegas!

Las Vegas 400

[*RACE #3 • LAS VEGAS MOTOR SPEEDWAY • MARCH 1, 1998]*

Fin. Pos.	Start Pos.	Car #	Driver	Team	Fin. Pos.	Start Pos.	Car #	Driver	Team
1	7	6	Mark Martin	Valvoline/Cummins Ford	23	20	77	Robert Pressley	Jasper Engines Ford
2	15	99	Jeff Burton	Exide Batteries Ford	24	21	40	Sterling Marlin	Coors Light Chevrolet
3	10	2	Rusty Wallace	Miller Lite Ford	25	22	98	Greg Sacks	Thorn Apple Valley Ford
4	16	26	Johnny Benson	Cheerios Ford	26	24	11	Brett Bodine	Paychex Ford
5	32	12	Jeremy Mayfield	Mobil 1 Ford	27	39	50	Ricky Craven	Budweiser Chevrolet
6	23	16	Ted Musgrave	PRIMESTAR Ford	28	35	91	Kevin Lepage	Little Joe's Auto Chevrolet
7	29	23	Jimmy Spencer	Winston/No Bull Ford	29	34	31	Mike Skinner	Lowe's Chevrolet
8	26	3	Dale Earnhardt	GM Goodwrench Service Plus Chevrolet	30	18	36	Ernie Irvan	M&M's Pontiac
9	4	94	Bill Elliott	McDonald's Ford	31	9	30	Derrike Cope	Gumout Pontiac
10	17	97	Chad Little	John Deere Ford	32	43	9	Lake Speed	Cartoon Network Ford
11	6	75	Rick Mast	Remington Arms Ford	33	31	29	Jeff Green	Team Monte Carlo Chevrolet
12	19	10	Ricky Rudd	Tide Ford	34	33	96	David Green	Caterpillar Chevrolet
13	2	7	Geoff Bodine	Philips Consumer Comm. Ford	35	27	17	Darrell Waltrip	SpeedBlock/Builders Square Chevrolet
14	36	21	Michael Waltrip	CITGO Ford	36	38	28	Kenny Irwin	Texaco/Havoline Ford
15	28	5	Terry Labonte	Kellogg's Corn Flakes Chevrolet	37	8	42	Joe Nemechek	BellSouth Chevrolet
16	12	90	Dick Trickle	Heilig-Meyers/Simmons Ford	38	25	46	Wally Dallenbach	First Union Chevrolet
17	5	24	Jeff Gordon	DuPont Refinishes Chevrolet	39	40	41	Steve Grissom	Kodiak Chevrolet
18	3	22	Ward Burton	MBNA America Pontiac	40	1	88	Dale Jarrett	Quality Care/Ford Credit Ford
19	11	18	Bobby Labonte	Interstate Batteries Pontiac	41	30	43	John Andretti	STP Pontiac
20	41	4	Bobby Hamilton	Kodak MAX Film Chevrolet	42	13	81	Kenny Wallace	Square D Ford
21	37	33	Ken Schrader	Skoal Bandit Chevrolet	43	42	8	Hut Stricklin	Circuit City Chevrolet
22	14	44	Kyle Petty	Hot Wheels Pontiac					

PRIMESTAR 500

It took just a single day after the Las Vegas 400 for NASCAR officials to make the decision to take a quarter-inch off the top of the rear spoilers of the Ford Tauruses in an effort to equalize competition on the race track. The move prompted immediate responses from the Ford teams.

The history of the sport has been marked by change after change as NASCAR has tried to make all the marques competitive with each other, providing optimum competition on the track for the fans. And, as in years past, when one side felt it was penalized unduly the fussing began.

It fell on deaf ears.

By the time the teams arrived at Atlanta Motor Speedway, the Fords had their spoilers trimmed to the proper 4 3/4-inch height, and two of the Blue Oval teams found themselves with new crew chiefs. Marc Reno had been released from Robert Yates Racing after the chemistry between himself and driver Kenny Irwin obviously wasn't working to Yates' satisfaction, and Donnie Richeson was gone from Brett Bodine's Paychex team. Brett's decision was an extremely difficult one, because Richeson was not only an employee, but also Brett's brother-in-law and a minority owner in the team. Brett's wife, Diane, and Donnie's wife, Donna, are twin sisters. Reno and Richeson were the fourth and fifth crew chiefs to be changed in the first four races of the season. Obviously, the pressure to perform was at an all-time high on the circuit.

(Right) *After spending the majority of the event making adjustments to the car, the Interstate Batteries crew turned Bobby Labonte's Pontiac into a rocket ship that propelled him into the lead for the first time with 47 laps remaining. No one would catch him from there.*

(Below) *What remains of the Lowe's Chevrolet is towed to the garage area after Mike Skinner nailed the wall shortly following a restart on lap 17, bringing out the second of seven cautions during the race.*

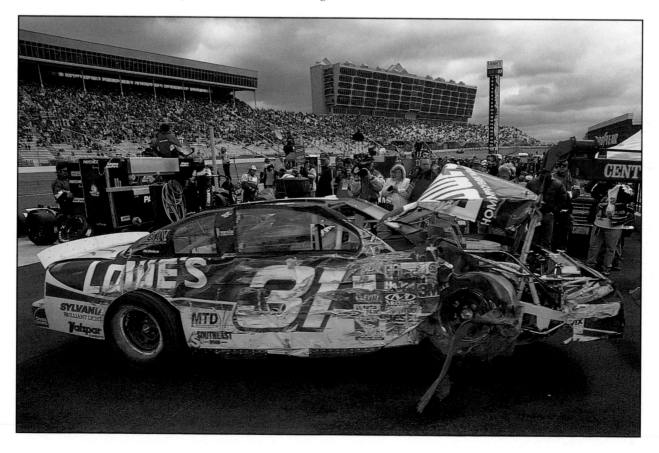

Rusty Wallace's third place at Las Vegas padded his point lead, and the Miller Ford driver found himself 56 points ahead of Dale Earnhardt when the teams unloaded at Ed Clark's immaculate Atlanta Motor Speedway. Jeremy Mayfield was now third in the standings, a mere three points behind Earnhardt as he continued his torrid early-season performances. Jimmy Spencer had moved to fourth place, where he held a two-point advantage over Bill Elliott, and Jeff Gordon found himself in sixth, 15 points behind Elliott and just three markers ahead of Las Vegas winner Mark Martin. Terry Labonte was 15 points behind Martin and 14 points ahead of Chad Little, while Bobby Hamilton held 10th place by 14 points over Geoff Bodine.

Atlanta was the final race in which provisionals from the final 1997 car owner standings would be used, and like every race in the early portion of 1998, qualifying would be of utmost importance, particularly to the new teams in the sport. They would have to make the field on their times, having no 1997 point provisionals to use.

Weather also needed to be factored in, with rain forecast for Saturday. It meant that the single session would probably be the one that determined the majority of the starting grid, and piled even more pressure on the teams to perform well during the Bud Pole qualifying session. And when Steve Park crashed heavily in the fourth turn late in practice, the time needed to extricate him from the car and clean up the track caused the practice session to be cut short.

When first-round qualifying was completed, John Andretti was surprised to find that he had turned the fastest lap and claimed the inside of the front row for the race. He hadn't felt the lap was an outstanding one while circling the track, but his speed of 192.956 mph was good enough to put the STP Pontiac on the pole. There would be no invitation to the Bud Shootout, however, as Petty

(Above) *Richard "Slugger" Labbe served double duty at Atlanta, performing his usual job as tire changer for Dale Jarrett on the "88" team, and assuming the interim crew chief's position on Kenny Irwin's "28" car after the departure of former crew chief Marc Reno.*

Enterprises does not run the Bud Pole decal on the Pontiac. Instead, the invitation went to Todd Bodine's Tabasco Pontiac, which claimed the outside of the front row.

Dick Trickle and Dale Jarrett turned in solid runs to grab the second row, with Irwin and Martin just a tick faster than a surprising Robert Pressley. Terry Labonte was in the fastest Chevrolet, marginally faster than Hendrick teammate Gordon, and Jeff Burton beat Jimmy Spencer for the final position in the top 10. With the second round of qualifying rained out, as predicted, the remainder of the field was filled with first-session times. Ken Schrader, Ted Musgrave, Kyle Petty, Steve Grissom, Bobby Hamilton, Ernie Irvan and Darrell Waltrip were all awarded provisionals.

Sterling Marlin, who had struggled with a malfunctioning steering box during his qualifying run, found himself on the sidelines for the race. Car owner points from 1997 were

(Above) *Kenny Irwin makes a move for the lead on teammate Dale Jarrett, one of several times the two Yates drivers swapped the point during the race. Irwin took the race's lap-leader bonus before finishing fifth, while Jarrett wound up in second place behind Labonte.*

(Below) *Jeff Burton forces the Exide Ford around the track after smacking the wall with just over one lap left in the race. Despite the damage, Burton managed to stay on the lead lap and take home an eighth-place finish.*

not high enough on the list to get his Sabco Coors Light Chevrolet in the field. Also missing the race were Chad Little, Morgan Shepherd (in his own car), Andy Hillenburg, Dave Marcis, Phil Parsons (substituting for Park in the Pennzoil Chevrolet) and Jeff Green.

A torrential downpour that caused flooding of some parking lots meant that Sunday's race was postponed, and teams readied to run the PRIMESTAR 500 on Monday. With just 45 minutes of Friday practice on the track, and none since, drivers were a little apprehensive about what the 500-miler would bring. Mike Skinner and Derrike Cope would each have grinding accidents, but for the most part, common sense prevailed on the track, with competitors taking their time and using their heads early in the race. As the field worked rubber into the track, washed off during the near constant two-days of rain, the race turned into a battle for victory that included Irwin, Jarrett, Martin, Mayfield, Wallace and Dick Trickle.

Many expected Bobby Labonte to be a huge factor in the race, but for the first two-thirds of the event, his was merely another car in the lead pack. Finally, after his team made change after change to his Interstate Batteries Pontiac, the crew got it right during his final pit stop on lap 270 of the 325-lap event. The speedy stop turned him back onto the track in second place, and leader Jarrett spurted to a lead of nearly two seconds over Bobby before the tires came in on the Pontiac.

Within five laps Labonte chopped the margin to a car-length, and on lap 279, Bobby moved to Jarrett's outside and took the lead. With Dale worried about his tire wear and needing a solid finish, Labonte eased away and stretched his margin at the point. Jeff Burton's wall-smacking on the next to last lap meant that the race would finish under caution, but Labonte was well in control of the event at that point. The victory was the third in the last four Atlanta races for the young Texan and was worth more than $106,000 to Joe Gibbs' team.

One week after a flawless performance at Las Vegas, the Valvoline crew had this mishap on pit road when the jackman dropped the car too early and Martin nailed the throttle before the stop was completed. The error cost the team four laps and resulted in a 25th-place finish.

Another trip to Atlanta - another trophy for the mantle. Bobby Labonte picks up his third trophy in his last four visits to AMS, and remains the only driver to win on the track since it was reconfigured midway through the 1997 season.

Jarrett was second ahead of another stout performance from the Penske twins, Mayfield and Wallace. Jeremy finished third and Rusty fourth in their white-and-blue Tauruses. Irwin had a superb race for the Yates team, bringing his Texaco Ford home fifth and leading the most laps in the race, while Trickle finished sixth, despite having the motor go sour in the final five laps. The Heilig-Meyers team was without its owner at the track, with Junie Donlavey home in Richmond, preparing for surgery to replace an aortic valve. Trickle hoped his finish was "good medicine" for Donlavey, one of the most popular owners in the sport.

Kenny Wallace came home seventh ahead of Jeff Burton, who continued around the track and remained on the lead lap, despite bringing out the race-ending yellow. Johnny Benson and Todd Bodine were ninth and 10th, the first drivers a lap behind.

PRIMESTAR 500
[*RACE #4 • ATLANTA MOTOR SPEEDWAY • MARCH 9, 1998*]

Fin. Pos.	Start Pos.	Car #	Driver	Team
1	14	18	Bobby Labonte	Interstate Batteries Pontiac
2	4	88	Dale Jarrett	Quality Care/Ford Credit Ford
3	26	12	Jeremy Mayfield	Mobil 1 Ford
4	22	2	Rusty Wallace	Miller Lite Ford
5	5	28	Kenny Irwin	Texaco Havoline Ford
6	3	90	Dick Trickle	Heilig-Meyers/Simmons Ford
7	24	81	Kenny Wallace	Square D Ford
8	10	99	Jeff Burton	Exide Batteries Ford
9	15	26	Johnny Benson	Cheerios Ford
10	2	35	Todd Bodine	Tabasco Pontiac
11	31	94	Bill Elliott	McDonald's Ford
12	8	5	Terry Labonte	Kellogg's Corn Flakes Chevrolet
13	30	3	Dale Earnhardt	GM Goodwrench Service Plus Chevrolet
14	34	91	Kevin Lepage	First Union Chevrolet
15	42	36	Ernie Irvan	Skittles Pontiac
16	40	41	Steve Grissom	Kodiak Chevrolet
17	37	33	Ken Schrader	Skoal Bandit Chevrolet
18	32	21	Michael Waltrip	CITGO Ford
19	9	24	Jeff Gordon	DuPont Refinishes Chevrolet
20	1	43	John Andretti	STP Pontiac
21	41	4	Bobby Hamilton	Kodak MAX Film Chevrolet
22	18	7	Geoff Bodine	Philips Consumer Comm. Ford
23	23	10	Ricky Rudd	Tide Ford
24	17	22	Ward Burton	MBNA America Pontiac
25	6	6	Mark Martin	Valvoline/Cummins Ford
26	27	11	Brett Bodine	Paychex Ford
27	7	77	Robert Pressley	Jasper Engines Ford
28	13	9	Lake Speed	Cartoon Network Ford
29	38	16	Ted Musgrave	PRIMESTAR Ford
30	33	96	David Green	Caterpillar Chevrolet
31	29	98	Greg Sacks	Thorn Apple Valley Ford
32	35	13	Jerry Nadeau	FirstPlus Financial Ford
33	25	75	Rick Mast	Remington Arms Ford
34	36	50	Ricky Craven	Budweiser Chevrolet
35	21	42	Joe Nemechek	BellSouth Chevrolet
36	39	44	Kyle Petty	Hot Wheels Pontiac
37	28	8	Hut Stricklin	Circuit City Chevrolet
38	19	30	Derrike Cope	Gumout Pontiac
39	12	46	Wally Dallenbach	First Union Chevrolet
40	43	17	Darrell Waltrip	SpeedBlock/Builders Square Chevrolet
41	11	23	Jimmy Spencer	Winston/No Bull Ford
42	16	31	Mike Skinner	Lowe's Chevrolet
43	20	78	Gary Bradberry	Pilot Travel Services Ford

TranSouth Financial 400

At the conclusion of the PRIMESTAR 500 at Atlanta, Dale Jarrett, race-winner Bobby Labonte, Rusty Wallace and Hendrick Motorsports teammates Jeff Gordon and Terry Labonte had all said goodbye to their race mounts. NASCAR officials impounded the five cars and took them to the Lockheed wind tunnel at nearby Marietta in hopes of further equalizing competition between the three makes of cars for the remainder of the season.

Within a matter of days NASCAR officials issued the latest changes, mandating that the Ford Tauruses lose two inches in width from their rear spoilers prior to the TranSouth Financial 400 at Darlington Raceway. It was the third change to the spoilers in the last four races, and hopefully, the sanctioning body noted, it would be the final move that would make all of the cars as equal as possible, enhancing competition on the race tracks.

While NASCAR officials were in the wind tunnel, Steve Park, Derrike Cope and Mike Skinner were beginning the road back from their collisions with the concrete

(Right) *Upon their arrival at Darlington, Ford crews went right to work trimming an inch off both sides of their rear spoilers, the latest change mandated in an effort to even the competition between car makes.*

(Below) *Dale Jarrett and crew chief Todd Parrott celebrate their first win of the season. The victory continued their rise through the standings since their poor finish at Daytona, and put them in the top 10 for the first time this year.*

(Above) *In lieu of an active sponsor, Darrell Waltrip painted his car in tribute to Tim Flock. When he arrived at Darlington, Waltrip's car carried Flock's old number, 300, but it was changed to the familiar "17" before Sunday's race.*

(Below) *Teammates Mark Martin (6) and Jeff Burton (99) share the front row for the start of the race. Despite losing even more rear spoiler, Fords swept the first five qualifying spots at Darlington.*

walls at Atlanta Motor Speedway. Park was in the worst shape of the trio, with a broken right femur and shoulder blade, as well as a broken left collarbone. The injuries would keep him out of a race car for several months, and car owners Dale and Teresa Earnhardt put their NASCAR Craftsman Truck Series driver, Ron Hornaday, in the Pennzoil Chevrolet for the Darlington race. Cope, with cracked ribs, and Skinner, beaten and bruised, would be in their Gumout Pontiac and Lowe's Chevrolet, respectively, at Darlington, with Morgan Shepherd enlisted to help Skinner in a relief-driving role.

In the Budweiser Chevrolet camp, regular driver Ricky Craven had stepped from the seat, suffering from recurring balance problems that his doctors felt went back to his accident at Texas in the spring of last year. NASCAR Busch Series champion Randy LaJoie would substitute for Craven until he was ready to resume his driving duties.

In the days prior to Darlington, Darrell Waltrip had stripped the SpeedBlock and Builder's Square decals from his Chevrolets, saying SpeedBlock had "grossly failed" to fulfill the financial terms of its agreement. He also appeared to have found a buyer for his race team, and his Chevrolet showed up at Darlington painted white and carrying the number 300 in honor of Tim Flock.

Flock, a two-time NASCAR Winston Cup champion, winner of 40 races in his career, one of the sport's pioneer drivers and still one of the most popular faces in the sport, had been at the Georgia Sports Hall of Fame dinner in Atlanta in late January when he felt short of breath. His wife, Frances, took him to the hospital, and subsequent

(Above) *Three wide at Darlington?! Bobby Hamilton (4) and Ted Musgrave get very close together behind Kevin Lepage (91) and Kenny Irwin (28), as Jeff Gordon (24) dares to try to scoot past on the outside, bringing Rusty Wallace (2) along with him. Remarkably, everyone made it through the turn without incident.*

(Right) *With an empty gas can sailing through the air, Dale Jarrett's crew finishes a green-flag pit stop for tires, fuel and a chassis adjustment. Great stops like this one helped Jarrett remain among the leaders while getting his car dialed in for the end of the race.*

tests showed that Tim was suffering from lung and liver cancer. He took a handful of chemotherapy sessions, went to Daytona, and in the few weeks since his return, had seen his health fail. At 73, and without medical insurance, the bills were mounting in the Flock household. Darrell hoped to call attention to Tim's problems with the paint scheme on his Chevrolet at Darlington, prompting donations to the trust and medical funds that had been established for Flock.

With the spoilers now 55 inches wide on the rear of the Tauruses instead of the former 57-inch width, Mark Martin sailed onto the tricky egg-shaped oval during his Bud Pole qualifying run in hopes of merely turning a lap that would give him a spot in the top 28 qualifiers, and keep his Valvoline Ford team in a frontstretch pit area for Sunday's race. What he got, after flat-footing the throttle more than he cared to, was a lap

that was good enough to gain an invitation to next February's Bud Shootout at Daytona.

Martin's white-knuckled ride just nipped the lap previously turned by his stablemate, Jeff Burton, with the two Roush Racing teammates claiming the front row for the 400-mile Sunday challenge. Dale Jarrett and Dick Trickle grabbed the second-row spots, with Kenny Irwin posting the fifth-fastest lap, his second strong showing with Richard Labbe as his new crew chief. Bobby Labonte was sixth fastest in the Interstate Batteries Pontiac, the fastest General Motors lap, while Michael Waltrip qualified seventh with the Wood Brothers' CITGO Ford, and found Sterling Marlin on his right for the start of the race. Ward Burton claimed the inside of the fifth row, while Kevin Lepage surprised many with a solid run to claim the final top-10 position.

With the car finally adjusted to his liking, Dale Jarrett (88) makes his move on race-leader Jeff Burton (99) with 19 laps remaining in the event. Jeff Gordon (24) prepares to follow Jarrett, and the two would fight it out for the win.

Only three front-side pit positions remained after the first round was completed, and 11 drivers ran in the second round, hoping to claim one of the three. Kenny Wallace was the fastest driver, while Dale Earnhardt and Joe Nemechek claimed the final pit stalls along the frontstretch. Those forced to use provisionals for the event were Jeremy Mayfield, Bobby Hamilton, Ernie Irvan, Kyle Petty, Todd Bodine, Jeff Green and Darrell Waltrip, while those who failed to make the race were Wally Dallenbach, Dave Marcis, Hut Stricklin, Gary Bradberry and Morgan Shepherd, trying for the second race to make the field with his own car. Hornaday, who crashed the primary Pennzoil Chevrolet in practice, failed to get the backup Monte Carlo into the race, as well.

Martin led the field under the green, but by the third lap, began drifting backward through the top 10. Although he was competitive throughout the day, Mark could not move his Ford back to a challenging position throughout the remainder of the race. It was not, however, the same way for some of the other Taurus drivers in the field.

Jarrett, Burton, Rusty Wallace and Mayfield all found a way to move to the point, and for the longest time, it looked like Burton would win his first race of the season in the Exide Ford. Jarrett looked strong, but was trapped in traffic, and Mayfield was pitting on the backstretch, hampering his chances for victory.

When the final caution of the race flew on lap 250 after LaJoie spun, Jarrett's Quality Care crew found the right combination for his red-white-and-blue Taurus. He emerged behind Burton and lined up for the restart. Jarrett tried and tried to get past the Exide Ford, and on lap 275, he made the inside move stick in the third and fourth turns and powered past Burton. Jeff's Taurus had chosen the final stages of the race to lose the edge in its handling, and the young Virginian could only watch as he drifted away from the point.

Jarrett was leading — but he had all he could handle in his mirrors. Gordon, always strong at Darlington, finally had the DuPont Chevrolet tuned to his satisfaction and he began to make his run at Jarrett. On the final lap, Jeff made his last-gasp, banzai move, diving to the inside of Jarrett as Dale slid slightly up the track. But Jarrett recovered, maintained the momentum, and whipped to a two car-length victory by the time the two leaders fought to the finish line, scoring the 16th triumph of his NASCAR Winston Cup career.

The Penske twins had another outstanding race, with Wallace finishing third behind Gordon and barely ahead of Mayfield. Jeremy's run through the field had been complimented with some outstanding pit crew work and strategy from crew chief Paul Andrews that allowed him to lead the race at one point, and remain in contention for the victory despite his backstretch pit position.

Jeff Burton was disappointed with his fifth-place finish after his dominant performance in the race, while Terry Labonte came home sixth in his Kellogg's Chevrolet. Martin was seventh, with Johnny Benson and Kenny Wallace the final drivers on the lead lap — both solid performances by the drivers and the teams. Ted Musgrave claimed the final top-10 position, giving the Roush team four drivers in the top 10 at the conclusion of the race.

Reigning two-time NASCAR Busch Series Champion Randy LaJoie, in his first outing as Ricky Craven's substitute, slides the Budweiser Chevrolet to a stop after backing it into the wall. Johnny Benson (26) and Derrike Cope (30) take evasive action on the apron.

(Right) LaJoie's flat-spotted Goodyears clearly illustrate why a spin will generally necessitate pitting for new tires.

TranSouth Financial 400

[RACE #5 • DARLINGTON RACEWAY • MARCH 22, 1998]

Fin. Pos.	Start Pos.	Car #	Driver	Team	Fin. Pos.	Start Pos.	Car #	Driver	Team
1	3	88	Dale Jarrett	Quality Care/Ford Credit Ford	23	6	18	Bobby Labonte	Interstate Batteries Pontiac
2	24	24	Jeff Gordon	DuPont Refinishes Chevrolet	24	4	90	Dick Trickle	Heilig-Meyers Ford
3	14	2	Rusty Wallace	Miller Lite Ford	25	34	9	Lake Speed	Cartoon Network Ford
4	37	12	Jeremy Mayfield	Mobil 1 Ford	26	13	96	David Green	Caterpillar Chevrolet
5	2	99	Jeff Burton	Exide Batteries Ford	27	41	35	Todd Bodine	Tabasco Pontiac
6	33	5	Terry Labonte	Kellogg's Corn Flakes Chevrolet	28	19	31	Mike Skinner	Lowe's Chevrolet
7	1	6	Mark Martin	Valvoline/Cummins Ford	29	40	44	Kyle Petty	Hot Wheels Pontiac
8	21	26	Johnny Benson	Cheerios Ford	30	43	17	Darrelll Waltrip	Tim Flock Special Chevrolet
9	26	81	Kenny Wallace	Square D Ford	31	25	13	Jerry Nadeau	FirstPlus Financial Ford
10	20	16	Ted Musgrave	PRIMESTAR Ford	32	42	29	Jeff Green	Team Monte Carlo Chevrolet
11	9	22	Ward Burton	MBNA America Pontiac	33	18	10	Ricky Rudd	Tide Ford
12	27	3	Dale Earnhardt	GM Goodwrench Service Plus Chevrolet	34	10	91	Kevin Lepage	Little Joe's Auto Chevrolet
13	16	43	John Andretti	STP Pontiac	35	38	4	Bobby Hamilton	Kodak Film MAX Chevrolet
14	8	40	Sterling Marlin	Coors Light Chevrolet	36	39	36	Ernie Irvan	Skittles Pontiac
15	30	94	Bill Elliott	McDonald's Ford	37	28	42	Joe Nemechek	BellSouth Chevrolet
16	7	21	Michael Waltrip	CITGO Ford	38	23	50	Randy LaJoie	Budweiser Chevrolet
17	29	97	Chad Little	John Deere Ford	39	5	28	Kenny Irwin	Texaco Havoline Ford
18	32	33	Ken Schrader	Skoal Bandit Chevrolet	40	31	30	Derrike Cope	Gumout Pontiac
19	36	41	Steve Grissom	Kodiak Chevrolet	41	11	7	Geoff Bodine	Philips Consumer Comm. Ford
20	17	77	Robert Pressley	Jasper Engines Ford	42	12	98	Greg Sacks	Thorn Apple Valley Ford
21	35	23	Jimmy Spencer	Winston/No Bull Ford	43	15	75	Rick Mast	Remington Arms Ford
22	22	11	Brett Bodine	Paychex Ford					

Food City 500

There was electricity in the air when the teams arrived at Bristol Motor Speedway, but it had nothing to do with lightning storms. With Richmond's date moved to later in the spring, the Food City 500 was the initial short-track race of the season, and the first time the cars and drivers had been on a bullring in six months.

There's simply something special about Bristol. And the fact that it now looks more like the football stadium at the University of Michigan, with high grandstands circling the half-mile oval, only adds to the mystique. A field of 43 powerful cars on the high banks, the lore of races past in Thunder Valley, a huge crowd that becomes a sea of faces and colors ... well, let's just use the world "spectacular" to describe a normal weekend at Bristol.

This one held the promise to be even better than usual.

With Rusty Wallace and Jeremy Mayfield at the top of the point table following the Darlington event, it was clear that the two teams' association under the Penske banner was paying huge dividends. In years past, Wallace would still be fighting his way back from a point hole dug at Daytona. Instead, after the first five races of the season, Rusty

(Right) *Dale Earnhardt "leans" on Brett Bodine as they race around the high banks of Bristol - a track that invites contact. Earnhardt came to Thunder Valley in third place in the standings and, based on past success, was looking forward to a strong run.*

(Below) *Jeff Gordon cools off the quick and easy way in victory lane after a grueling afternoon that ended in a record-tying fourth straight spring win at Bristol. The victory moved Gordon to third in the standings, closing the gap considerably on point-leader Rusty Wallace.*

found himself on the top rung, 54 points ahead of Mayfield. Jeremy was in the middle of a solid string of four top-five finishes in the first five races that had surprised many, and he was enjoying the result of his hard work.

Dale Earnhardt was 76 points behind Mayfield and 130 behind Wallace in the early going, but looked forward to Bristol, knowing he had been extremely successful here in the past. Earnhardt may have carried a small smile entering Bristol, but it paled in comparison to the huge grin pasted over Jeff Gordon's face. Gordon had won the last three spring events at Bristol, and was just 17 markers behind Earnhardt in their battle for third, after jumping from seventh to fourth place as a result of his Darlington finish.

Bill Elliott was fifth in the standings, eight points behind Gordon and just four ahead of Terry Labonte, while Mark Martin was seventh, 23 points behind Labonte. Jeff Burton was now eighth, 19 behind Martin, with Bobby Labonte falling from sixth place to ninth after Darlington. He was 15 points behind Burton. Dale Jarrett's hard-fought Darlington victory had moved him from 15th in the standings to 10th, just four

Randy LaJoie rests between practice rounds, preparing to start his second event behind the wheel of the Budweiser Chevrolet. His hard work in practice paid off in the race, when he improved on his 17th-place qualifying effort to finish 10th.

points behind Labonte and 40 ahead of Ken Schrader.

During the days between Darlington and Bristol, Darrell Waltrip had confirmed the sale of his race team to Tim Beverly, a Texas businessman who specializes in the sale of corporate jet aircraft. Beverly would reorganize the team, Darrell said, and he would return as the driver when the team resumed racing. In the meantime, Waltrip had taken Earnhardt's offer to drive the Pennzoil Chevrolet while Steve Park mended from his Atlanta accident. The deal seemed perfect. Darrell would bring a level of experience (and former champion's provisionals) to the fledgling team, while his own ride was being reorganized.

Morgan Shepherd was enlisted as the driver of the First Union Chevrolet while Wally Dallenbach took a break to tend to an aggravated hernia. Randy LaJoie was back for his second race in Ricky Craven's Budweiser Chevrolet, and Gere Kennon had left the shop foreman's job at the Skittles team to join Brett Bodine as the crew chief on the Paychex Ford.

A total of 47 cars were on hand to qualify for the 43 available positions when the first qualifying session began on Friday.

John Andretti (43) and Greg Sacks (98) rub fenders, while Jimmy Spencer (23) and Ted Musgrave (16) close in from behind. Of the four, Musgrave would fare best, taking home his third top-10 finish of the year.

Jerry Nadeau, currently tied with Kevin Lepage in the rookie standings, experiences a slight flame-out entering the turns. Although he continued in the race and was running at the finish, the mechanical problems left him 101 laps off the winning pace.

Fast during the practice sessions, Gordon was comfortable with the setup under his DuPont Chevrolet, but during his first lap around the half-mile oval, he found that the track had changed just slightly. He had to adjust the tiniest bit, and although he turned the fastest lap to that point in the session, he knew the speed was vulnerable. And it was.

Wallace, who knew the time he needed to post after Gordon's run, drove his Miller Lite Ford deep into the first turn and rocketed out of the second, gaining the tenth of a second he needed. When his lap was over, he had won his fourth Bristol pole and the 19th of his career, claiming the Bud Pole Award by just .064 seconds. Gordon was relegated to the outside of the front row, with Terry Labonte and Mike Skinner claiming the second-row positions. Jeff Burton and Dale Jarrett formed a Ford third row, with Bobby Labonte and Johnny Benson in seventh and eighth positions for the start of the race. Mark Martin and Mayfield completed the top 10, barely beating the times turned by Greg Sacks and Shepherd.

Jimmy Spencer led second-round qualifying, and when the remainder of the field was listed, three former NASCAR Winston Cup champions found themselves needing provisionals to make the starting lineup. Earnhardt's qualifying problems continued, while Elliott and Waltrip also were forced to start from the back of the pack. Ward Burton, Bobby Hamilton, Dick Trickle and Steve Grissom were the other provisional starters, while Jeff Green, Joe Nemechek, Gary Bradberry and Dave Marcis all failed to make the grid and were forced to load their cars into the transporters and watch the race on ESPN.

For the longest time, the battle for the Food City 500 victory was between Terry Labonte and Wallace, with the Kellogg's Chevrolet and the Miller Lite Ford trading the point back and forth. But as the event neared the final 100 laps, Wallace began drifting backward after losing the edge in the engine bay of the blue-and-white Taurus. Just 40 laps later, Wallace's hopes for a solid finish ended in crumpled sheetmetal when he ran over some debris on the track, cut the right-front tire and whacked the wall, brining out the 12th caution of the race.

Former champions and fierce competitors Darrell Waltrip and Dale Earnhardt laugh about old times at Bristol. Beginning this week, Waltrip would be driving for Earnhardt with Steve Park on the mend.

53

(Above) *Pole-winner Rusty Wallace (2) jumps to the lead in the opening laps, with Jeff Gordon (24) who qualified second and third-place starter Terry Labonte (5) staying close behind. Wallace and Labonte pulled away and spent much of the race swapping the lead between them.*

(Left) *Wallace sticks his Miller Lite Ford on the yellow line after regaining the lead from Chad Little (97), who drops in behind and goes to school on the six-time Bristol winnner*

On pit road the complexion of the event changed. Labonte had been the leader, with Jarrett second and Gordon third when the yellow flew for the Wallace incident. With his Rainbow Warriors putting together a brilliant stop, Gordon fired off pit road. Behind him, Labonte was watching in his mirror to see if he would beat Jarrett out of the pits, and Terry's momentary hesitation when the jack dropped cost him. Gordon claimed the lead, and Jarrett beat Labonte out of the pits for second place. It took Terry until lap 455 to get past Jarrett and take the position behind Gordon.

Despite two more yellow flags during the final 50 laps, including one caused by Gordon when he clipped slow-running Greg Sacks with just 14 laps left in the race, no one had an an-

swer for the DuPont Chevrolet. Gordon cruised to a record-tying fourth straight spring Bristol victory, writing his name into the record book alongside Waltrip's, who won in 1981-84 while driving for Junior Johnson.

Labonte finished second, while Jarrett remained in third after fighting back from a cut tire early in the race. Jeff Burton finished fourth, and Benson claimed fifth place ahead of Schrader, while Martin fought his way to seventh place, beating Ted Musgrave for the position. Michael Waltrip, driving a backup CITGO Ford after crashing the primary car in Friday's practice, claimed ninth place, the final driver on the lead lap. LaJoie was 10th, just in front of Brett Bodine, with Trickle 13th behind Mayfield, who fell to 12th when he spun while trying to pass Jarrett in the late going.

The victory was the 31st of Gordon's career, and he made it clear that he would not have won the race without the help of his crew. He had a mount that was not quite good enough to win the race by itself, but his crew had turned the stop on pit road when it was needed most, pushing him into the lead at a critical time.

Bett Bodine's crew performs on pit road under the direction of crew chief Gere Kennon, who had just joined the team after leaving the Skittles effort. Their first outing together resulted in a respectable 11th-place finish for Bodine

Food City 500

[RACE #6 • BRISTOL MOTOR SPEEDWAY • MARCH 29, 1998]

Fin. Pos.	Start Pos.	Car #	Driver	Team	Fin. Pos.	Start Pos.	Car #	Driver	Team
1	2	24	Jeff Gordon	DuPont Refinishes Chevrolet	23	43	1	Darrell Waltrip	Pennzoil Chevrolet
2	3	5	Terry Labonte	Kellogg's Corn Flakes Chevrolet	24	12	46	Morgan Shepherd	First Union Chevrolet
3	6	88	Dale Jarrett	Quality Care/Ford Credit Ford	25	19	75	Rick Mast	Remington Arms Ford
4	5	99	Jeff Burton	Exide Batteries Ford	26	15	30	Derrike Cope	Gumout Pontiac
5	8	26	Johnny Benson	Cheerios Ford	27	23	91	Kevin Lepage	Little Joe's Auto Chevrolet
6	14	33	Ken Schrader	Skoal Bandit Chevrolet	28	31	77	Robert Pressley	Jasper Engines Ford
7	9	6	Mark Martin	Valvoline/Cummins Ford	29	16	35	Todd Bodine	Tabasco Pontiac
8	29	16	Ted Musgrave	PRIMESTAR Ford	30	35	10	Ricky Rudd	Tide Ford
9	32	21	Michael Waltrip	CITGO Ford	31	36	9	Lake Speed	Cartoon Network Ford
10	17	50	Randy LaJoie	Budweiser Chevrolet	32	4	31	Mike Skinner	Lowe's Chevrolet
11	20	11	Brett Bodine	Paychex Ford	33	1	2	Rusty Wallace	Miller Lite Ford
12	10	12	Jeremy Mayfield	Mobil 1 Ford	34	7	18	Bobby Labonte	Interstate Batteries Pontiac
13	41	90	Dick Trickle	Heilig-Meyers Ford	35	34	97	Chad Little	John Deere Ford
14	26	23	Jimmy Spencer	Winston/No Bull Ford	36	11	98	Greg Sacks	Thorn Apple Valley Ford
15	38	94	Bill Elliott	McDonald's Ford	37	22	13	Jerry Nadeau	FirstPlus Financial Ford
16	42	41	Steve Grissom	Kodiak Chevrolet	38	33	44	Kyle Petty	Hot Wheels Pontiac
17	39	22	Ward Burton	MBNA America Pontiac	39	18	7	Geoff Bodine	Philips Consumer Comm. Ford
18	40	4	Bobby Hamilton	Kodak MAX Film Chevrolet	40	24	40	Sterling Marlin	Coors Light Chevrolet
19	21	43	John Andretti	STP Pontiac	41	25	8	Hut Stricklin	Circuit City Chevrolet
20	28	36	Ernie Irvan	Skittles Pontiac	42	13	81	Kenny Wallace	Square D Ford
21	30	96	David Green	Caterpillar Chevrolet	43	27	28	Kenny Irwin	Texaco Havoline Ford
22	37	3	Dale Earnhardt	GM Goodwrench Service Plus Chevrolet					

Texas 500

Rusty Wallace and Jeremy Mayfield arrived at Texas Motor Speedway separated by a single point at the top of the NASCAR Winston Cup standings following the Bristol event. Wallace was at the top of the ladder, but for all intents and purposes, the two were in a virtual deadlock for the lead.

Obviously things were working between the two teams, but the problems both had suffered at Bristol – Rusty's engine woes and the late-race spin by Mayfield that cost him a fifth top-five finish in the first six events of the season – had allowed Jeff Gordon to close to within 41 points of Wallace.

The point battle may have claimed the headlines, but many competitors came to Texas with a heavy heart. Nearly all were friends with Tim Flock, one of the sport's most prolific winners and a two-time champion in the early years of NASCAR racing. Flock succumbed to his battle with cancer two days after the Bristol race, and all were pleased that Darrell Waltrip had painted his Chevrolet like Flock's old Chryslers at Darlington, something that Tim had been able to enjoy during his final days.

(Right) *With seven cautions during the Texas 500, there was plenty of action on pit road. After completing their stops, Robert Pressley (77), Rusty Wallace (2) and Joe Nemechek (42) come out three abreast in their fight for track position.*

(Below) *Mark Martin stalks Chad Little, setting up on the inside to make the pass for the lead - and ultimately the win - which he accomplished with 30 laps remaining in the event. Little maintained second place to nail down his best career finish in NASCAR Winston Cup competition.*

NASCAR Vice President for Competition Mike Helton (black jacket), TMS President Eddie Gossage (facing Helton in gray jacket) and NASCAR Winston Cup Director Gary Nelson (kneeling in red shirt) are joined by Mark Martin and other race officials in the area of the first turn where there were recurring water problems.

Behind Rusty, Jeremy and Jeff sat Terry Labonte, whose first top-five finish of the season at Bristol had moved him into fourth, just 17 points behind his Hendrick Motorsports teammate. Bill Elliott remained fifth in the standings, while Dale Earnhardt fell from third to sixth, trailing Elliott by just a single marker. Mark Martin moved to within three points of Earnhardt, with Jeff Burton eighth, five points behind Martin. After a 34th place at Daytona, Dale Jarrett had marched through the point standings to move to ninth, nine points behind Burton, while Ken Schrader, sixth at Bristol, had moved to 10th in the standings. The biggest loser in the Bristol event was Bobby Labonte, who fell from ninth to 14th in the points.

Still, it was early in the season, and many of the contenders felt that the 500-miler at Texas would be the proper place to begin a run toward the top of the standings.

For some it would be. But for others, the second annual event at Texas would become a huge nightmare.

Last year's inaugural event had been beset with problems including a long and steady rainfall that turned parking lots into oozing quagmires, creating traffic jams that were unprecedented in the history of the sport. Everyone hoped that

This bottle, spotted in the garage area, evoked chuckles among the competitors.

this year would be a successful event for the huge number of fans who would attend, but El Niño had something to say about things. The weather had created a high water table at the track that resulted in moisture being trapped beneath the racing surface, some of which began to seep through the asphalt in the first turn. Despite attempts to correct the problem, qualifying day for both the NASCAR Busch Series and NASCAR Winston Cup teams was less than smooth, and qualifying was halted. An inspection showed that moisture had resumed seeping through the asphalt, and qualifying was cancelled for the remainder of the day. Track officials had denied any problem with the track, saying the drivers were simply trying to go too fast, but finally were forced to admit there was a problem. Competitors and media members were in an uproar about the way the situation was handled.

Qualifying was held Saturday morning after crews worked on the track during the night, and Mayfield became the seventh different Bud Pole winner of the season by turning a lap more than a mile per hour faster than Joe Nemechek. It was the second pole of his NASCAR Winston Cup career, and the Mobil 1 corporate executives in attendance couldn't have been more pleased. Ward Burton and Kenny Irwin

shared the second row, with Chad Little and point-leader Wallace in the third row. Martin and Robert Pressley claimed the fourth row, ahead of David Green and Gary Bradberry, while Bobby Labonte and Mike Skinner found themselves just outside the top 10. With just a single session of qualifying, and with the laps of the nine drivers who ran Friday counting, the starting grid held some surprises. Terry Labonte and Bill Elliott needed provisionals, as did Jimmy Spencer, Michael Waltrip, Dick Trickle and Steve Grissom. Lake Speed was the final provisional in the field, leaving Todd Bodine, Jerry Nadeau, Billy Standridge, Andy Hillenburg and Derrike Cope out of the race.

With 11 NASCAR Busch Series cars heavily damaged in accidents during the running of the Coca-Cola 300 — the first NASCAR Busch Series victory for Dale Earnhardt Jr. — no one knew quite what to expect on Sunday. Prior to the start of the Texas 500, 28 drivers had been involved in various incidents.

Last year's inaugural event had been clouded by a first-turn, multi-car accident that took several potential winners from the field before the first lap was finished. This year it took just a little longer.

A lap longer, to be exact.

One of Jeremy Mayfield's crew members stands ready with a huge tape patch after a cut tire damaged the Mobile 1 Taurus. The patch is applied to the right-front fender in an attempt to salvage the car's aerodynamics. Mayfield, who started on the pole and led the most laps in the race, wound up losing three laps and finishing 23rd.

With the field rumbling into the first turn at full gallop to begin the second lap, Bradberry was bumped from behind. He corrected and drove on, but behind him, a chain-reaction accident occurred. When the smoke cleared, Darrell Waltrip, Earnhardt, Gordon, Ernie Irvan, John Andretti, Rick Mast, Hut Stricklin, Kenny Wallace and Ted Musgrave were among the victims.

After a 33-minute red flag to clean up the debris, the race restarted and Mayfield took command, eventually leading more than 100 laps. Jeff Burton, winner of the inaugural event here last year, emerged to challenge, but both drivers would see their luck turn sour. Mayfield cut a tire on lap 177, dropping him off the pace, and Burton cut a tire and hit the fourth-turn wall just nine laps later while leading the race.

Martin, Little and Dale Jarrett took up the battle for victory until Jarrett lost a cylinder and fell away from the fight at the front, leaving Martin and Little, Roush Racing teammates, to contend for the win. The outcome of the event was ultimately determined on pit road, when Little took four tires during the final pit stop, while Martin took just right-sides from his Valvoline crew, putting him back onto the track at the point. He never relinquished it.

(Above) *John Andretti (43), Ernie Irvan (36) and Rick Mast (75) tangle hard against the wall in the first turn, ending their days after completing just one lap of the race. Jeff Gordon (24) was also involved, along with Brett Bodine, Earnhardt, Musgrave, Waltrip, Kenny Wallace and Kevin Lepage, all of whom returned after repairs were made.*

(Below) *Hut Stricklin was also involved in the second-lap incident, seen here consulting with crew chief Jim Long (left). Stricklin returned to the track, but completed just 10 more laps before parking the Circuit City Chevrolet for the rest of the day.*

His margin over Little at the end of the event was a solid half-second, with Chad posting his career-best NASCAR Winston Cup finish. With Johnny Benson coming home fifth behind Robert Pressley and Joe Nemechek, three Roush Fords were in the top five. Terry Labonte was sixth ahead of Jimmy Spencer, with Bobby Labonte and Michael Waltrip eighth and ninth, ahead of Grissom. Jarrett's engine problems dropped him to 11th at the conclusion of the event, just ahead of Rusty Wallace, the final driver to finish on the lead lap.

Mayfield's promising race resulted with a 23rd-place finish, three laps behind as a result of his tire problems.

Texas Motor Speedway officials were told in no uncertain terms by NASCAR to fix the problems at the race track. By Sunday night, the track's owners and management had pledged to make whatever changes were necessary to solve the track's problems before the June NASCAR Craftsman Truck Series event, which went well.

Mark Martin gives a Texas-sized yell after emerging from his car in the winner's circle. Martin notched his second win of the year, and jumped from seventh to fourth in the championship standings

Texas 500

[RACE #7 • TEXAS MOTOR SPEEDWAY • APRIL 5, 1998]

Fin. Pos.	Start Pos.	Car #	Driver	Team	Fin. Pos.	Start Pos.	Car #	Driver	Team
1	7	6	Mark Martin	Valvolino/Cummins Ford	23	1	12	Jeremy Mayfield	Mobil 1 Ford
2	5	97	Chad Little	John Deere Ford	24	10	78	Gary Bradberry	Pilot Travel Centers Ford
3	8	77	Robert Pressley	Jasper Engines Ford	25	24	50	Randy LaJoie	Budweiser Chevrolet
4	2	42	Joe Nemechek	BellSouth Chevrolet	26	25	4	Bobby Hamilton	Kodak MAX Film Chevrolet
5	27	26	Johnny Benson	Cheerios Ford	27	20	10	Ricky Rudd	Tide Ford
6	37	5	Terry Labonte	Kellogg's Corn Flakes Chevrolet	28	36	71	Dave Marcis	Realtree Camouflage Chevrolet
7	39	23	Jimmy Spencer	Winston/No Bull Ford	29	23	99	Jeff Burton	Exide Batteries Ford
8	11	18	Bobby Labonte	Interstate Batteries Pontiac	30	30	16	Ted Musgrave	PRIMESTAR Ford
9	40	21	Michael Waltrip	CITGO Ford	31	17	24	Jeff Gordon	DuPont Automotive Refinishes Chevrolet
10	42	41	Steve Grissom	Kodiak Chevrolet	32	29	7	Geoff Bodine	Philips Consumer Comm. Ford
11	13	88	Dale Jarrett	Quality Care/Ford Credit Ford	33	12	31	Mike Skinner	Lowe's Chevrolet
12	6	2	Rusty Wallace	Miller Lite Ford	34	31	81	Kenny Wallace	Square D Ford
13	38	94	Bill Elliott	McDonald's Ford	35	34	3	Dale Earnhardt	GM Goodwrench Service Plus Chevrolet
14	21	40	Sterling Marlin	Coors Light Chevrolet	36	35	1	Darrell Waltrip	Pennzoil Chevrolet
15	3	22	Ward Burton	MBNA America Pontiac	37	16	91	Kevin Lepage	Little Joe's Auto Chevrolet
16	18	11	Brett Bodine	Paychex Ford	38	28	98	Greg Sacks	Thorn Apple Valley Ford
17	26	44	Kyle Petty	Hot Wheels Pontiac	39	4	28	Kenny Irwin	Texaco Havoline Ford
18	9	96	David Green	Caterpillar Chevrolet	40	33	8	Hut Stricklin	Circuit City Chevrolet
19	22	46	Wally Dallenbach	First Union Chevrolet	41	14	75	Rick Mast	Remington Arms Ford
20	43	9	Lake Speed	Cartoon Network Ford	42	15	43	John Andretti	STP Pontiac
21	32	33	Ken Schrader	Skoal Bandit Chevrolet	43	19	36	Ernie Irvan	Skittles Pontiac
22	41	90	Dick Trickle	Heilig-Meyers Ford					

Goody's Headache Powder 500

While transporters were hauling the remains of 39 damaged or destroyed NASCAR Busch Series and NASCAR Winston Cup cars back to the shops on the East Coast following the events in Texas, Speedway Motorsports Chairman O. Bruton Smith pledged that the appropriate changes would be made to Texas Motor Speedway.

Teams fell to work immediately on the cars that could be repaired, with some of the chassis slated for competition in the upcoming event in California. For the majority of teams, the cars for Martinsville were already sitting in the shop, ready for action at Clay Earles' paper clip-shaped track in Southern Virginia.

For three of the drivers injured at Texas, however, substitutes were sought. By the time the teams assembled at the splendid little bullring next to the famed duck pond, Morgan Shepherd found himself in a Lowe's uniform to fill in for Mike Skinner. Rich Bickle had been hired on an interim basis by Cale Yarborough Motorsports to drive the Thorn Apple Valley Fords while Greg Sacks recovered from his Texas injuries, and Jeff Green was asked to stand by and assist the Gumout team. Derrike Cope doubted

(Right) *Jeff Gordon (24) sticks a fender inside of Rusty Wallace (2), trying to gain the position in the corner. Ted Musgrave (16) and Joe Nemechek (42) look to follow Gordon through, while Ken Schrader (33) drifts out of the groove on the outside.*

(Below) *The huge crowd that turned out at Martinsville on Monday was treated to bright sunshine and an exciting 500 laps of NASCAR Winston Cup short-track competition.*

Pole-winner Bobby Hamilton paces Rusty Wallace and rest of the starting field through the first turn in preparation for the initial green flag. This would be the fifth time in Hamilton's career that he started from the pole.

whether his injured ribs could take the pounding at the stand-on-the-gas, stand-on-the-brakes, 500-lap enduro around the half-mile track.

The three substitute drivers sliding through their car windows weren't the only new faces among some teams. Corrie Stott, son of former ARCA and NASCAR Winston Cup competitor Ramo Stott, had been signed as the new crew chief for Sterling Marlin in the Sabco stable. Jim Long, recently of Ricky Rudd's team, had been named the new crew chief for the struggling Stavola Brothers and their Circuit City Chevrolets.

As teams prepared for first-round qualifying, Rusty Wallace found himself with a 24-point lead over Penske-Kranefuss teammate Jeremy Mayfield, although neither of the Ford drivers had fared well at Texas. Wallace finished 12th, while Jeremy's tire troubles late in the race dropped him to 23rd in the final rundown.

The second-lap, multi-car accident at Texas had cost some of the other challengers, as well. Despite continuing after their crews made repairs, Jeff Gordon finished 31st and fell to fifth in the point standings, 98 markers behind Wallace. Dale Earnhardt struggled to a 35th-place finish and found himself falling from sixth to ninth place in the standings. Terry Labonte was now third, 11 points behind Mayfield and just 35 behind Wallace, while Mark Martin's victory boosted him to fourth place in the points, 41 ahead of Gordon and 22 behind Terry.

Bill Elliott had dropped from fifth to sixth behind Gordon, while Dale Jarrett continued his impressive climb through

With the crowd gone and the sun low in the sky, Martinsville's wall shows evidence of the day's competition. There were 14 cautions during the event, 12 of which were for spins or accidents.

the standings to seventh, seven points behind the McDonald's Ford driver. Jeff Burton, now 45 points behind Jarrett, remained eighth while Johnny Benson moved all the way to 10th place, just 17 points behind Earnhardt. Benson's rise was even more impressive when one considered the fact that he had missed the Daytona 500 and was counting only his finishes in the six races he had run, rather than the seven others could count.

With just 22 pit stalls available on the frontstretch at Martinsville, qualifying took on even more importance than usual. The chances of winning a race from the backstretch are long, and everyone knew they had to make their best efforts during the first qualifying session. With a car his Morgan-McClure team built in three days of intensive work, Bobby Hamilton claimed the first Bud Pole for a Chevrolet this season, needing every bit of speed he could squeeze out of the Kodak Monte Carlo to do it. He clocked a 20.323-second lap to beat Rusty Wallace by .002 seconds, and found himself with his fifth career pole and the first for his team since 1995.

Gordon and Ricky Rudd posted identical laps to share the second row, with Gordon earning the inside because he was higher in the point standings. David Green put the Caterpillar Chevrolet on the inside of the third row, with Ken Schrader on his right, while Elliott and John Andretti made up the fourth row, ahead of Joe Nemechek and Bobby Labonte. Chevrolets claimed three of the first five positions for the start of the race, and when the scoring sheets were handed out at the conclusion of the session, Ernie Irvan found himself with the final spot on the frontstretch pits.

Dale Jarrett and Lake Speed led those pitting on the backstretch, and when a light rain began falling before the second session was scheduled to begin, the hopes of Wally Dallenbach, Dave Marcis and Gary Bradberry all washed down the drains in Martinsville's infield along with the raindrops. First-session times set the remainder of the field, with provisionals going to Benson, Chad Little, Dick Trickle, Geoff Bodine, Jeff Green in the Gumout Pontiac, Jerry Nadeau and Terry Labonte, who used a former champion's provisional to claim the final position on the grid.

The weather front enveloping the middle of the East Coast battered the area with heavy rains and high winds, causing the Goody's 500 to be postponed. On Monday under sunny skies, a huge throng of fans filled the seats to see if Hamilton could make good on the promise his Kodak Chevrolet had shown during qualifying. That he could run Martinsville well was no question. He had finished third or better in the last three events at the track, but the Morgan-McClure team had never claimed a short-track victory.

Sterling Marlin's Coors Chevrolet made hard contact with the No Bull Ford of Jimmy Spencer in an early-race incident that also included Mast, Grissom and Shepherd. Although Marlin took the brunt of the damage, he continued after repairs were made and finished the race in 36th position.

(Left) *By taking four fresh tires at every opportunity, Bobby Hamilton (4) was able to pass when and where he needed to. Here, he uses the outside to take the lead from John Andretti.*

(Below Left) *Although Hamilton ran a clean race, his Kodak Chevrolet still picked up a few doughnuts, an inevitable consequence of 500 laps at Martinsville.*

For the first half of the event, it was a Hamilton runaway. He led all but 29 of the first 250 laps and was clearly the dominant driver in the field. In the second half of the event, he continued to run well, although at times he found himself needing to fight his way back to the front after yellow-flag pit stops. While other teams took two tires to gain track position, Hamilton and his crew took the extra seconds to bolt four new Goodyears on the yellow Monte Carlo, and every time it paid off.

After the 13th caution of the event, Hamilton emerged 10th from pit road and immediately started nosing his way to the front. With just over 75 laps remaining, he passed Jarrett for second place, and then passed John Andretti for the lead with 62 laps left in the race. He had been saving the car, the brakes and the motor throughout the day, and put everything to use during "show time." He pulled away to win by more than six seconds over Ted Musgrave, who brought his PRIMESTAR Ford to its best finish of the young season. The victory made Hamilton the sixth different driver to win a race in the first eight races of the season.

Rusty Wallace gets a little loose coming off the corner, allowing Jeff Gordon (24) to slip to the inside and take the position away. Ted Musgrave (16) avoids the trouble, and would eventually move up to second place, tying his career-best finish for the fourth time.

Andretti, gambling at the end, ran out of fuel with four laps left while he was just over a second behind Hamilton, and saw his sure second place become an 18th-place finish in the final results.

Jarrett came home third, ahead of a rock-solid performance by Earnhardt that brought back memories of Dale's vaunted short-track heroics of the past. Both drivers were pleased with their performances after working from the backstretch pits throughout the race. Randy LaJoie, who also pitted on the back-stretch in the Budweiser Chevrolet, worked his way to a strong fifth-place finish, losing his fourth-place battle to Earnhardt with 11 laps to go. Rusty Wallace was the final driver on the lead lap, taking sixth place in his Miller Lite Ford.

Mayfield was right behind the senior partner of the Penske troops, finishing seventh, while Gordon was eighth and Ernie Irvan grabbed his first top-10 finish of the season with the Skittles Pontiac, taking ninth place. Schrader posted his third top-10 finish of the season with the Skoal Chevrolet, while Morgan Shepherd finished 11th in his stand-in role with the Lowe's Chevrolet.

The Martinsville trophy brings Hamilton's career win total to three, and marks the first victory for the Morgan-McClure team to come on a short track.

Goody's Headache Powder 500

[*RACE #8 • MARTINSVILLE SPEEDWAY • APRIL 20, 1998*]

Fin. Pos.	Start Pos.	Car #	Driver	Team	Fin. Pos.	Start Pos.	Car #	Driver	Team
1	1	4	Bobby Hamilton	Kodak MAX Film Chevrolet	23	29	77	Robert Pressley	Jasper Engines Ford
2	12	16	Ted Musgrave	PRIMESTAR Ford	24	9	42	Joe Nemechek	BellSouth Chevrolet
3	23	88	Dale Jarrett	Quality Care/Ford Credit Ford	25	32	41	Steve Grissom	Kodiak Chevrolet
4	31	3	Dale Earnhardt	GM Goodwrench Service Plus Chevrolet	26	43	5	Terry Labonte	Kellogg's Corn Flakes Chevrolet
5	36	50	Randy LaJoie	Budweiser Chevrolet	27	42	13	Jerry Nadeau	FirstPlus Financial Ford
6	2	2	Rusty Wallace	Miller Lite Ford	28	20	22	Ward Burton	MBNA America Pontiac
7	13	12	Jeremy Mayfield	Mobil 1 Ford	29	18	6	Mark Martin	Valvoline/Cummins Ford
8	3	24	Jeff Gordon	DuPont Automotive Refinishes Chevrolet	30	26	23	Jimmy Spencer	Winston/No Bull Ford
9	22	36	Ernie Irvan	Skittles Pontiac	31	25	8	Hut Stricklin	Circuit City Chevrolet
10	6	33	Ken Schrader	Skoal Bandit Chevrolet	32	15	99	Jeff Burton	Exide Batteries Ford
11	30	31	Morgan Shepherd	Lowe's Chevrolet	33	28	75	Rick Mast	Remington Arms Ford
12	7	94	Bill Elliott	McDonald's Ford	34	16	44	Kyle Petty	Hot Wheels Pontiac
13	19	11	Brett Bodine	Paychex Ford	35	40	7	Geoff Bodine	Philips Consumer Comm. Ford
14	4	10	Ricky Rudd	Tide Ford	36	21	40	Sterling Marlin	Coors Light Chevrolet
15	10	18	Bobby Labonte	Interstate Batteries Pontiac	37	39	90	Dick Trickle	Heilig-Meyers Ford
16	38	97	Chad Little	John Deere Ford	38	37	26	Johnny Benson	Cheerios Ford
17	41	30	Jeff Green	Gumout Pontiac	39	34	35	Todd Bodine	Tabasco Pontiac
18	8	43	John Andretti	STP Pontiac	40	14	1	Darrell Waltrip	Pennzoil Chevrolet
19	35	28	Kenny Irwin	Texaco Havoline Ford	41	11	98	Rich Bickle	Thorn Apple Valley Ford
20	24	9	Lake Speed	Cartoon Network Ford	42	33	91	Kevin Lepage	Little Joe's Auto Chevrolet
21	27	21	Michael Waltrip	CITGO Ford	43	5	96	David Green	Caterpillar Chevrolet
22	17	81	Kenny Wallace	Square D Ford					

DieHard 500

For Bobby Hamilton and his Kodak teammates at Morgan-McClure Racing, it seemed as though they had barely returned to their Abingdon, Va., shop before they were busy loading the superspeedway Monte Carlo for the trek to Alabama, giving them precious little time to savor the rich Martinsville victory.

The win at Martinsville had paid more than $227,000 to Hamilton and his team, bolstered by $106,400 from the 76 Challenge that had rolled and rolled and rolled in increments of $7,600 since last September when Mark Martin won from the pole at Dover. Hamilton, however, had little time to worry about how he would spend his share of the huge payday. Four days after the Martinsville victory that had also provided him with a long-sought grandfather clock, symbolic of victory at the southern Virginia half mile, he was walking through the garage gate at the biggest track on the tour.

R.J. Reynolds, sponsor of the spring Winston 500 since 1971, and Sears' DieHard brand, sponsor of Talladega's fall race since 1988, swapped event names beginning this year. The move put the Winston 500 toward the end of the season, when the final event

(Right) *After finishing third, then second at Talladega last year, Bobby Labonte finally gets to uncork the champagne after winning from the pole in the DieHard 500. With the victory, Labonte joined Jeff Gordon and Mark Martin as two-time winners and became the only driver to notch two poles in the season's first nine races.*

(Below) *Bill Elliott waits for fuel after taking left-side tires on the McDonald's Ford. Under green, pit road is filled with most of the cars from the lead group, as no one wanted to be left alone and out of the lead draft.*

of the No Bull 5 would focus attention on that particular race. It also moved DieHard into network television on CBS, rather than on ESPN, which would continue to telecast the fall event at the mammoth 2.66-mile superspeedway.

The machinations of swapping sponsor names mattered little to competitors as they worked their way through practice toward the first qualifying session. Most important to all of the drivers and crews was a good, solid finish that would move them closer to their goals of being at the top of the point standings when the season ended in November.

Rusty Wallace continued to lead the standings, now enjoying a 33-point margin over stablemate Jeremy Mayfield. Terry Labonte found himself 72 points behind Mayfield and in a virtual tie for third with Hendrick Motorsports teammate Jeff Gordon, who was just a single marker behind the Kellogg's Chevrolet driver. Dale Jarrett's ascent through the point standings continued at Martinsville, and he found himself tied with Gordon for fourth place.

Mark Martin slipped from fourth to sixth place behind the Gordon/Jarrett tie, but he was just 30 points behind the two

(Top) *NASCAR Busch Series regular Dennis Setzer relaxes in the garage with Bill Elliott, who entered a car for Setzer in a special promotion for sponsor McDonald's.*

(Above) *Randy LaJoie, who continued his role as interim driver of the Budweiser Chevrolet, has a serious conversation with veteran Ernie Irvan. LaJoie had a strong run to 10th place in the DieHard 500, and Irvan brought the Skittles Pontiac home in sixth.*

(Right) *Terry Labonte fronts the lead draft consisting of eight cars lined up in single file, hoping to break away from the pack. Labonte led on four different occasions, but was passed by brother Bobby just two laps from the end, a move that dropped Terry to fourth place at the finish.*

(Opposite Page) *Wally Dallenbach (46) eases ahead of Ken Schrader (33) through the tri-oval with the two cars literally inches apart at nearly 200 miles per hour. John Andretti (43) holds his own on the outside, but drifts up a bit to give the two Chevrolets some room to race.*

Ken Schrader moved from 12th to ninth following the Martinsville race, 61 points behind Earnhardt and holding a 22-point bulge over Jeff Burton. Bobby Labonte was a mere two points outside the top 10 as the crews prepared for the freight-train test of Talladega.

With 52 cars on hand and just 36 positions to be earned by speed, the Bud Pole session began with every team in the garage area walking on eggshells. A single mistake by the crew or a single slip on the track by the driver would mean the difference between being in the field for Sunday's race and watching it on television.

For the longest time, it looked like Earnhardt would claim his first pole since 1996 after he posted a lap at 195.194 miles per hour early in the session. But he had been looking at the time sheets from practice, and when media members asked him if his speed would stand up, he shook his head gently. Who, then, he was asked, would beat that speed? "That green-and-black car," he said, meaning the Interstate Batteries Pontiac.

and locked in furious battle with Bill Elliott, just a single point behind the Valvoline Ford driver. Dale Earnhardt's fighting fourth place at Martinsville helped him stop his slide, and he moved from ninth to eighth place in the standings, now 29 points behind Elliott and 166 behind point-leader Wallace.

About two hours later, the seven-time champion's prediction became reality. Bobby Labonte, driving the same Grand Prix he had taken to the pole for the Daytona 500 in February, was just a tick of the watch faster than Earnhardt and the only driver to break the 49-second barrier, and grabbed his second Bud Pole of the season. Still, the outside of the front row was the best qualifying effort for the Goodwrench Chevrolet driver so far this season, improving on his fourth-place Daytona 500 start that had resulted in his first victory in the classic event.

Right behind the Pontiac, older brother Terry Labonte put his Kellogg's Chevrolet on the inside of the second row with Ken Schrader on his right. Morgan Shepherd, still in the Lowe's Chevrolet for Mike Skinner, claimed the inside of the third row, and Gordon turned the sixth-fastest lap of the session. Derrike Cope, back in the Gumout Pontiac, injured ribs and all, was seventh fastest, giving General Motors' products a sweep of the top seven positions on the starting grid. The fastest Ford in qualifying belonged to Lake Speed, while Dale Jarrett and Randy Lajoie, still in the Budweiser Chevrolet, beat Joe Nemechek and Jerry Nadeau for the final positions in the top 10.

Dennis Setzer, driving a Ford Thunderbird with McDonald's McRib sponsorship for the single event, was the fastest second-round qualifier, with Rick Mast grabbing the final position in the field based on speed. Mayfield, Martin, Johnny Benson, Ted Musgrave, Brett Bodine, Steve Grissom and Robert Pressley all made the field by using provisionals, but nine other drivers weren't as lucky. Todd Bodine, Jeff Green, Hut Stricklin, Matt Kenseth, Rich Bickle, Dan Pardus, Gary Bradberry, Geoff Bodine and Bob Strait all were forced to watch their cars being loaded into the transporters at the conclusion of the second qualifying session.

(Above) *The defining moment of the race came on lap 141 when this accident sent Bill Elliott and Dale Earnhardt into the wall on their sides. Kyle Petty (44) also sustained heavy damage in the incident that ultimately involved 20 of the 43 cars in the field.*

(Below) *The wide racing surface gives drivers enough room to form three drafting lines all the way around the track, a feature of Talladega's that adds measurably to the overall excitement at NASCAR's largest superspeedway.*

Most expected Bobby Labonte to be a threat at Talladega, but few expected him to win the DieHard 500. After all, he was in a Pontiac, and the last time a Pontiac had been to victory lane at Talladega was when Richard Petty rolled into the Winston 500 winner's circle in 1983. And, a Pontiac had never won a restrictor-plate race since NASCAR instituted them in 1988.

The first 140 laps of the DieHard 500 were stirring, to say the least. Bobby and Terry had their turns at the point, but they also shared the lead with the likes of Earnhardt, Jarrett, Sterling Marlin, Gordon and Michael Waltrip before the incident that shaped the finish of the race occurred.

On lap 141, the smallest nudge by Ward Burton sent Earnhardt's Chevrolet into Elliott's Taurus, and instantly, the accident was underway. Elliott and Earnhardt slammed into the concrete, the two cars locked together. Both drivers walked away from the accident, and some 20 cars were also involved, including contenders Martin, Shepherd, Schrader, John Andretti, Ricky Rudd, Waltrip, Cope, Hamilton and Kyle Petty.

The accident had happened behind Labonte, and after a 27-minute red flag to clean up the debris, Bobby found himself leading, with Jarrett, Gordon, Kenny Wallace, Jimmy Spencer and brother Terry still in contention for the victory.

As the laps wound down, Gordon and Kenny Wallace fell away from the draft, and it became evident that one of four drivers — Jarrett, Spencer or the Labontes — would win the race. On the penultimate lap, Bobby made his move, driving to the outside of brother Terry in the first and second turns. Spencer and Jarrett went with him, providing the boost he needed to pass the Kellogg's Chevrolet, and from that point on,

Back in the garage, the crew throws a tarp over the battered McDonald's Taurus. Elliott had been leading the race just six laps before the wreck, but left Talladega with a dismal 39th-place finish that cost him dearly in the point standings.

Bobby drove as hard as he could. Spencer tried every way he knew to pass the Pontiac and claim the victory, but came up just a couple of car-lengths short.

Jarrett held on for third place, with Terry taking fourth, while Gordon finished fifth and Ernie Irvan brought the Skittles Pontiac home in sixth place. Kenny Wallace and Ward Burton were seventh and eighth, while Marlin and LaJoie claimed the final top-10 positions, just ahead of Brett Bodine, Rusty Wallace and Jeremy Mayfield.

DieHard 500

[*RACE #9 • TALLADEGA SUPERSPEEDWAY • APRIL 26, 1998*]

Fin. Pos.	Start Pos.	Car #	Driver	Team	Fin. Pos.	Start Pos.	Car #	Driver	Team
1	1	18	Bobby Labonte	Interstate Batteries Pontiac	23	38	6	Mark Martin	Valvoline/Cummins Ford
2	22	23	Jimmy Spencer	Winston/No Bull Ford	24	13	10	Ricky Rudd	Tide Ford
3	9	88	Dale Jarrett	Quality Care/Ford Credit Ford	25	8	9	Lake Speed	Cartoon Network Ford
4	3	5	Terry Labonte	Kellogg's Corn Flakes Chevrolet	26	21	46	Wally Dallenbach	First Union Chevrolet
5	6	24	Jeff Gordon	DuPont Automotive Refinishes Chevrolet	27	28	71	Dave Marcis	Realtree Camouflage Chevrolet
6	19	36	Ernie Irvan	Skittles Pontiac	28	31	47	Billy Standridge	FCR/Philips Consumer Comm. Ford
7	35	81	Kenny Wallace	Square D Ford	29	4	33	Ken Schrader	Skoal Bandit Chevrolet
8	20	22	Ward Burton	MBNA America Pontiac	30	30	4	Bobby Hamilton	Kodak MAX Film Chevrolet
9	14	40	Sterling Marlin	Coors Light Chevrolet	31	43	77	Robert Pressley	Jasper Engines Ford
10	10	50	Randy LaJoie	Budweiser Chevrolet	32	11	42	Joe Nemechek	BellSouth Chevrolet
11	41	11	Brett Bodine	Paychex Ford	33	15	43	John Andretti	STP Pontiac
12	23	2	Rusty Wallace	Miller Lite Ford	34	34	97	Chad Little	John Deere Ford
13	37	12	Jeremy Mayfield	Mobil 1 Ford	35	5	31	Morgan Shepherd	Lowe's Chevrolet
14	29	91	Kevin Lepage	Dare County Tourism Chevrolet	36	2	3	Dale Earnhardt	GM Goodwrench Service Plus Chevrolet
15	24	1	Darrell Waltrip	Pennzoil Chevrolet	37	12	13	Jerry Nadeau	FirstPlus Financial Ford
16	42	41	Steve Grissom	Kodiak Chevrolet	38	32	44	Kyle Petty	Hot Wheels Pontiac
17	27	96	David Green	Caterpillar Chevrolet	39	17	94	Bill Elliott	McDonald's Ford
18	36	75	Rick Mast	Remington Arms Ford	40	25	28	Kenny Irwin	Texaco Havoline Ford
19	26	89	Dennis Setzer	McDonald's McRib Ford	41	39	26	Johnny Benson	Cheerios Ford
20	16	90	Dick Trickle	Heilig-Meyers Ford	42	40	16	Ted Musgrave	PRIMESTAR Ford
21	33	21	Michael Waltrip	CITGO Ford	43	18	99	Jeff Burton	Exide Batteries Ford
22	7	30	Derrike Cope	Gumout Pontiac					

California 500 Presented by NAPA

Within hours after finishing 25th in the DieHard 500 at Talladega Superspeedway, Wally Dallenbach had been given his walking papers by Sabco Racing, and Morgan Shepherd had been nominated to drive the First Union Chevrolet in the second running of the California 500 just five days later.

While Wally scrambled to find a ride for the remainder of the season, Geoff Bodine and the Mattei Motorsports team decided it was time to make a change in the crew chief department. Geoff had failed to qualify for the DieHard 500, and Tim Brewer found himself packing his toolbox Monday following the Talladega race.

Last year when the teams arrived at the emerald oasis in the dusty industrial zone of Fontana, Calif., they were stunned with the sheer beauty and attention to detail that had gone into building the two-mile oval on the site of a former Kaiser steel mill. The memories of the wide roads and sidewalks, the acres of sod and resort-style landscaping had remained with them through the year, and they were delighted to return to Roger Penske's immaculate facility. The track's owners had added 15,777 seats since last year,

(Right) *Waiting for the last drops of fuel to fill the tank, the Rainbow Warriors prepare to send Jeff Gordon back into action on the first pit stop of the day. The defending race champion was running second at the time after leading the first 21 laps from the pole.*

(Below) *Mark Martin takes the checkered flag in a convincing win at California to become the first three-time winner of the 1998 season.*

bringing the total to nearly 86,500, and the sold-out crowd made it obvious that additional seats would be put in place before the third running of the California 500.

With Shepherd behind the wheel of the First Union Chevrolet, and with Mike Skinner still recovering from injuries, Lowe's Chevrolet owner Richard Childress nominated NASCAR Busch Series regular Mike Dillon to drive the blue-and-yellow Monte Carlo at California.

Dale Earnhardt and Bill Elliott, battered and beaten from their Talladega crash, returned to action, with Elliott trying not to take deep breaths to aggravate his bruised sternum. Earnhardt had suffered second-degree burns on his neck and face in the flash fire from Elliott's Ford during that Talladega wreck, and although uncomfortable from the itching and burning, he was determined to start his climb back through the point standings.

Rusty Wallace brought his 36-point lead to California, with Penske stablemate Jeremy Mayfield continuing to surprise many with his second place in the point standings. He was 26 markers ahead of Terry Labonte, while Dale Jarrett had moved to fourth place, just a single point behind Labonte. Jeff Gordon, hoping to duplicate his victory in the inaugural California 500, was fifth in the standings, 10 points behind Jarrett and a solid 96 points ahead of sixth-place Mark Martin.

Bobby Labonte's Talladega victory had moved him from 11th in the standings to seventh, where he trailed Martin by 29 points but held a 15-point bulge over Elliott, now eighth. Earnhardt had fallen to ninth place, 20 points behind Elliott, while Jimmy Spencer had moved from 14th to 10th place following his runner-up finish at Talladega.

Dallenbach, helmet bag in hand, was wandering through the garage area when he heard a screech and a thump that brought a halt to Friday morning's practice session. When the Tabasco Pontiac was towed back to the garage area and driver Todd Bodine was taken to a nearby hospital to be checked out, it became apparent that another driver would be needed for the backup Tabasco Pontiac. Wally was pressed into service, and although Bodine could have competed in the race, he was extremely stiff and sore when he returned to the track after his hospital visit. He was the first to admit that the team's efforts would be in better hands for the rest of the weekend if Wally were the pilot of the car.

With the starting field lined up on the grid, crews stand at attention along pit road for the singing of the National Anthem.

The importance of drawing an early number for the first qualifying session cannot be underscored. The later in the session a driver runs, the higher the temperature is in the Southern California sun. Gordon, who pulled the number four qualifying slot, pasted a 39.610-second "come-and-beat-that" lap on the board early in the session and then sat back to see if anyone could.

The answer was a resounding "no!" and when the time sheets were handed out at he conclusion of the session, Gordon was a full two-tenths of a second ahead of the second-fastest driver, Mayfield, and had claimed his first Bud Pole of the season, the 19th of his career. Mark Martin and Rusty Wallace made up the second row, while Johnny Benson and Joe Nemechek grabbed the third-row spots ahead of Bobby Labonte and Ward Burton. Terry Labonte and Shepherd were ninth and 10th, in front of a solid-running Darrell Waltrip and the stiff and sore Elliott. Dale Jarrett crashed while trying to put together a strong qualifying lap, and Brett Bodine crashed his Paychex Ford in almost the same place as Jarrett's mishap.

Dillon struggled in the first round of qualifying, so Skinner shuffled over to the Lowe's Chevrolet and put it in the field in the 27th starting position during the second round. He then worked on the car's race setup before handing the wheel back to Dillon for the race. Jarrett worked the backup Quality Care Taurus into good enough shape to earn the final position in the field based on speed, while Michael Waltrip, Brett Bodine, Randy LaJoie, Chad Little, Steve Grissom, Dallenbach and Earnhardt were forced to take provisionals to make the grid. Hut Stricklin, Dave Marcis, Rich Bickle and Tony Raines in Kurt Roehrig's Ford, were unable to run fast enough to make the field.

Part of the California experience is, of course, Hollywood, and competitors, media members and a throng of other guests made their way to the Wiltern Theater in Hollywood on Friday evening to be part of a nationally televised celebration of NASCAR's 50th anniversary season. One of the many highlights of the evening was the presentation to Richard Petty of NASCAR's Lifetime Achievement Award, and the selection of five "Driver of the Decade" winners. Herb Thomas, Petty, Cale Yarborough, Darrell Waltrip and Dale Earnhardt were the worthy recipients of those honors.

With choreographed precision, the Budweiser crew provides service for driver Randy LaJoie. Unfortunately, the team would wind up packing early after LaJoie was involved in an accident 40 laps before the finish of the event.

While work crews were still sweeping up the bits of confetti that filled the theater during the finale, drivers walked to their cars and slid through the windows for the start of the second annual California 500. Gordon was the home-state favorite to win his third event of the season. A native Californian, Jeff led the field for the first 21 laps before Mayfield shouldered his way past with his Mobil 1 Taurus. Jeremy was headed for another strong performance, but on lap 35, the future of the race became obvious to the 100,000 fans on hand. Martin, his red-white-and-blue Valvoline Taurus at full song, thundered past Mayfield down the frontstretch, and Mark began to stamp his insignia all over the event.

Last year, he seemed to have the race in hand, but was forced to pit in the wan-

The Labonte brothers, both sporting special paint schemes, started nose to tail with Bobby qualifying seventh and Terry in ninth. Their finishes, on the other hand, were much different: Terry drove the Kellogg's Chevrolet to third place, while Bobby fell to 38th after the engine failed in the Interstate Pontiac.

ing laps for a splash of fuel, handing the victory to Gordon. This time, however, the race didn't come down to fuel mileage, and when it was over, Mark had pounded his way to a 1.2-second victory over Mayfield. He became the first driver to win three events this year, putting the California 500 trophy on the shelf beside those won at Las Vegas and Texas. His win, along with his victory in Saturday's second round of the IROC series, made it a clean sweep in California for the Arkansas native.

Terry Labonte turned in another workmanlike performance behind the wheel of his Kellogg's Chevrolet to claim third place ahead of Gordon, while Darrell Waltrip surprised everyone but himself with a heady run to fifth place in the Pennzoil Pontiac. Chad Little finished sixth ahead of a strong run by Geoff Bodine, while Benson was eighth and Earnhardt ninth. Jeff Burton claimed the final position in the top 10 ahead of Ricky Rudd, who struggled with clutch problems.

For the second straight race, Earnhardt and Elliott were involved in a grinding crash, with Elliott getting the worst of this one. His McDonald's Ford was totaled, and the accident also collected Kyle Petty and Mike Dillon. The wreck was triggered when oil spilled from Jarrett's blown engine right in front of Petty and Elliott. Jarrett was relegated to 41st place in the race results, costing him valuable points in the battle for the championship. Earnhardt's crew, on the other hand, kept him on the lead lap with some excellent pit work, and Dale responded with a vigilant drive that, at one point, saw him battling Gordon for fourth place before he faded to ninth.

Mark Martin throws a fist in the air in triumph and, possibly, vindication. Last year he appeared to have the car to beat but ran out of fuel, handing the victory to Gordon.

California 500 Presented by NAPA

[RACE #10 • CALIFORNIA SPEEDWAY • MAY 3, 1998]

Fin. Pos.	Start Pos.	Car #	Driver	Team	Fin. Pos.	Start Pos.	Car #	Driver	Team
1	3	6	Mark Martin	Valvoline/Cummins Ford	23	35	78	Gary Bradberry	Pilot Travel Centers Ford
2	2	12	Jeremy Mayfield	Mobil 1 Ford	24	10	46	Morgan Shepherd	First Union Chevrolet
3	9	5	Terry Labonte	Kellogg's Corn Flakes Chevrolet	25	30	75	Rick Mast	Remington Arms Ford
4	1	24	Jeff Gordon	DuPont Automotive Refinishes Chevrolet	26	33	13	Jerry Nadeau	FirstPlus Financial Ford
5	11	1	Darrell Waltrip	Pennzoil Chevrolet	27	31	4	Bobby Hamilton	Kodak MAX Film Chevrolet
6	40	97	Chad Little	John Deere Ford	28	38	11	Brett Bodine	Paychex Ford
7	26	7	Geoff Bodine	Philips Consumer Comm. Ford	29	42	35	Wally Dallenbach	Tabasco Pontiac
8	5	26	Johnny Benson	Cheerios Ford	30	41	41	Steve Grissom	Kodiak Chevrolet
9	43	3	Dale Earnhardt	GM Goodwrench Service Plus Chevrolet	31	25	43	John Andretti	STP Pontiac
10	21	99	Jeff Burton	Exide Batteries Ford	32	16	9	Lake Speed	Cartoon Network Ford
11	23	10	Ricky Rudd	Tide Ford	33	24	16	Ted Musgrave	PRIMESTAR Ford
12	8	22	Ward Burton	MBNA America Pontiac	34	4	2	Rusty Wallace	Miller Lite Ford
13	22	36	Ernie Irvan	Skittles Pontiac	35	27	31	Mike Dillon	Lowe's Chevrolet
14	14	40	Sterling Marlin	Coors Light Chevrolet	36	39	50	Randy LaJoie	Budweiser Chevrolet
15	15	33	Ken Schrader	Skoal Bandit Chevrolet	37	29	90	Dick Trickle	Heilig-Meyers Ford
16	18	28	Kenny Irwin	Texaco Havoline Ford	38	7	18	Bobby Labonte	Interstate Batteries Pontiac
17	20	77	Robert Pressley	Jasper Engines Ford	39	32	30	Derrike Cope	Gumout Pontiac
18	19	96	David Green	Caterpillar Chevrolet	40	13	91	Kevin Lepage	Fluidyne Automotive Chevrolet
19	34	81	Kenny Wallace	Square D Ford	41	36	88	Dale Jarrett	Quality Care/Ford Credit Ford
20	37	21	Michael Waltrip	CITGO Ford	42	17	44	Kyle Petty	Hot Wheels Pontiac
21	28	23	Jimmy Spencer	Winston/No Bull Ford	43	12	94	Bill Elliott	McDonald's Ford
22	6	42	Joe Nemechek	BellSouth Chevrolet					

May 16, 1998

The Winston

Since the inaugural event at Charlotte in 1985, when the engine in the Junior Johnson-owned Budweiser Chevrolet exploded just yards after Darrell Waltrip crossed the finish line to grab the victory, The Winston has been full of surprises. The fact that the winner receives $200,000 and that, with no points at stake, drivers take a different tack than they do on a normal Sunday have led to on-track fireworks that have made the event one of the most popular on the circuit each season.

The format of The Winston has evolved through the years, and this year the three segments consisting of 30, 30 and 10 laps remained the same, but with a tweak added at the conclusion of the first segment of the race. In past years, the finishing positions of the first 30-lap segment have been inverted for the second 30, and at times, it appeared that drivers worked their way to the back of the field in the first 30 laps to have a good starting position for the second 30.

This year, however, race officials made a slight change, rolling a roulette wheel out to the start/finish line. The spin of the wheel would determine the number of positions

(Right) *Mark Martin declares victory in Charlotte's winner's circle after streaking past the coasting Jeff Gordon on the final lap of the prestigious all-star event.*

(Below) *For The Winston, sponsor DuPont formulated this very unusual paint for Jeff Gordon's Monte Carlo that made the car appear to change colors as it moved under the bright lights at Charlotte Motor Speedway. Unfortunately for Gordon, the new paint didn't improve his fuel mileage.*

that would be inverted. Whatever number came up — no less than three, nor more than 12 — would be the number of drivers changing positions for the second 30-lap segment.

A second little tweak came at the conclusion of the second segment. In the past, all drivers were allowed to make a stop on pit road, allowing crews to make whatever changes were needed for the final 10-lap shootout. Drivers returned to the positions they had earned on the track at the conclusion of the second 30 laps for the start of the final 10 laps.

That, too, was changed for this year's running of the all-star race. Drivers could pit if they wished during that caution, but if they did, they would rejoin the field in the position they exited the pits. The decision to pit and lose position, or stay on the

and apparel sales. This year would be no different, with Jeff Gordon's DuPont Chevrolet sporting paint that changed colors depending on how the light struck it. Dale Earnhardt's black Goodwrench Chevrolet was gold with Bass Pro Shops on the hood, and Mark Martin's familiar red-white-and-blue Valvoline Ford had become a black-yellow-and-red Taurus with Eagle

Jimmy Spencer (23) and Jeremy Mayfield (12), winners of their respective No Bull 25 qualifying races, work past Ward Burton (22) during the Winston Open. Mayfield had little trouble completing the pass on Spencer and rolled all the way to victory lane before transferring to the night's main event.

track on old tires and improve track position, would be one that would add another wrinkle to the event's closing moments.

The Winston Open also had a tweak added this year. Competitors would race in No Bull 25 qualifying races to determine the starting positions for the Winston Open, much the same as the Gatorade Twin 125s shape the starting lineup for the Daytona 500. The winner of the Winston Open, the preliminary event to the all-star race, would advance to the final starting position in The Winston.

In the last few years, the all-star weekend has also offered teams and sponsors the opportunity to change their regular paint schemes for the "one-off" event, and capitalize on the special appearances from the standpoint of increased souvenir

One, normally an associate sponsor on the car, becoming the primary sponsor for the event. Other cars, including those of Mike Skinner, Lake Speed, Terry Labonte, Brett and Geoff Bodine and Ward Burton, also had paint schemes that were changed for the weekend in one form or another.

With 10 days between the California race and the opening of practice for The Winston weekend, most drivers had the opportunity to rest up and recharge the batteries after 10 races in the last 12 weekends. Mike Skinner returned to the cockpit of the Lowe's Chevrolet, and Wally Dallenbach was enlisted as the driver of the Budweiser Chevrolet, while Rich Bickle was still handing the controls of Cale Yarborough's Thorn Apple Valley Ford. In perhaps the worst shape of the drivers in the garage area at Charlotte was Bill Elliott, who had suffered fractures in his left foot and one in his left middle finger in the crash at California.

However, when pole qualifying was completed under the Charlotte lights, it was Elliott and his McDonald's crew who produced the magic needed to claim the inside of the front row for the start of the prestigious event. The Winston's pole qualifying rules bring the entire team into play. The driver makes three laps and must make a right-side, two-tire stop during those three laps. Cumulative time counts, with penalties involved if the team doesn't get the lug nuts tightened correctly. With just one car at a time on pit road, there are no speed limits, and it becomes white-knuckle time for drivers and crew members as each competitor whistles onto pit road for that crucial two-tire stop.

Elliott screamed onto pit road, his crew whipped a 9.41-second stop on the Ford and Bill blasted back around the track, posting an average speed of 142.084 miles per hour to win his second straight pole for The Winston. He was also aided by drivers like Earnhardt, Jeff Burton, John Andretti, Dale Jarrett and others who made mistakes on pit road.

Terry Labonte claimed the outside of the front row, with Bobby Labonte and Jeff Gordon in the second row ahead of Martin and Sterling Marlin. Jarrett and Michael Waltrip made up the fourth row, while Darrell Waltrip and Kenny Irwin were ninth and 10th for the start of the race. Geoff Bodine and Ricky Rudd made up the sixth row, Bobby Hamilton and Jeff Burton were right behind them, and Ernie Irvan and Rusty Wallace comprised the eighth row. Bickle and Andretti were in the ninth row, with Earnhardt on the inside of the 10th row in the final qualifying position after he slid through his pit and did not complete his qualifying run.

Jeremy Mayfield and Jimmy Spencer won the No Bull 25s, each pocketing $25,000, before Mayfield laid waste to the Winston Open field by leading nearly half of the laps and beating Joe Nemechek's Chevrolet to the line to earn the final starting position in The Winston.

Mayfield's dream of sweeping the night's events came to an end with engine failure, and the hopes of other drivers ended with losing arguments on the racetrack. Darrell Waltrip and Ernie Irvan touched in the second turn on the third lap, and the Skittles Pontiac smacked the concrete wall. On lap 10, the engine in Waltrip's Pennzoil Chevrolet exploded, and behind

(Left) *Mark Martin's traditional Valvoline colors were replaced with those of Eagle One for the special event, and Mark gave them their money's worth by taking them to victory lane.*

(Below) *Dale Earnhardt also displayed a one-time paint job for Bass Pro Shops, but his night yielded disappointing results when Dale was caught up in an accident that ended his night just nine laps into the event.*

him, Earnhardt hit the oil and slammed into the wall, his third hard crash in six weeks. Terry Labonte would also whack the wall, and Wallace was involved in that incident, which ended any hope he had of victory.

Gordon won the first segment easily, and the roulette wheel came up "4", putting Marlin on the pole for the start of the second 30 laps. Martin flashed to the front immediately and swept the second 30 laps, setting up the vital decision for crew chiefs and drivers whether or not to pit for the final segment of the race. The need for new tires was most critical, and the entire field rolled onto pit road.

Martin took four tires and returned to the track in sixth place behind those who took only right sides. Gordon was at the point, the beneficiary of a great pit stop by his Rainbow Warriors, and when the green flag waved, Jeff hot-footed it away from the pack. He was brought to heel immediately, however, by a yellow flag signaling a false start. The field lined up again, and when the green flew the second time, Gordon hesitated long enough to make it a clean start, but immediately bolted to a lead that looked invincible.

Behind him, Martin began fighting his way to the front, using the four fresh tires to his advantage, but Gordon had checked out on the field and Mark was merely trying to get as far forward in the finishing order as possible. As the field rolled out of the fourth turn to take the white flag for the final lap, Martin passed Bobby Labonte for second place, but Gordon was well ahead, and Martin knew he had nothing under the hood of the Taurus that could cut that gap in the 1.5 remaining miles.

(Above) *Mark Martin and Bobby Labonte lead Jeff Gordon and Sterling Marlin toward the line for a restart during the second segment of The Winston. After jumping to the early lead in the second 30-lap run, Martin stayed in front to win the segment easily.*

(Below) *A capacity crowd packs the grandstands at Charlotte Motor Speedway in what has proven to be one of the most popular events each season. Given the history of the all-star race, they're nearly assured to have an exciting evening under the lights, with plenty of fireworks on, and above, the track.*

Gordon looked set to win his third all-star race, but as he dove into the first turn, he ran out of fuel and slowed. Martin, astonished at the turn of events, buried the throttle and rocketed around the track, streaking under the checkered flag and winning The Winston for the first time in his nine tries at the event. Bobby Labonte finished second, Jarrett third, Jeff Burton fourth and Wallace fifth, with Gordon relegated to a 12th-place finish. Marlin was sixth ahead of Elliott and Geoff Bodine, while Hamilton, Bickle and Michael Waltrip finished ahead of Gordon.

The entire Valvoline crew joins car owner Jack Roush and Mark Martin in victory lane to celebrate the win and the accompanying payday worth more than a quarter of a million dollars. The win came in Martin's ninth consecutive appearance in The Winston.

The Winston

[CHARLOTTE MOTOR SPEEDWAY • MAY 16, 1998]

Fin. Pos.	Driver	Fin. Pos.	Driver	Fin. Pos.	Start Pos.	Car #	Driver	Team
SEGMENT 1 (30 LAPS)		**SEGMENT 2 (30 LAPS)**		**SEGMENT 3 (10 LAPS)**				
1	Jeff Gordon	1	Mark Martin	1	5	6	Mark Martin	Eagle One Ford
2	Bobby Labonte	2	Jeff Gordon	2	3	18	Bobby Labonte	Interstate Batteries Pontiac
3	Mark Martin	3	Dale Jarrett	3	7	88	Dale Jarrett	Quality Care/Ford Credit Ford
4	Sterling Marlin	4	Bobby Labonte	4	14	99	Jeff Burton	Exide Batteries Ford
5	Dale Jarrett	5	Sterling Marlin	5	16	2	Rusty Wallace	Miller Lite Ford
6	Kenny Irwin	6	Jeff Burton	6	6	40	Sterling Marlin	Coors Light Chevrolet
7	Rusty Wallace	7	Rusty Wallace	7	1	94	Bill Elliott	McDonald's Ford
8	Terry Labonte	8	Geoff Bodine	8	11	7	Geoff Bodine	Philips Consumer Comm. Ford
9	Jeff Burton	9	Bill Elliott	9	13	4	Bobby Hamilton	Kodak MAX Film Chevrolet
10	Bill Elliott	10	Michael Waltrip	10	17	98	Rich Bickle	Thorn Apple Valley Ford
11	Ricky Rudd	11	Bobby Hamilton	11	8	21	Michael Waltrip	CITGO Ford
12	Michael Waltrip	12	Rich Bickle	12	4	24	Jeff Gordon	DuPont Automotive Refinishes Chevrolet
13	Geoff Bodine	13	Kenny Irwin	13	10	28	Kenny Irwin	Texaco Havoline Ford
14	Bobby Hamilton	14	Terry Labonte	14	2	5	Terry Labonte	Kellogg's Corn Flakes Chevrolet
15	Rich Bickle	15	Ricky Rudd	15	12	10	Ricky Rudd	Tide Ford
16	Jeremy Mayfield	16	Jeremy Mayfield	16	20	12	Jeremy Mayfield	Mobil 1 Ford
17	Darrell Waltrip	17	Darrell Waltrip	17	9	1	Darrell Waltrip	Pennzoil Chevrolet
18	John Andretti	18	John Andretti	18	18	43	John Andretti	STP Pontiac
19	Dale Earnhardt	19	Dale Earnhardt	19	19	3	Dale Earnhardt	Bass Pro Shops Chevrolet
20	Ernie Irvan	20	Ernie Irvan	20	15	36	Ernie Irvan	Skittles Pontiac

Coca-Cola 600

With The Winston weekend completed, Mark Martin found he had little time to think about his third victory in his last three outings (IROC, California 500 and The Winston). Instead, it seemed as though he had barely peeled off the Eagle One driver's suit and zipped back into his familiar Valvoline livery before practice began at Charlotte for the Coca-Cola 600.

The victory in the non-points all-star race had added another $257,500 to his total winnings, boosting it to more than $1.4 million for the season — and the year was less than one-third complete. Now Martin's attention, and that of his fellow competitors, was re-focused on the NASCAR Winston Cup championship and the longest race of the season that faced everyone in the garage area.

The importance of the Coca-Cola 600 at Charlotte can not be over emphasized. It is the event at nearly every team's home track, where families and friends of hard working crew members are in attendance to see how well their team fares. Because it is 100 miles longer than any other race on the schedule, it takes a mental and physical toll on the

(Right) Rusty Wallace, hoping to turn things around after tumbling to fourth place in the points as a result of his California finish, has his Miller Lite Ford flying ahead of Joe Nemechek (42) and Johnny Benson (26). Rusty held a strong late-race lead, but did not need the final caution that gave Gordon an opportunity to win.

(Below) The DuPont team pushes their Monte Carlo to the line wearing a collective look of determination after hearing about their fuel miscalculation in The Winston all week long. Before the night was over, their faces would reflect the satisfaction of victory — and vindication.

crews and drivers, and puts a premium on engine preparation and mechanical reliability. Everyone wants to win at Charlotte. To have notched the Coca-Cola 600 victory means bragging rights until the tour returns to the hometown track in October.

Martin hoped his fortunes would continue. He had climbed to fifth in the point standings following his California victory, and now trailed Rusty Wallace by 50 markers. Wallace's 34th-place finish at California due to engine failure had tumbled him from the point lead to fourth, while Jeremy Mayfield's career-best second-place finish at the Southern California two-mile oval had moved him into the point lead. He held a 36-point margin over Terry Labonte as the chase for the championship resumed, while Jeff Gordon had eased from fifth to third place as a result of his California 500 finish. Gordon was 11 points behind his Hendrick Motorsports teammate and just 47 points behind Mayfield.

The engine failure at California had also cost Dale Jarrett, who fell from fourth in the points to sixth and was now 39 behind Martin. Dale Earnhardt, despite being involved in an accident at California, moved up to seventh, 72 points behind Jarrett, but was steadily falling further behind in the overall point totals. He was now 234 behind Mayfield. Jimmy Spencer had climbed from 10th to eighth in the standings, 39 behind Earnhardt, while Bobby Labonte slipped slightly to ninth place, 15 behind Spencer. Ken Schrader moved up to 10th place, 11 points behind Bobby, while Bill Elliott fell from the top 10. The accidents that left him easing his way around the garage area had put him 11th entering the Charlotte race, 19 behind Schrader, a single point ahead of Michael Waltrip and just two points ahead of Ward Burton.

For Wallace, Bobby Labonte, Schrader, Earnhardt and point-leader Mayfield, the Coca-Cola 600 took on added importance. They were the top five finishers in the Daytona 500 and, as such, had qualified for Winston's No Bull 5 million-dollar bonus at Charlotte. If any of the five could win the Coca-Cola 600, he would collect an extra $1 million from the Series' sponsor, Winston. That, in itself, was more than enough to get everyone's attention.

While Martin and his Valvoline teammates held sway in the garage area, Gordon and the Rainbow Warriors were grim-faced as practice sessions unfolded prior to qualifying. The fact that Gordon had run out of fuel with less than a lap remaining

Mark Martin, back in his familiar Valvoline colors, tries to continue his winning streak that includes the California 500, the IROC event at Charlotte, The Winston and the NASCAR Busch Series race run on Saturday. He looked unbeatable in the 600, leading the most laps throughout the evening, but faded slightly near the end to a fourth-place finish.

in The Winston, and that it had cost the team and the driver the victory in an event they had dominated was not lost on the Hendrick Motorsports team. It was the kind of mistake that the team has seldom made over the past five years, and each of the crew members found themselves embarrassed when they thought of letting that event slip away.

It was no surprise, then, when Gordon hauled tail in the DuPont Monte Carlo during his qualifying lap, rocketing to a speed of 182.976 miles per hour. As at California, where he won his first pole of the season, the luck of the draw was helpful to Gordon. At California, he had drawn an early number, getting his lap in before the asphalt heated up from the Southern California sun. At Charlotte, he drew a late number (43 of 51) and, with the qualifying session beginning at 7 p.m., Gordon didn't venture onto the track until it had cooled off. Ward Burton's luck was just the opposite. His number in the qualifying line was seven, and the lap he turned was almost, but not quite, good enough to secure the pole. It did, however, put the MBNA Pontiac driver on the outside of the front row.

(Above) *The special paint schemes of Michael Waltrip (21) and Terry Labonte (5) didn't help them go fast in qualifying, as both were forced to use provisionals to make the starting field.*

(Below) *Jimmy Spencer jerks the wheel hard right to keep his Winston Ford from coming around after contact from behind. Jimmy was unable to save it, however, and the ensuing spin brought out the second of eight cautions during the night.*

John Andretti and Rusty Wallace claimed the second-row positions, while Martin and Bobby Labonte were right behind them. Dick Trickle and Gary Bradberry each turned in sparkling qualifying efforts to gather the fourth-row spots, while Rick Mast and Jarrett slipped into the fifth row, just in front of Randy LaJoie (back in the Budweiser Chevrolet for the 600) and Mayfield.

The second round of qualifying was held during the daytime hours, and with the track slower, the quest for a starting berth became even more intense. With Michael and Darrell Waltrip using provisionals along with Jeff Burton, Johnny Benson, Ted Musgrave, Bobby Hamilton and Kenny Wallace, it meant that eight drivers would not make the field. Among them were Andy Hillenburg, Dave Marcis, Randy MacDonald, Dan Pardus, Billy Standridge and Morgan Shepherd with the First Union Chevrolet from the Sabco stable. Also missing the race was Hut Stricklin, who soon found himself relieved of his driving duties by the Stavola Brothers team.

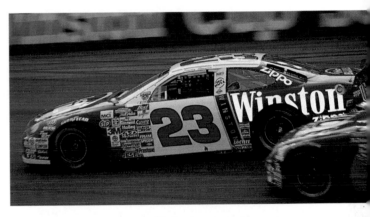

(Below) *The Exide crew hurdles the wall as Jeff Burton enters his pit under green. Aided by great stops on pit road, Burton was able to fight all the way from his 38th starting spot to finish 8th on the lead lap.*

Also missing the event was rookie Kenny Irwin, bringing long faces to the proud Texaco Havoline crew members as they packed away the famed "28." It took some scurrying through the record book to find out when the last time a Robert Yates Racing entry had missed a race. It turned out to be the August Michigan race in 1994, when driver Ernie Irvan was injured in practice.

In the days prior to the event, Bud Moore announced his team would return to a limited number of races this season with sponsorship from Rescue Engine Treatment, and with Blaise Alexander to drive some of the events. While Moore was talking about the new black-and-yellow colors on his Tauruses, Todd Bodine was sharing pictures of his newborn daughter, Ashlyn Marie, to anyone who wished to look.

For the battered and beaten Elliott, the season took another nightmarish turn. Still sore and hobbled from his accidents at Talladega and California, Elliott was hustling back and forth in his plane from Charlotte to Houston, Texas, where his 74-year-

Rusty Wallace (2) lines up behind the pace car with (in order) Bobby Labonte, Mark Martin and Dale Jarrett closing up from behind for the final restart of the race with just 16 laps remaining. Not pictured is Jeff Gordon, who lined up sixth on the outside for the dash to the checkers.

old father, George, was undergoing surgery for a brain tumor. Bill's year, which had begun so strongly, had become a physical and emotional struggle.

Despite having won the Bud Pole for the Coca-Cola 600, Gordon and his Rainbow Warriors remained stone-faced throughout the weekend. The cause wasn't helped by the fact that Jeff overslept and missed a practice session, and when Terry Labonte was pressed into service to drive the DuPont car in Jeff's absence, the Monte Carlo brushed the wall, meaning additional work for the Warriors. Gordon, arriving at the track as his car was being returned to the garage after the incident, became even more determined to put on a strong performance in the 600 to atone for his sleeping through the alarm clock at his Lake Norman home.

The longest race of the season saw Earnhardt in yet another accident when LaJoie and the black Chevrolet were involved in yet another wreck. When the field took the green flag following that caution and with less than 50 laps remaining in the event, it appeared that Rusty Wallace and Bobby Labonte were set to have a full-fledged rumble to decide which driver would win the No Bull 5 $1 million from Winston.

That plan went by the wayside when the final yellow flag of the night waved with just 21 laps left, sending all of the leaders to pit road. Wallace, Labonte, Jarrett and Martin all took two tires. Gordon, on the other hand, went for four and would line up sixth on the restart with only 16 laps remaining in the race. Three laps later, he moved past both Jarrett and Martin into third place. With 11 laps left, he whipped past Bobby Labonte into second place, and on lap 391, he found a way past Wallace to take the point, spoiling the million-dollar dreams of both Wallace and Labonte in the process. Gordon drove on to win by nearly a half-second.

Rusty was second and Bobby third, with Martin seeing his winning streak end at four after winning Saturday's NASCAR Busch Series event. Jarrett, Joe Nemechek, Andretti and Jeff Burton beat Johnny Benson to the line, while Schrader finished 10th, the first driver to complete 399 laps.

The victory made up for the embarrassment the Rainbow Warriors felt for the fuel problem that had cost them The Winston, and for Gordon's recalcitrant alarm clock. It also made him just the fifth driver in history to win back-to-back Coca-Cola 600s.

(Left) On the final caution of the night, the Rainbow Warriors give Jeff Gordon four fresh tires for the final sprint to the checkered flag. Bobby Labonte (18) tears away from his pit after taking just right-sides only.

(Below) The call for a full set of fresh rubber pays off for Gordon as he is able to keep the DuPont Chevrolet on the inside and work past both Bobby Labonte (18) and Rusty Wallace (2) in the closing laps, and continue on for the win.

Coca-Cola 600

[*RACE #11 • CHARLOTTE MOTOR SPEEDWAY • MAY 24, 1998*]

Fin. Pos.	Start Pos.	Car #	Driver	Team	Fin. Pos.	Start Pos.	Car #	Driver	Team
1	1	24	Jeff Gordon	DuPont Automotive Refinishes Chevrolet	23	13	7	Geoff Bodine	Philips Consumer Comm. Ford
2	4	2	Rusty Wallace	Miller Lite Ford	24	16	08	Rich Bickle	Thorn Apple Valley Ford
3	6	18	Bobby Labonte	Interstate Batteries Pontiac	25	42	81	Kenny Wallace	Square D Ford
4	5	6	Mark Martin	Valvoline/Cummins Ford	26	9	75	Rick Mast	Remington Arms Ford
5	10	88	Dale Jarrett	Quality Care/Ford Credit Ford	27	19	9	Lake Speed	Cartoon Network Ford
6	26	42	Joe Nemechek	BellSouth Chevrolet	28	20	35	Todd Bodine	Tabasco Pontiac
7	3	43	John Andretti	STP Pontiac	29	34	31	Mike Skinner	Lowe's Chevrolet
8	38	99	Jeff Burton	Exide Batteries Ford	30	29	44	Kyle Petty	Hot Wheels Pontiac
9	39	26	Johnny Benson	Cheerios Ford	31	35	10	Ricky Rudd	Tide Ford
10	14	33	Ken Schrader	Skoal Bandit Chevrolet	32	23	41	Steve Grissom	Kodiak Chevrolet
11	18	36	Ernie Irvan	Skittles Pontiac	33	25	30	Derrike Cope	Gumout Pontiac
12	41	16	Ted Musgrave	PRIMESTAR Ford	34	2	22	Ward Burton	MBNA America Pontiac
13	21	23	Jimmy Spencer	Winston/No Bull Ford	35	24	97	Chad Little	John Deere Ford
14	33	94	Bill Elliott	McDonald's Ford	36	15	91	Kevin Lepage	First Union Chevrolet
15	30	40	Sterling Marlin	Coors Light Chevrolet	37	8	78	Gary Bradberry	Pilot Travel Centers Ford
16	27	77	Robert Pressley	Jasper Engines Ford	38	11	50	Randy LaJoie	Budweiser Chevrolet
17	43	1	Darrell Waltrip	Pennzoil Chevrolet	39	28	3	Dale Earnhardt	GM Goodwrench Service Plus Chevrolet
18	37	21	Michael Waltrip	CITGO Ford	40	22	13	Jerry Nadeau	FirstPlus Financial Ford
19	12	12	Jeremy Mayfield	Mobil 1 Ford	41	36	5	Terry Labonte	Kellogg's Corn Flakes Chevrolet
20	40	4	Bobby Hamilton	Kodak MAX Film Chevrolet	42	31	92	Elliott Sadler	Op/Tower Clothing Chevrolet
21	7	90	Dick Trickle	Heilig-Meyers Ford	43	17	96	David Green	Caterpillar Chevrolet
22	32	11	Brett Bodine	Paychex Ford					

MBNA Platinum 400

Dover Downs is DuPont's "home track," located south of the corporate giant's Wilmington headquarters, and as far as Jeff Gordon was concerned, there was no better place to have next on the schedule.

With three victories in the last five events at Denis McGlynn's "Monster Mile," Gordon was sure his Rainbow Warriors would have a highly competitive mount for him to flash in front of the team's sponsors. More important to both Gordon and DuPont, the results of the Coca-Cola 600 put Gordon into the lead in the point standings as the defending NASCAR Winston Cup champion arrived in Delaware's Capital City.

During the first of two weekends at Charlotte, a fuel-mileage mistake had cost the Rainbow Warriors a victory in The Winston. A week later during the Coca-Cola 600, the same type of mistake ultimately cost Jeremy Mayfield the point lead. The Mobil 1 Ford had run out of fuel before quarter-distance in the longest race of the year, and had fallen off the lead lap as a result. Mayfield later had handling problems with the white-and-blue Taurus and ended up with a 19th-place finish.

(Right) Darrell Waltrip confers with Dale Earnhardt, his current car owner, before climbing aboard the Pennzoil Chevrolet. Waltrip could not squeeze enough speed out of the car during qualifying and had to take the former champion's provisional, but climbed to a 20th-place finish in the race.

(Below) Dale Jarrett lets the champagne fly in Dover's victory lane after scoring his second win of the season, which also moved him up a notch to fifth in the point standings.

The combination of Gordon's victory and Jeremy's finish vaulted Jeff into a 27-point lead over Mayfield as teams prepared for the Dover grinder. Rusty Wallace found himself just four points behind his Penske teammate, while Mark Martin trailed Wallace by 55 points. A problem with a wheel bearing at Charlotte caused Terry Labonte to fall from second place in the standings to fifth, where he now trailed Martin by 43 markers. Dale Jarrett was sixth in points, just six behind Terry, while holding a 116-point lead over Bobby Labonte. Jimmy Spencer held eighth place, with Ken Schrader moving to ninth, 22 behind Spencer. Dale Earnhardt fell from seventh to 10th place in the point standings after his Charlotte accident with Randy LaJoie.

Bill Elliott trailed Earnhardt by nine points, while Jeff Burton and Michael Waltrip were tied for 12th place, just eight points behind Elliott. Johnny Benson and Ward Burton completed the top 15 following the Charlotte race.

(Left) *Ward Burton, sporting a platinum-colored paint scheme for sponsor MBNA, leads Ted Musgrave (16), Derrike Cope (30) and Gary Bradberry through Dover's high banks.*

(Below) *Jeff Gordon rolls off pit road after a gas-and-go with just eight laps remaining in the race. The stop for fuel dropped Gordon to third place after he had dominated the event by leading all but 24 of the race's 400 laps.*

The Circuit City Chevrolet fielded by the Stavola Brothers had a new driver at Dover, following the dismissal of Hut Stricklin after he failed to qualify for the Coca-Cola 600. NASCAR Busch Series star Buckshot Jones was doing double duty on the Monster Mile, and there was talk that Buckshot might drive additional races in the Stavola car before the season was complete.

While Jones was sliding in and out of the window of the red-and-white Chevrolet, Morgan Shepherd was sharing information with Waddell Wilson, who had been named as a consultant and strategist on race weekends for the First Union Monte Carlo fielded by the Sabco organization. Team owner Felix Sabates hoped that some of Wilson's extensive knowledge would help get the team righted and moving in the proper direction after the green-black-and-silver car had struggled throughout the season. By the time qualifying was completed, however, Wilson found himself with nothing to do. Shepherd had failed to make the field.

After spending a day at DuPont headquarters signing autographs and having his picture taken with children of the employees, Gordon looked as though he would give the company even more reason to celebrate during the first round of Bud Pole qualifying. In the end, however, it was a superlative performance by Wallace and the Miller Lite Ford that claimed the inside of the front row for the start of the MBNA Platinum 400.

Throwing caution to the wind, Wallace buried his right foot and rocketed to a lap at 155.898 miles per hour around the one-mile oval, and in the process, he set an all-time single-lap qualifying record for the venerable facility. His lap broke the previous record of 155.229 mph set 29 years ago when Bobby Unser whistled a USAC Champ car around the track. Wallace knew that the speed wouldn't last long — Dover had an Indy Racing League event scheduled for mid-July — but for at least six weeks, Rusty could claim the fastest lap in the history of the track.

Martin and Jarrett claimed the second row ahead of Ricky Rudd and Joe Nemechek, while Rick Mast and Ernie Irvan made up the fourth row. Kenny Irwin rebounded from missing the Charlotte race to claim the ninth-fastest lap, just ahead of Ward Burton's platinum-colored MBNA Pontiac, carrying the silvery paint as part of MBNA's special promotion that weekend.

Lake Speed and Mayfield barely missed the top 10, and Dennis Setzer found himself pressed into service in the FirstPlus Financial Ford while Jerry Nadeau fought off nausea from a stomach disorder. Setzer failed to make the field, joining Shepherd and Todd Bodine on the sidelines. Jeff Burton, Bobby Hamilton, Chad Little, Randy LaJoie, Steve Grissom, Kevin Lepage and Darrell Waltrip all were forced to use provisionals to make the field for the MBNA Platinum 400.

With 10,000 new seats added and a record crowd of 107,000 jammed into the speedway for Sunday's 400-lapper, many expected the victory to go to either Gordon or Martin, the two hottest drivers on the tour. And for the longest time, Gordon looked as though the rainbow-painted DuPont

Buckshot Jones got the call to climb behind the wheel of the Circuit City Chevrolet at Dover, after Hut Stricklin's release following the events at Charlotte. Jones, shown here following Steve Grissom (41) on the outside of John Andretti (43) and Joe Nemechek (42), had a sparkling run, bringing the Stavola Brothers' entry home in eighth place.

The Tide guys swarm Ricky Rudd's Ford during a pit stop for tires, fuel and a chassis adjustment. Rudd, who started fifth in the race, fell one lap off the winning pace but still managed a sixth-place finish to gain his first top 10 of the season.

Chevrolet would be the car that would arrive in the Dover winner's circle for yet another time.

Over the years at Dover, fuel mileage has played a key role in determining who takes home the hardware at the conclusion of the events, and it turned out that this would be another one of those races. Gordon was thoroughly dominant in the event, leading 376 of the 400 laps and simply crushing the field with the strength and handling package under the Monte Carlo. But when teams made pit stops with just over 100 laps to go, Gordon knew he would be back on pit road before the end of the race.

He pitted on lap 295 and would need to go 105 laps on the tank of fuel if the race remained under green-flag conditions. His problem was that the mileage figures for the event showed that he could not go the distance. He could only hope for yellow flags.

Three laps later, both Dale Jarrett and Jeff Burton hit pit road and would need to go just 102 laps on their full fuel tanks. Jarrett immediately radioed crew chief Todd Parrott, asking if he had enough fuel to go the distance, and Parrott clicked off in Jarrett's ear that he was "good to go." A relieved Jarrett settled in and began pacing the Qualify Care Ford for the final quarter of the race.

Gordon, knowing he would be forced to stop, tried to open a lead on the field to give himself as much cushion as he could

before the fateful stop that loomed. He built a six-second margin over Jeff Burton, but Jarrett was on the move. Jarrett worked his way past the fellow Ford driver and set off after Gordon, closing to just under two seconds before settling in and letting Gordon ease back to a 2.5-second lead. It now was a matter of fate.

At Rockingham earlier in the season, Jarrett had been the dominant one, and had seen the race slip from his grasp in the closing laps. This time, if the race remained green, the win would go to the Ford driver, despite the dominance shown by Gordon throughout the event.

As the laps wound down, Gordon knew his fate was sealed. He peeled off the track onto pit road with just eight laps left in the race for the splash of fuel that would carry him to the end of the event, and handed the lead over to Jarrett. Well clear of everyone on the track, Jarrett eased the red-white-and-blue Ford to a 13-second victory over Burton, while Gordon returned to the track on the lead lap after his hasty stop and claimed third place. Bobby Labonte was the only other driver on the lead lap at the end, taking fourth place.

Mayfield led the lap-down drivers in fifth, while Rudd posted a strong sixth-place finish ahead of Martin. Buckshot Jones had an outstanding debut for the Stavolas coming home in eighth place, while Ernie Irvan and Terry Labonte finished ninth and 10th.

Dale Jarrett takes the checkered flag, scoring a 13-second victory over second-place Jeff Burton. Although the margin seems dominant, Jarrett took the lead for the first time on lap 393 when Gordon stopped for fuel, and led the final eight circuits for his first Dover victory.

MBNA Platinum 400

[*RACE #12 • DOVER DOWNS INTERNATIONAL SPEEDWAY • MAY 31, 1998*]

Fin. Pos.	Start Pos.	Car #	Driver	Team	Fin. Pos.	Start Pos.	Car #	Driver	Team
1	4	88	Dale Jarrett	Quality Care/Ford Credit Ford	23	26	7	Geoff Bodine	Philips Consumer Comm. Ford
2	37	99	Jeff Burton	Exide Batteries Ford	24	15	23	Jimmy Spencer	Winston/No Bull Ford
3	2	24	Jeff Gordon	DuPont Automotive Finishes Chevrolet	25	34	3	Dale Earnhardt	GM Goodwrench Service Plus Chevrolet
4	36	18	Bobby Labonte	Interstate Batteries Pontiac	26	6	42	Joe Nemechek	BellSouth Chevrolet
5	12	12	Jeremy Mayfield	Mobil 1 Ford	27	18	31	Mike Skinner	Lowe's Chevrolet
6	5	10	Ricky Rudd	Tide Ford	28	42	91	Kevin Lepage	Little Joe's Auto Chevrolet
7	3	6	Mark Martin	Valvoline/Cummins Ford	29	10	22	Ward Burton	MBNA America Pontiac
8	19	8	Buckshot Jones	Circuit City Chevrolet	30	33	71	Dave Marcis	Realtree Camouflage Chevrolet
9	8	36	Ernie Irvan	Skittles Pontiac	31	27	98	Rich Bickle	Thorn Apple Valley Ford
10	17	5	Terry Labonte	Kellogg's Corn Flakes Chevrolet	32	41	41	Steve Grissom	Kodiak Chevrolet
11	7	75	Rick Mast	Remington Arms Ford	33	9	28	Kenny Irwin	Texaco Havoline Ford
12	16	43	John Andretti	STP Pontiac	34	35	78	Gary Bradberry	Pilot Travel Centers Ford
13	24	94	Bill Elliott	McDonald's Ford	35	32	30	Derrike Cope	Gumout Pontiac
14	21	21	Michael Waltrip	CITGO Ford	36	11	9	Lake Speed	Cartoon Network Ford
15	25	33	Ken Schrader	Skoal Bandit Chevrolet	37	39	97	Chad Little	John Deere Ford
16	29	11	Brett Bodine	Paychex Ford	38	30	96	David Green	Caterpillar Chevrolet
17	38	4	Bobby Hamilton	Kodak MAX Film Chevrolet	39	23	77	Robert Pressley	Jasper Engines Ford
18	1	2	Rusty Wallace	Miller Lite Ford	40	31	81	Kenny Wallace	Square D Ford
19	20	40	Sterling Marlin	Coors Light Chevrolet	41	14	26	Johnny Benson	Cheerios Ford
20	43	1	Darrell Waltrip	Pennzoil Chevrolet	42	28	44	Kyle Petty	Hot Wheels Pontiac
21	13	90	Dick Trickle	Heilig-Meyers Ford	43	40	50	Randy LaJoie	Budweiser Chevrolet
22	22	16	Ted Musgrave	PRIMESTAR Ford					

Pontiac Excitement 400

Although disappointed that his dominating performance at Dover had not resulted in a victory, his third-place finish combined with Jeremy Mayfield's fifth place provided Jeff Gordon with a 47-point margin when the teams arrived at Richmond for the Pontiac Excitement 400.

The date switch from previous years allowed the Richmond event to be run under the lights in the Capital of the Confederacy. It was the first short-track event since Martinsville, and the last until the pressure-packed stretch run to the title included Bristol in August. It also guaranteed a full-scale sellout of the grandstands for the Sawyer family, who have spent the last several years building the three-quarter mile mini-superspeedway into one of the most fabulous stops on the circuit.

It's not just the meticulous preparation and work that went into designing the track, or the grandstands that now encircle the venue, making it look more like a football stadium. It doesn't end with the caring attitude of the staff, the workers and the management that begins with Patriarch Paul and spreads down through his children and grandchildren. The

(Right) *Drivers race side by side under the flagstand as the field fans out in the early laps on Richmond International Raceway's smooth, roomy racing surface.*

(Below) *Rich Bickle (right) and Cale Yarborough ponder their strategy for the Pontiac Excitement 400 in Richmond's garage area. Bickle, continuing to drive for Yarborough in Greg Sacks' absence, clicked off a qualifying lap that was good enough to put him on the front row for the start of the race, his best career NASCAR Winston Cup start.*

(**Top Left**) *On Friday night during the NASCAR Busch Series companion event, the Miller Lite and Kellogg's teams work under portable lights in Richmond's garage area, converting their cars from qualifying trim to race setups for Saturday's activities.* (**Above Left**) *As daylight turns to darkness behind the colorful sunset, Richmond's beautiful three-quarter-mile speedway comes to life under the lights.* (**Above Right**) *Two-time Richmond winner Ernie Irvan stands by while the Skittles crew prepares his Pontiac for competition.*

pleasure of the event also comes from the people and the city of Richmond, which have made strategic efforts to ensure that the hotels and restaurants carry fan-friendly prices during race weekends. All in all, it is one of the best stops on the tour, and drivers, teams, media members and fans are delighted to have the event in the summer, rather than in February or March, which had been the traditional date in the past.

Frustration levels were on the rise with several teams. Dale Earnhardt, fighting handling problems all day at Dover, had been lapped five times and now found himself down to 13th in the point standings. Rusty Wallace, with a car he felt capable of easily scoring the Dover victory, had been trapped on pit road during a stop when a yellow came out and had lost two laps, falling to 92 points behind Gordon in the chase for the championship.

Jeff Green found himself in the First Union Chevrolet after Morgan Shepherd was unable to make the field at Dover. His brother, David, was struggling with a sore shoulder after a Dover accident, and ultimately would miss the race at Richmond when Kevin Lepage became available after failing to make the race in qualifying.

Mark Martin remained solidly in fourth place in the point standings, just 18 markers behind Wallace, and Dale Jarrett's second victory of the season moved him to fifth place, 20 points behind Martin. Jarrett was 40 points ahead of Terry Labonte, while Bobby Labonte now found himself 96 points behind his brother. Jeff Burton's second place and newfound consistency on the track shoved the Exide Ford driver upward on the ladder, where he was now eighth, 72 points behind the younger Labonte.

In ninth place, Ken Schrader continued his solid performances and trailed Jeff Burton by 17. Jimmy Spencer was just a single point behind Schrader and just 25 ahead of Bill Elliott, more comfortable now that his father had been transferred from the Houston hospital to one in Atlanta following his recent surgery.

After the conclusion of practice, a look at the speed sheets raised eyebrows throughout the garage area. In several instances, drivers and cars not usually at the top of the sheet were listed, and if those numbers translated into laps during Bud Pole qualifying, the grid for Saturday night's Pontiac Excitement 400 would have an unusual look.

Sterling Marlin ran hard, put up a 124.997-mile per hour lap and emerged from the Coors Light Chevrolet with a smile. It remained pasted on his face even after Jeff Gordon picked up four-tenths of a second during his second lap to claim his third Bud Pole of the season. But the smiles of Gordon and Marlin could not be compared to the beaming delight on Rich Bickle's face as he slid through the window of his Thorn Apple Valley Ford following his run. After running well at Richmond in the NASCAR Craftsman Truck Series for two races, Bickle had put Cale Yarborough's Ford on the outside of the front row for his best career NASCAR Winston Cup start.

Dale Jarrett found himself fourth fastest, barely ahead of Kenny Wallace. Jeff Green's debut in the First Union Chevrolet put him sixth fastest, giving the Sabco team two cars in the top six for the start of the event. Ken Schrader posted yet another solid qualifying run, taking the inside of the fourth row, while

Waddell Wilson (top) returned as a consultant to Sabco's "46" team with driver Jeff Green behind the wheel for the first time. Wilson put a strong package under the Chevrolet and Green responded with a sixth-place qualifying effort. During the race, however, this spin and subsequent meeting with the fourth-turn wall ended his night in the garage.

Johnny Benson stirred up the Cheerios and put his Jack Roush Ford alongside Schrader. Chad Little and Ted Musgrave responded with solid laps, making Roush cars 8th, 9th and 10th on the starting grid.

Where were the championship contenders? Mayfield qualified 15th, Terry Labonte 16th, Mark Martin 19th and Rusty Wallace found himself 22nd for the start of the race. Spencer, Earnhardt, Bobby Hamilton, Rick Mast, Geoff Bodine, Darrell

Waltrip and Derrike Cope all took provisionals to make the field, leaving Lepage on the outside looking in. Even more disastrous was the fact that Buckshot Jones, after his eighth-place finish at Dover, failed to make the field with the Stavola Brothers' Circuit City Chevrolet. The worst part for all was that Richmond is the corporate home of Circuit City, and to fail to make the field with the company's top executives in attendance was a nightmare turned reality.

It got better. With many of the leaders pitting under the yellow for Gordon, Jarrett, Schrader and Ricky Rudd remained on the track, moving up to the front of the line. With 17 laps left, the green flew and Rudd began trying to win his first race of the season. Halfway through the first green-flag lap, however, he spun down the backstretch, bringing out another yellow when seven cars were involved in the melee.

Every driver in the field at Richmond had spent the early part of their careers racing on Saturday nights, being involved in more shootouts than they cared to remember. For the fans watching the Richmond event — whether in the grandstand seats at the track or on their television screens at home — the final 50 laps of the Pontiac Excitement 400 were properly named.

The early portion of the event merely set the stage for the final 50 circuits, with Michael Waltrip's accident from a cut tire bringing out the caution flag on lap 344. When the green flag waved on lap 350, Rusty Wallace was at the point, with Gordon, Terry Labonte, Jarrett, Jeff Burton and Bobby Labonte all in the hunt for the victory.

Gordon began working Rusty for the point, and with less than 30 laps to go, Jeff dove into the first turn on the outside of Wallace, almost clearing the Miller Lite Ford. Rusty's right front clipped the left rear of Gordon's Chevrolet, sending the DuPont Monte Carlo spinning into the concrete wall. Gordon's evening was finished.

On lap 390, the green flew again, but a radiator hose broke loose from Lepage's Caterpillar Chevrolet, spraying water on the track and creating a problem that collected four more cars. The flag that flew from the flagstand wasn't the yellow that leader Dale Jarrett expected. Instead, it was red, thrown by race officials to give cleanup crews time to attend to the fluid on the track.

The red flag meant a stoppage of the event, and when the green finally waved again, there were just three laps to go. It would be a war between Jarrett, Terry Labonte, Wallace and Schrader for the victory, with Jarrett starting at the point.

With just over two laps to go, Labonte made his move, slashing under Jarrett in the third turn, bouncing up off the apron and slapping the Ford's sheetmetal, moving Jarrett out of the groove just enough to gain the lead. While Jarrett and Labonte were fighting for the lead, Benson crashed along the frontstretch, bringing out the yellow and white flags as the leaders flashed under-

Andy Graves (right) makes his first trip to a NASCAR Winston Cup victory lane as a crew chief, helping Terry Labonte celebrate his first win of the season.

neath. Labonte and Jarrett saw them, knowing the event would now finish under yellow. Jarrett eased out of the throttle, but Wallace rocketed alongside Labonte, racing him all the way back to the checkered flag. Labonte maintained his margin to win his first race of the year and give new crew chief Andy Graves his first NASCAR Winston Cup victory.

Although Wallace finished behind the Kellogg's car, he was moved back to third in the results for having passed Jarrett under the yellow flag. Schrader finished fourth, while Martin brought his Valvoline Ford home in fifth place.

Mayfield was sixth, with Burton seventh after Exide officials announced that they would continue sponsorship of the driver and team through the year 2001. Bobby Labonte, Kenny Irwin and Sterling Marlin completed the top 10 finishers.

Jeff Gordon (24) edges past race-leader Rusty Wallace in the first turn just moments before Gordon's Chevrolet went spinning into the wall. Gordon, who would not return to the race, wound up listed in 37th place. Wallace finished third.

Pontiac Excitement 400

[*RACE #13 • RICHMOND INTERNATIONAL RACEWAY • JUNE 6, 1998*]

Fin. Pos.	Start Pos.	Car #	Driver	Team	Fin. Pos.	Start Pos.	Car #	Driver	Team
1	16	5	Terry Labonte	Kellogg's Corn Flakes Chevrolet	23	5	81	Kenny Wallace	Square D Ford
2	4	88	Dale Jarrett	Quality Care/Ford Credit Ford	24	27	44	Kyle Petty	Hot Wheels Pontiac
3	22	2	Rusty Wallace	Miller Lite Ford	25	21	94	Bill Elliott	McDonald's Ford
4	7	33	Ken Schrader	Skoal Bandit Chevrolet	26	12	9	Lake Speed	Cartoon Network Ford
5	19	6	Mark Martin	Valvoline/Cummins Ford	27	2	98	Rich Bickle	Thorn Apple Valley Ford
6	15	12	Jeremy Mayfield	Mobil 1 Ford	28	41	7	Geoff Bodine	Philips Consumer Comm. Ford
7	13	99	Jeff Burton	Exide Batteries Ford	29	23	36	Ernie Irvan	Skittles Pontiac
8	14	18	Bobby Labonte	Interstate Batteries Pontiac	30	34	31	Mike Skinner	Lowe's Chevrolet
9	11	28	Kenny Irwin	Texaco Havoline Ford	31	28	50	Randy LaJoie	Budweiser Chevrolet
10	3	40	Sterling Marlin	Coors Light Chevrolet	32	42	1	Darrell Waltrip	Pennzoil Chevrolet
11	26	10	Ricky Rudd	Tide Ford	33	30	96	Kevin Lepage	Caterpillar Chevrolet
12	18	42	Joe Nemechek	BellSouth Chevrolet	34	43	30	Derrike Cope	Gumout Pontiac
13	9	97	Chad Little	John Deere Ford	35	31	35	Todd Bodine	Tabasco Pontiac
14	37	23	Jimmy Spencer	Winston/No Bull Ford	36	35	71	Dave Marcis	Realtree Camouflage Chevrolet
15	10	16	Ted Musgrave	PRIMESTAR Ford	37	1	24	Jeff Gordon	DuPont Automotive Finishes Chevrolet
16	39	4	Bobby Hamilton	Kodak MAX Film Chevrolet	38	36	13	Jerry Nadeau	FirstPlus Financial Ford
17	20	90	Dick Trickle	Heilig-Meyers Ford	39	32	41	Steve Grissom	Kodiak Chevrolet
18	8	26	Johnny Benson	Cheerios Ford	40	33	21	Michael Waltrip	CITGO Ford
19	24	22	Ward Burton	MBNA America Pontiac	41	17	77	Robert Pressley	Jasper Engines Ford
20	25	11	Brett Bodine	Paychex Ford	42	6	46	Jeff Green	First Union Chevrolet
21	38	3	Dale Earnhardt	GM Goodwrench Service Plus Chevrolet	43	40	75	Rick Mast	Remington Arms Ford
22	29	43	John Andretti	STP Pontiac					

Miller Lite 400

The 400-mile sprints at Roger Penske's immaculate two-mile oval in the Irish Hills of Michigan have traditionally been among the most hotly contested races of the season. The track's wide straights and corners offer the opportunity for drivers to race three and four abreast if they are brave enough, and the crowds have jammed the facility since the initial NASCAR Winston Cup race was held there in 1969. Michigan Speedway is the closest venue for many of the fans in the Midwest, and they are just as knowledgeable and vocal as any NASCAR Winston Cup follower from the Southeast where the sport was born.

By the time the teams unloaded in the Michigan garage area, crews and fans alike had plenty to talk about with all that had occurred during the days since Terry Labonte's Richmond victory. First, of course, was the altercation between Rusty Wallace and Jeff Gordon that sent the rainbow-hued Chevrolet into the wall, ending his night. Steam was coming out of Gordon's ears as he walked the length of pit road after the event, and Rusty shrugged it off as a racing incident. Video replays from a variety of angles were

(Right) Mark Martin flashes a satisfied smile in Michigan's victory lane. After working with his car for three-quarters of the race to make the proper adjustments, Martin took the point from Jeff Gordon and led 39 of the final 50 laps to become the first four-time winner of the season and move to within 28 points of first place in the standings.

(Below) The starting lineup poses for a group picture during pre-race ceremonies with a plaque presented by Michigan Speedway to commemorate NASCAR's 50th Anniversary Celebration.

inconclusive, but the end result remained the same: The bump and slam into the concrete wall had dropped Gordon from the point lead.

Then there was the red flag near the end of the race — an unusual occurrence. Normally, an incident that close to the end of an event will result in the race finishing under caution. Dale Jarrett was in command at the time the red came out, and when the race was restarted with three laps remaining, Jarrett was still the leader. But, with two to go, Terry Labonte rooted Jarrett out of the groove using a bodyslam that would have made Sting proud, and Jarrett responded after the event was over by whacking the sheet metal of the Kellogg's Chevrolet.

(Above) *Kevin Hamlin, talking with car owner Richard Childress, dons a black-and-white Goodwrench uniform for the first time, having swapped crew-chief positions with Larry McReynolds.*

(Left) *Crew chief Ray Evernham keeps the watch on his driver, Jeff Gordon, during practice at Michigan. With their car dialed-in perfectly, Gordon dominated the first half of the event until a caution allowed his competitors to make the necessary adjustments to challenge him.*

(Below Left) *Wally Dallenbach (in white shirt) walks the Budweiser Chevrolet up pit road prior to making his qualifying attempt. Wally, in his first points-race appearance in the car after Randy LaJoie made nine starts for the injured Ricky Craven, qualified eighth fastest and finished 10th in the race.*

Immediately following the Richmond race, team owner Richard Childress made the announcement that he was switching crew chiefs for his two NASCAR Winston Cup efforts, with Larry McReynolds moving to the Lowe's team to work with driver Mike Skinner, and Kevin Hamlin taking over with Dale Earnhardt's Goodwrench team. The expected magic between McReynolds and Earnhardt had not occurred, other than the Daytona 500 victory, and Earnhardt was struggling, now in 12th place in the point standings. He had finished 39th, 25th and 21st in his last three outings, had qualified in the top five just twice, and had an average starting position of 28th, having been forced to use four provisionals already this season. Richard's decision set tongues wagging in the garage area.

Wally Dallenbach was in the Budweiser Chevrolet at Michigan for Hendrick Motorsports, and Morgan Shepherd was enlisted to drive the Circuit City Chevrolet for the Stavola

Rookie Kenny Irwin (28) gives Lake Speed (9) a little push along the frontstretch, hoping to beat Chad Little (97) and Dick Trickle (90) into the first turn. Jeff Green, making his second appearance in the First Union Chevrolet, finds himself in the unenviable position of being surrounded by a pack of Fords.

Brothers. Hut Stricklin found himself employed as the driver of Buzz McCall's Caterpillar Chevrolet, and Terry Labonte found himself in a Chevrolet carrying a paint scheme heralding Kellogg's new Marshmallow Blasted Fruit Loops.

In all, much had occurred during those few days between the conclusion of the night race at Richmond and the opening of practice at Michigan.

As teams prepared for the first round of qualifying, Mayfield and his Mobil 1 team found themselves 45 points ahead of their Penske mates, with Rusty now second in the standings. Gordon had fallen to third, 21 points behind Wallace and 66 out of the lead, while Mark Martin and Dale Jarrett were tied for fourth place, just seven points behind the defending NASCAR Winston Cup champion.

Terry's Richmond victory helped him move to 40 points behind the Martin/Jarrett combo, while younger brother Bobby now trailed Terry by 134. Jeff Burton and Ken Schrader were in hot pursuit of the Interstate Batteries Pontiac driver, with Jimmy Spencer 10th and Bill Elliott 11th in the standings. Earnhardt held 12th place ahead of Michael Waltrip, Bobby Hamilton and Ernie Irvan.

With John Andretti having to switch to a backup car after a practice accident, and with a broken engine fitting that required a change in the maw of the Goodwrench Chevrolet, drivers lined up for the first round of qualifying. When it was over, Ward Burton had claimed his first Bud Pole of the season in his MBNA Pontiac, beating the lap posted by Jarrett. Ironically, Wallace and Gordon would line up side by side in the second row for the start of the Miller Lite 400, and Kevin Lepage claimed the fifth starting position with a strong run in the Chevrolet fielded by LJ Racing.

Ward Burton (22) and Dale Jarrett (88) share the front row as they head for the initial green flag of the race. Burton, who won his first Bud Pole of the year, had a strong run to eighth place to post his second top-10 finish, while Jarrett wound up right where he started - in second.

Bill Elliott, whose record at Michigan rates among the best in the history of the track, put the McDonald's Ford on the outside of the third row, with Martin and Dallenbach claiming the seventh- and eighth-fastest laps ahead of Ricky Rudd and Jeff Burton. Terry Labonte and Darrell Waltrip, in a strong showing with the Pennzoil Chevrolet, barely missed positions in the top 10.

Earnhardt was the final qualifier during the first day, and after his run he let a small smile flit across his face. "Well, I made the race the first day," the seven-time champion said. "I know 25th isn't first, but it's a major improvement over 43rd!"

In the second round of qualifying, Shepherd and the Stavola team figured out the handling of the Circuit City Chevrolet, and aided by cooler, overcast conditions, ripped a lap three-tenths of a second faster than the pole winner to claim the 26th starting spot for the Michigan race. Chad Little, Dick Trickle, Steve Grissom, Robert Pressley, Mike Skinner, Kyle Petty and Hut Stricklin used provisionals to make the field, forcing Derrike Cope, Tony Raines, Dave Marcis and Todd Bodine to the sidelines for the 400-lap race.

When the green flag dropped on the field Sunday afternoon, it took just seven laps for Gordon to fight his way to the point, and once there, he began easing away from the frantic

battle behind him. Lap by lap, tenth of a second by tenth, he began to build his lead, and by the halfway point of the race, it appeared that he was headed for his fourth victory of the season. Seemingly on cruise control in the green-flag race, Gordon moved to more than nine seconds in front of the second-place struggle.

Then the yellow waved. Gordon was ready to lap Jimmy Spencer, Darrell Waltrip and Bobby Labonte when NASCAR officials saw a black piece of debris on the racing surface and called for the first caution of the event. It turned out to be a piece of roll bar padding, which Gordon later said he saw fly out of the window of a car he could not identify. The field headed for pit road, and when the green flag waved again, Gordon's lead had disappeared.

He would lead again in the race, from laps 121-149, but the yellow had allowed his competitors to make changes in their chassis settings and tire air pressures, negating Jeff's advantage.

Martin mounted a charge and raced side by side with the DuPont Chevrolet for more than a lap before finally making the pass stick. Once at the point, Martin was not to be denied. He built his lead car-length by car-length, with a final round of green-flag pit stops looming for everyone. A mistake on tire pressure, a problem with lug nuts, a miscue with the fuel can,

(Right) *Chad Little challenges Kenny Irwin (28) on the inside as he charges through the field from his 37th starting spot, gaining 21 positions during the day to finish 16th.*

(Below) *Irwin brings his car to a halt while the Texaco team begins a pit stop for fresh tires and fuel. Irwin was the top-finishing rookie in the race, taking a 13th-place finish.*

a broken jack — anything could go wrong during that final, frantic scramble on pit road.

But Martin's Valvoline crew performed flawlessly, and Mark regained the lead once the green-flag stops were completed. Behind him, Jarrett and Gordon were having a hammer-and-tongs battle for second place. Gordon was trying everything he could to maintain the position, and Jarrett was determined to get past the defending Series champion and set sail for the Valvoline Ford. Eventually, Jarrett won the battle, but it was too late to try to chase down Martin.

Gordon was forced to settle for third place, while Jeff Burton came home fourth ahead of Mayfield. Elliott equaled his best finish of the season with his sixth place, beating Bobby Labonte, while Ward Burton finished eighth ahead of Joe Nemechek and Dallenbach, who claimed a top 10 in his first points-race in the Budweiser Chevrolet.

Spencer finished 11th, a lap behind, with Waltrip 12th. At a post-race inspection, the cars of Spencer, Waltrip and Bobby Labonte, who were ahead of Gordon when the piece of roll bar padding appeared on the track, were checked thoroughly by NASCAR officials. None of the three were missing any parts of the roll bar padding that is mandatory in the machines.

Under gray skies and with a stiff breeze blowing, the capacity crowd on hand at Michigan stands and cheers as the starting field rumbles under the green flag to begin the Miller Lite 400.

Miller Lite 400

[*RACE #14 • MICHIGAN SPEEDWAY • JUNE 14, 1998*]

Fin. Pos.	Start Pos.	Car #	Driver	Team	Fin. Pos.	Start Pos.	Car #	Driver	Team
1	7	6	Mark Martin	Valvoline/Cummins Ford	23	20	7	Geoff Bodine	Philips Consumer Comm. Ford
2	2	88	Dale Jarrett	Quality Care/Ford Credit Ford	24	38	90	Dick Trickle	Heilig-Meyers Ford
3	4	24	Jeff Gordon	DuPont Automotive Finishes Chevrolet	25	13	9	Lake Speed	Cartoon Network Ford
4	10	99	Jeff Burton	Exide Batteries Ford	26	22	16	Ted Musgrave	PRIMESTAR Ford
5	15	12	Jeremy Mayfield	Mobil 1 Ford	27	18	98	Rich Bickle	Thorn Apple Valley Ford
6	6	94	Bill Elliott	McDonald's Ford	28	34	33	Ken Schrader	Skoal Bandit Chevrolet
7	17	18	Bobby Labonte	Interstate Batteries Pontiac	29	41	31	Mike Skinner	Lowe's Chevrolet
8	1	22	Ward Burton	MBNA America Pontiac	30	31	46	Jeff Green	First Union Chevrolet
9	16	42	Joe Nemechek	BellSouth Chevrolet	31	28	75	Rick Mast	Remington Arms Ford
10	8	50	Wally Dallenbach	Budweiser Chevrolet	32	40	77	Robert Pressley	Jasper Engines Ford
11	30	23	Jimmy Spencer	Winston/No Bull Ford	33	29	11	Brett Bodine	Paychex Ford
12	12	1	Darrell Waltrip	Pennzoil Chevrolet	34	35	78	Gary Bradberry	Pilot Travel Centers Ford
13	14	28	Kenny Irwin	Texaco Havoline Ford	35	27	13	Jerry Nadeau	FirstPlus Financial Ford
14	32	36	Ernie Irvan	Skittles Pontiac	36	42	44	Kyle Petty	Hot Wheels Pontiac
15	25	3	Dale Earnhardt	GM Goodwrench Service Plus Chevrolet	37	9	10	Ricky Rudd	Tide Ford
16	37	97	Chad Little	John Deere Ford	38	19	4	Bobby Hamilton	Kodak MAX Film Chevrolet
17	3	2	Rusty Wallace	Miller Lite Ford	39	23	81	Kenny Wallace	Square D Ford
18	36	40	Sterling Marlin	Coors Light Chevrolet	40	5	91	Kevin Lepage	Boyd's Ultraviolet Chevrolet
19	11	5	Terry Labonte	Kellogg's Corn Flakes Chevrolet	41	39	41	Steve Grissom	Kodiak Chevrolet
20	33	43	John Andretti	STP Pontiac	42	43	96	Hut Stricklin	Caterpillar Chevrolet
21	24	21	Michael Waltrip	CITGO Ford	43	26	8	Morgan Shepherd	Circuit City Chevrolet
22	21	26	Johnny Benson	Cheerios Ford					

Pocono 500

There was no question that the upstart team of the first half of the 1998 season wore blue-and-white uniforms. And it wasn't the Miller Lite team surrounding the No. 2 car in the garage area. Rather, it was the Mobil 1 team that worked on the "12" car.

Jeremy Mayfield had stormed out of the gate at Daytona with a hard-fought third place, but it was a "ho-hum, it's the first race of the season and a restrictor-plate race at that, so anything can happen" kind of conversation in the garage area.

The Kranefuss-Haas team was formed in 1994, with Jeff Gordon and Geoff Brabham each making single appearances for team owners Michael Kranefuss and Carl Haas. The team ran full time in 1995 with John Andretti behind the controls of its Thunderbirds. Andretti remained the driver until mid-season in 1996 when, in a bizarre mid-season driver swap between the Kranefuss-Haas team and Cale Yarborough's effort, Mayfield wound up driving the No. 12 Fords.

Tim Brewer, who had been the crew chief since the team's inception, left during the 1996 season, as well. With Mayfield on board, most expected the team to continue run-

(Right) *Jeremy Mayfield swings the victory towel after emerging from his car in Pocono's winner's circle, celebrating the first win of his NASCAR Winston Cup career in his 125th start. The win was hugely popular for the likeable Kentucky native, and increased his lead in the points to 36 over Jeff Gordon.*

(Below) *Mayfield flashes under the flagstand to take the checkers ahead of Jeff Gordon. In an eight-lap dash from the final restart of the race, Mayfield fought off the challenges of both Gordon and Dale Jarrett, maintaining his lead and posting the win.*

Sterling Marlin (40) hugs the inside through the third turn ahead of a line of challengers led by Kyle Petty (44). Marlin brought the Coors Light Chevrolet home in ninth place to gain his third top-10 finish of the year.

ning in the middle of the pack, but those who felt that way overlooked one important factor.

Kranefuss, the former worldwide racing boss at Ford Motor Company, is an extremely genial man, one who fits well into the NASCAR world despite his German heritage and accent. But under that pleasant smile, extended hand and ever-present cordiality is the competitive steel forged in the blazing cauldrons of international motorsports, including the no-holds-barred world of Formula One and world endurance racing. He was the man behind the rebirth of Ford's domestic racing activities, and he has long been considered one of the best judges of young driving talent.

When he made the decision to leave Ford and form a NASCAR Winston Cup team, he knew the going would be difficult. He also felt that, in Mayfield, he had found the raw talent that could be refined into a winner, much the same as when he had plucked Jeff Gordon from the sprint-car ranks and put him into the Ford pipeline in Bill Davis' NASCAR Busch Series team.

The missing link now, Kranefuss felt, was the team's crew chief. Brewer was a good start, but Kranefuss realized the team needed something different, someone who could work with young talent and lead by example, someone who had been through the fire, understood the sport and the chemistry within a team. Paul Andrews was his man.

Andrews, dissatisfied with the progress of Geoff Bodine's effort, packed his toolbox and moved across town to the Kranefuss team. He had several offers at the end of the 1997 season, but knew long before the public did that Haas was selling his interest in the team to Roger Penske. The new Penske-Kranefuss team would work directly with Wallace and the Miller team this season in a solid alliance that would benefit both organizations. He decided to stay and work with Mayfield.

Andrews? Paul Andrews? Haven't we heard that name before? The answer is a quiet yes.

As Alan Kulwicki's crew chief in Alan's championship season of 1992, Andrews led a group of underdog teammates to one of the most hard-fought and surprising NASCAR Winston Cup championships in history. He had remained with the "7" team after Alan's death, but finally decided it was time to go somewhere else.

The fit couldn't have been more perfect with Mayfield, Kranefuss and Penske. And now, as the teams arrived at Pocono for the first of two stops at Drs. Rose and Joe Mattioli's triangular superspeedway, Mayfield was in command of the NASCAR Winston Cup point standings after the first 14 races of the season. The team had yet to win, but seven top fives and nine top 10s had given Mayfield a 26-point lead over Gordon. Mark Martin was just two points behind the DuPont Chevrolet driver, while Dale Jarrett was mere five points behind Martin. Wallace was fifth in the standings, 35 behind Jarrett, and Terry Labonte found himself sixth, 74 behind Rusty and 142 out of the point lead. Although it was still early in the season, it appeared that the battle for the championship was rounding into form, and those six drivers would contend for the title.

Bobby Labonte was another 94 points behind his brother, while Jeff Burton, Jimmy Spencer and Ken Schrader made up the rest of the top 10, with Bill Elliott 11th, 22 points behind Schrader.

In the days between the events at Michigan and Pocono, Circuit City told the Stavola Brothers it was pulling its sponsorship for the rest of the season, and MBNA informed Bill Davis it would not return in 1999 as the sponsor of the Ward Burton-driven Pontiac team. At Mattei Motorsports, Waddell Wilson was hired as the team's vice president of racing operations in an effort to get Geoff Bodine and the Philips-sponsored team on track.

Weather in the Pocono Mountains is always one of the variables teams have to plan for. It can be hot and sultry, or cold enough to pull out the winter jackets used at Daytona in February and Atlanta in November. And in the past it has been all of that in a single weekend. In first-round qualifying at Pocono for this event, it was sunny and hot with clouds building and then passing overhead, returning the bright sunshine within minutes.

Jeff Gordon caught a cloud. He said afterward that he felt it cooled the track enough to give him a tenth or two during his flat-out qualifying run, and despite slapping the third-turn wall during his lap, the cloud was just enough to give him his

The Cheerios team scrambles to replace four tires on Johnny Benson's Ford during the first caution period, which came just seven laps into the race. There were a total of nine cautions during the day, with four yellow flags appearing in the final 50 laps.

fourth Bud Pole in the last six races. He nipped Wallace by less than two-tenths of a second for the pole, putting the two drivers side by side for the second straight race after their Richmond altercation.

Mayfield and Schrader made up the second row ahead of Ward Burton and Mark Martin, with Joe Nemechek and Ted Musgrave in the fourth row ahead of Dale Jarrett and Chad Little. Dale Earnhardt posted the 11th-fastest lap, the best start for him this season on a non restrictor-plate track. Those taking provisionals to make the field were Johnny Benson, Steve Grissom, Geoff Bodine, Lake Speed, Derrike Cope, Kevin Lepage and Todd Bodine. Dave Marcis and Buckshot Jones, trying to make the field with his own team's Pontiac, did not make the starting field.

Mayfield bolted to the lead on the first lap of Sunday's race, and while most felt it was refreshing to see a new driver at the point, they sat back and waited for Gordon to take over. But Mayfield had the horses under the hood of his Mobile 1 Taurus, and with teammate Wallace forced to pit road for a stop-and-go penalty after jumping the start, Jeremy went about his business of leading the race.

His day was not without drama, however. Mayfield also was assessed a stop-and-go penalty for speeding on pit road, and, along with the rest of the field, was forced to wait out a rain delay that stopped the event for more than an hour.

(Top) *Rusty Wallace (2) beats pole-winner Jeff Gordon (24) into the first turn after taking the initial green flag to start the race, but Rusty immediately was black-flagged for jumping the start.*

(Above) *While trying to catch back up to the leaders after his stop-and-go penalty, the engine lets go in the Miller Ford, sending Wallace to the garage after completing just 13 laps.*

(Below) *Jeff Gordon leads the pack off pit road after wholesale stops on the second caution of the day, which came on lap 35. The work of Gordon's crew allowed him to leave the pits first, taking the lead away from Dale Jarrett, who comes out in second.*

On the last restart of the race, Mayfield held the lead with Gordon and Jarrett right behind, looking through their windshields and measuring the Kentucky native for the final dash to the cash. When the green flag dropped with eight laps to go, everyone expected the "24" and the "88" to blow Mayfield away. But with Andrews in his ear and with his attention totally focused on the job at hand, Mayfield did exactly what he needed to do and brought the Taurus home three car-lengths ahead of Gordon. Jarrett finished third ahead of Jeff Burton, while Mark Martin finished fifth.

Mayfield's victory overshadowed one of the most impressive runs in recent years by the driver he called his hero, Darrell Waltrip. Mayfield hails from Waltrip's hometown of Owensboro, Ky., and Darrell was the driver Jeremy most wanted to emulate when he started racing go-karts early in his career. At Pocono, the two raced door to door in the closing 25 laps, with Darrell fading from the lead to sixth in the final stages of the race on used tires. It was an outstanding performance by Waltrip, who finished ahead of Dallenbach, Earnhardt, Sterling Marlin and Jimmy Spencer.

"Oh, I wish he wouldn't do that!" Not Mayfield's idea of the ideal victory-lane kiss, car owner Michael Kranefuss lays one on his driver after scoring the first win for the team since its inception in 1995. The victory came in Kranefuss' 109th start as a team owner.

Pocono 500

[*RACE #15 • POCONO RACEWAY • JUNE 21, 1998*]

Fin. Pos.	Start Pos.	Car #	Driver	Team	Fin. Pos.	Start Pos.	Car #	Driver	Team
1	3	12	Jeremy Mayfield	Mobil 1 Ford	23	38	41	Steve Grissom	Kodiak Chevrolet
2	1	24	Jeff Gordon	DuPont Automotive Finishes Chevrolet	24	5	22	Ward Burton	MBNA America Pontiac
3	9	88	Dale Jarrett	Quality Care/Ford Credit Ford	25	40	9	Lake Speed	Cartoon Network Ford
4	28	99	Jeff Burton	Exide Batteries Ford	26	41	30	Derrike Cope	Gumout Pontiac
5	6	6	Mark Martin	Valvoline/Cummins Ford	27	21	90	Dick Trickle	Heilig-Meyers Ford
6	18	1	Darrell Waltrip	Pennzoil Chevrolet	28	25	96	Hut Stricklin	Caterpillar Chevrolet
7	14	50	Wally Dallenbach	Budweiser Chevrolet	29	20	31	Mike Skinner	Lowe's Chevrolet
8	11	3	Dale Earnhardt	GM Goodwrench Service Plus Chevrolet	30	10	97	Chad Little	John Deere Ford
9	15	40	Sterling Marlin	Coors Light Chevrolet	31	17	44	Kyle Petty	Hot Wheels Pontiac
10	34	23	Jimmy Spencer	Winston/No Bull Ford	32	27	98	Rich Bickle	Thorn Apple Valley Ford
11	36	28	Kenny Irwin	Texaco Havoline Ford	33	26	46	Jeff Green	First Union Chevrolet
12	12	5	Terry Labonte	Kellogg's Corn Flakes Chevrolet	34	31	36	Ernie Irvan	Skittles Pontiac
13	19	43	John Andretti	STP Pontiac	35	7	42	Joe Nemechek	BellSouth Chevrolet
14	29	21	Michael Waltrip	CITGO Ford	36	37	26	Johnny Benson	Cheerios Ford
15	23	18	Bobby Labonte	Interstate Batteries Pontiac	37	22	94	Bill Elliott	McDonald's Ford
16	32	77	Robert Pressley	Jasper Engines Ford	38	24	75	Rick Mast	Remington Arms Ford
17	8	16	Ted Musgrave	PRIMESTAR Ford	39	13	81	Kenny Wallace	Square D Ford
18	35	11	Brett Bodine	Paychex Ford	40	39	7	Geoff Bodine	Philips Consumer Comm. Ford
19	42	91	Kevin Lepage	Boyd's Ultra Violet Chevrolet	41	33	10	Ricky Rudd	Tide Ford
20	16	4	Bobby Hamilton	Kodak MAX Film Chevrolet	42	2	2	Rusty Wallace	Miller Lite Ford
21	30	13	Jerry Nadeau	FirstPlus Financial Ford	43	4	33	Ken Schrader	Skoal Bandit Chevrolet
22	43	35	Todd Bodine	Tabasco Pontiac					

Save Mart/Kragen 350

Jeremy Mayfield's first career NASCAR Winston Cup victory and the brilliant run by Darrell Waltrip in the Pocono 500 were the television highlights Sunday evening following the rain-delayed event. Only a few people had wandered over to the back of a black transporter where a Chevrolet Monte Carlo was being loaded for the trip back to North Carolina.

Those who made the walk saw Dale Earnhardt with a smile on his face at the conclusion of a race for the first time in a long while. He had finished eighth — still a good distance from the front of the field where he wanted to be, but that eighth-place finish was, in his estimation, another step along the road toward victory.

The crew chief switch made by team owner Richard Childress two races ago had resulted in solid qualifying and race performances by Earnhardt and the Goodwrench team, and it was also clear that Mike Skinner and Larry McReynolds were beginning to work well together at the Lowe's effort. Earnhardt's Pocono finish boosted him to 10th place in the standings, and although he was almost 500 points behind the battle at the

(Right) *The crews of Dale Jarrett and Jeff Gordon go head to head in their battle on pit road. Uncharacteristically, Gordon's Rainbow Warriors had a few problems at Sears Point, forcing Gordon to fight traffic from the middle of the field on his way back to the front.*

(Below) *Rounding the second turn, the middle of the field uses the entire track in a mad scramble that lies in the aftermath of Jerry Nadeau's opening-lap bobble.*

top of the ladder, it was an improvement for the team. One step at a time, crew members seemed to be saying to each other. One step at a time.

Mayfield held a 36-point lead over Gordon as teams arrived in the Sonoma Valley north of San Francisco. He had led the most laps at Pocono, and added 10 markers to his margin in the process. Even so, the Kentuckian knew that he would be at a disadvantage on the Sears Point road course. Gordon, on the other hand, came to his native state ready to do battle at the track just 30 miles from his hometown of Vallejo. He finished second at the road course in 1997, and was third in 1995. The

DuPont team also won at Watkins Glen last August, and Gordon knew he would have a strong mount as he sought to win for the fourth time this season.

Dale Jarrett was third in the standings, 12 points behind Gordon after Pocono and just five points ahead of Mark Martin in the battle for the championship. Terry Labonte, although fifth in the standings, finished 12th at Pocono and now found himself 200 points behind in his endeavor to win a third career NASCAR Winston Cup title. With the season approaching the halfway mark, Labonte knew it was time to get things moving in an upward direction, or he would find himself out of the hunt.

For the first time, competitors used this new high-speed chute that eliminated the famed Carousel and shortened the track by slightly over a half mile. The new section does, however, open a new passing lane and increases visibility for the fans.

(Top) *A veteran of off-road and open-wheel racing, Robby Gordon, returned to the seat of a NASCAR Winston Cup car at Sears Point, taking the wheel of Buzz McCall's CAT-sponsored Chevrolet. Gordon qualified 18th, but suffered suspension problems that put him out of the race in 37th place.*

(Above) *Former NASCAR Craftsman Truck Series Champion and California native Ron Hornaday entered this Chevrolet on the road course and, despite suffering some damage during the event, managed a 14th-place finish after starting 33rd.*

Engine woes at Pocono had cost Rusty Wallace dearly. He was now in sixth place, 16 points behind Terry and 82 points ahead of Bobby Labonte. The Interstate Batteries Pontiac driver was beginning to look over his shoulder, where a hard-charging Jeff Burton now was just seven points behind Bobby, with Jimmy Spencer only four points behind Burton. Bill Elliott was 11th in the standings, just four points behind Earnhardt.

The track the teams faced had seen considerable change since Speedway Motorsports took over just prior to last year's event. Bruton Smith's company built more grandstands, but more importantly, moved hundreds of thousands of yards of dirt, changing the sight-lines and opening up the vistas for those seated on the hillsides around the track. The configuration had changed, as well. Gone was the famed downhill, left-hander known as the Carousel, which provided a daring passing area in the past. Also eliminated with the Carousel was Kulwicki Corner, where Alan had deposited his Hooters Thunderbird on top of a tire barrier, prompting corner workers to create a sign overnight at the site.

Instead, the track's management had built a high-speed semi-banked turn at the end of the top straight, sending competitors directly into the flat right-hander at the far end of the track. For practical purposes, it opened up the track for more "NASCAR-like" competition for both drivers and fans, but it eliminated three of the most challenging turns on the track for competitors. It also chopped just over a half mile off the track, turning what had been a 2.52-mile circuit into a 1.949-mile road course.

Several teams opted to employ "road-course" drivers for the event. Wally Dallenbach was in the Budweiser Chevrolet for the third straight week, and hoped his road-racing background would bring a victory to the Hendrick Motorsports entry. Felix Sabates hired Tommy Kendall to drive the First Union Chevrolet, and Buzz McCall brought Robby Gordon from the CART circuit to drive the Caterpillar Chevrolet. Tom Hubert, shop foreman for Kurt Roehrig's Pennzoil-sponsored NASCAR Craftsman Truck Series team, had a Ford the team had built in its spare time, and he hoped to make the field at Sears Point. Ron Hornaday was in a NAPA-sponsored Chevrolet in hopes of putting on a strong performance in front of the West Coast fans who had watched him make mincemeat of the NASCAR Winston West circuit over the years.

Outside front-row starter Jerry Nadeau got a quick jump on Jeff Gordon after taking the green flag, but couldn't get his Taurus slowed down in time to make the second turn. Nadeau, after a quick trip through the grass, slides high and gathers up his car while the rest of the field bears down on the inside.

(Right) *Mark Martin (6) puts the heat on Bobby Labonte (18) in their chase behind the leaders. Trans-Am champion Tommy Kendall, enlisted to drive the LJ Racing Chevrolet carrying sponsorship from First Union, follows the NASCAR Winston Cup regulars and eventually managed a 16th-place finish.*

(Below Right) *In a flurry of activity aimed at helping their driver make up positions on the track, the DuPont crew heads for the right side in a four-tire stop for Jeff Gordon.*

With so many changes to the track, several teams had decided to take advantage of the California 500 near Los Angeles in May to spend a few days in Northern California at Sears Point in preparation for the 16th race of the season. Among them was Gordon, whose DuPont effort leaves no stones unturned in its quest for championships.

Already knowing what gear selection was needed, and with the basic chassis setup under the DuPont Chevrolet upon their arrival at the track, Gordon and the Rainbow Warriors were left with just the fine-tuning during the practice sessions prior to the first round of qualifying. Although he spun early in the first session, Gordon found his Monte Carlo to be one of the fastest cars on the list at the end of practice. He knew he had a shot at his first career pole on a road course, and he drew an early number for his qualifying run. Gordon put the lap together, and when he returned to pit road, his number was atop the leader board. When Mark Martin reached for too much on his lap and spun, Gordon was home free, winning his fifth Bud Pole in the last seven races.

The surprises were behind him. Jerry Nadeau called on the road-racing background from his early career and slapped the FirstPlus Financial Ford on the outside of the front row ahead of Jarrett and Geoff Bodine. Mayfield was on the inside of the third row with Bobby Hamilton alongside, while Rick Mast, after attending road-racing school, qualified seventh fastest, better than Kyle Petty, Bobby Labonte and Hubert, who was delighted to have won a place in the field, let alone the top 10!

Martin led second-round qualifying with a lap that would have put him fourth fastest, and when the second session was completed, Dallenbach, Dick Trickle, Steve Grissom, Derrike Cope, Kevin Lepage and Bill Elliott were forced to use provisionals. Harry Melling's Cartoon Network team also used a

provisional, and with Lake Speed physically struggling after a practice crash, Butch Gilliland was nominated to drive the Ford. Lepage, signed to a contract to become a Roush driver in the future, parted company with LJ Racing after practice, and Kendall, who failed to make the field in the First Union Chevrolet, became the driver of the "91" car for the race. Dave Marcis, Todd Bodine, Rick Ware and Chris Raudman failed to make the field.

Nadeau, in his eagerness to lead, all but crashed at the top of the hill on the first lap, bunching the field behind him as drivers scrambled to avoid a multi-car accident at the outset of the race. Jerry's miscue enabled Gordon to spurt into the lead, where he stayed for the first 37 laps.

But when Gordon's crew struggled on a pair of pit stops, he found himself unusually deep in the field. A caution when Jeff Burton's Exide Ford punched a hole in the concrete wall after being shunted in a tangle with Jarrett, left Gordon 17th in line when the race went back to green with 38 laps remaining. At the front, Ricky Rudd held sway, with a hard charging Bobby Hamilton nipping at the rear bumper of the Tide Ford.

Hamilton wasn't the only one charging. Gordon had the bit in his teeth and began clicking off cars one by one. Hamilton finally took the lead, moving past Rudd on lap 85. In his ear, Hamilton could hear that Gordon was coming and was told, lap by lap, that Gordon was passing cars and moving ever closer. In front of him, Rudd and Geoff Bodine tangled, moving Jeff to fourth place. He slipped past Mast to take third on lap 92, and four laps later, passed Andretti to

claim the runner-up position. With 16 laps left in the race, he knew he had plenty of time to get Hamilton. On lap 102, Gordon made his move, diving inside Hamilton in the final turn, banging sheet metal between the two Chevrolets. Again, the cars touched before Gordon sprung free, taking the lead after a spectacular charge through half the field.

He eased away and eventually won by nearly 2.5 seconds, leaving Hamilton in second, Andretti in third and Bobby Labonte charging to fourth place. Rusty Wallace and Martin were fifth and sixth, ahead of Sterling Marlin, Mast and Kenny Irwin. Steve Grissom claimed his second top 10 of the season with his 10th-place finish.

Wife Brooke joins Jeff Gordon in his first victory lane celebration on the road course at Sonoma. Although his margin of victory was nearly three seconds, his win from the pole was hard fought, having to slice his way through the field after falling back during pit stops. The victory, his fourth of the year, returned the defending champion to the point lead after falling to third three weeks ago at Richmond.

Save Mart/Kragen 350

[*RACE #16* • *SEARS POINT RACEWAY* • *JUNE 28, 1998*]

Fin. Pos.	Start Pos.	Car #	Driver	Team	Fin. Pos.	Start Pos.	Car #	Driver	Team
1	1	24	Jeff Gordon	DuPont Automotive Finishes Chevrolet	23	35	97	Chad Little	John Deere Ford
2	6	4	Bobby Hamilton	Kodak MAX Film Chevrolet	24	40	9	Butch Gilliland	Cartoon Network Ford
3	21	43	John Andretti	STP Pontiac	25	14	42	Joe Nemechek	BellSouth Chevrolet
4	9	18	Bobby Labonte	Interstate Batteries Pontiac	26	8	44	Kyle Petty	Hot Wheels Pontiac
5	28	2	Rusty Wallace	Miller Lite Ford	27	37	50	Wally Dallenbach	Budweiser Chevrolet
6	26	6	Mark Martin	Valvoline/Cummins Ford	28	15	10	Ricky Rudd	Tide Ford
7	16	40	Sterling Marlin	Coors Light Chevrolet	29	34	23	Jimmy Spencer	Winston/No Bull Ford
8	7	75	Rick Mast	Remington Arms Ford	30	36	77	Robert Pressley	Jasper Engines Ford
9	12	28	Kenny Irwin	Texaco Havoline Ford	31	31	98	Rich Bickle	Thorn Apple Valley Ford
10	39	41	Steve Grissom	Kodiak Chevrolet	32	30	11	Brett Bodine	Paychex Ford
11	17	3	Dale Earnhardt	GM Goodwrench Service Plus Chevrolet	33	38	90	Dick Trickle	Heilig-Meyers Ford
12	43	94	Bill Elliott	McDonald's Ford	34	11	21	Michael Waltrip	CITGO Ford
13	13	1	Darrell Waltrip	Pennzoil Chevrolet	35	4	7	Geoff Bodine	Philips Consumer Comm. Ford
14	33	17	Ron Hornaday	NAPA Auto Parts Chevrolet	36	32	36	Ernie Irvan	Skittles Pontiac
15	3	88	Dale Jarrett	Quality Care/Ford Credit Ford	37	18	96	Robby Gordon	Caterpillar Chevrolet
16	42	91	Tommy Kendall	Boyd's Ultra Violet Chevrolet	38	41	30	Derrike Cope	Gumout Pontiac
17	24	31	Mike Skinner	Lowe's Chevrolet	39	23	99	Jeff Burton	Exide Batteries Ford
18	5	12	Jeremy Mayfield	Mobil 1 Ford	40	25	22	Ward Burton	MBNA America Pontiac
19	20	16	Ted Musgrave	PRIMESTAR Ford	41	10	19	Tom Hubert	Bradford White Ford
20	27	33	Ken Schrader	Skoal Bandit Chevrolet	42	29	5	Terry Labonte	Kellogg's Corn Flakes Chevrolet
21	19	26	Johnny Benson	Cheerios Ford	43	2	13	Jerry Nadeau	FirstPlus Financial Ford
22	22	81	Kenny Wallace	Square D Ford					

Jiffy Lube 300

For every team and fan, the July Fourth Pepsi 400 at Daytona International Speedway held the promise of being one of the most spectacular events of the season, with the first-ever night race at The Beach scheduled to be run during prime time on CBS.

Those plans became part of history, however, when wildfires raged through the forests of northern Central Florida, threatening Daytona Beach, overrunning huge portions of Volusia County and, in some cases, creeping to within shouting distance of the track. The Speedway's management postponed the Pepsi 400 at the last minute and turned the track, its facilities, hospitality tents and stockpiled food and beverages into shelters and meals for those forced from their homes by the fires. Firefighters and emergency personnel on hand for the event turned their skills and equipment to battle the raging blazes while thick clouds of smoke blotted the sun from the sky for days.

The Pepsi 400 was rescheduled for October 17, previously the open date between the Winston 500 at Talladega and the Dura Lube 500 at Phoenix. The rescheduling meant that teams would run back-to-back restrictor-plate races in the fall, but more im-

(Right) Defending race champion Jeff Burton (99) pulls to the inside after taking the lead from Jeff Gordon and prepares to set sail, leaving all challengers in his wake. After taking the lead for the first time on lap 80, Burton laid waste to the rest of the field, eventually winning by more than seven seconds over teammate Mark Martin.

(Below) Kyle Petty's Hot Wheels crew rips through a late-race pit stop, helping their driver stay among the leaders in the race. Petty, after a strong qualifying run to start sixth, finished in eighth place and picked up his first top-10 finish of the season.

portantly to every team, it meant that beginning with the second Pocono race, there would be no break in the schedule for 16 consecutive races.

Jeff Gordon thus had an extra week to savor his fourth victory of the season, his first at Sears Point in front of many friends from his childhood days, and a return to the top of the point standings. Jeremy Mayfield's 18th place at Sears Point dropped him from first place to second, 40 points behind Gordon, and allowed Mark Martin to close to within 12 points of second place. Dale Jarrett was fourth in the standings, just 22 points behind Martin as teams arrived at the Bahre family's New Hampshire International Speedway.

Rusty Wallace was now fifth in points, 136 behind Jarrett and more than 175 behind Gordon. Wallace knew that if he were to be a factor in the championship chase he would need to turn things around beginning with the Jiffy Lube 300. Bobby Labonte was now sixth in points, 77 behind Rusty and 25 ahead of his slumping older brother. Jeff Burton remained eighth in points, 96 behind Terry after the wall-banging episode at Sears Point, while Jimmy Spencer was ninth, 74 points behind Burton. Dale Earnhardt was now 10th in the standings, 33 behind Spencer and 46 points ahead of Bill Elliott.

Things were changing in the Tabasco Pontiacs. The team had hired Loy Allen to drive at Daytona, but when the Pepsi 400 was postponed, the immediate word was that Todd would be in the car at New Hampshire. A couple of days later, he was released from the team and Gary Bradberry was named to drive at New Hampshire, although no one knew who would drive the car after the Jiffy Lube 300. Ted Musgrave's situation at Roush Racing began to have some clarity when Ted was told he would be out of the PRIMESTAR Ford after the upcoming race at Watkins Glen, and would be replaced by new Roush signee Kevin Lepage. At LJ racing, where Lepage had shown his wares during the first half of the season, musical driver seats began. Andy Hillenburg was named as the driver for the New Hampshire event.

(Top) *Ricky Craven receives congratulations from Hendrick teammate Jeff Gordon following Craven's run to the pole in the Budweiser Chevrolet. Craven's pole was also a moral victory, coming in his return to the car after sitting out the last 12 events.*

(Left) *Darrell Waltrip (1) gets some heat from his car owner, Dale Earnhardt (3), with Ken Schrader (33) pressuring Earnhardt from behind. Waltrip gave the Pennzoil Monte Carlo another good ride, finishing in 13th place. Schrader, usually strong at New Hampshire, scored a top-10 finish after posting the fastest lap in second-round qualifying.*

Pit road is a flurry of activity during an early-race caution that brought nearly the entire field in for service. The Jiffy Lube 300 had six cautions for a total of 40 laps.

In the Budweiser Chevrolet camp, there was renewed enthusiasm. After being sidelined since March with what doctors said was post-concussion syndrome, Ricky Craven returned to his spot behind the wheel at what many consider to be his "home" track. The Maine native drew the final number in qualifying and was just happy to be back in his car. With qualifying delayed both before and during by rain, Craven's stomach was full of double-parked butterflies as his turn approached.

Kyle Petty stopped alongside Craven after the third-generation driver made his qualifying run and told Ricky that the track was slick. He suggested that if Craven spun his tires on his way off of pit road, the resulting heat would help the Goodyears grip better during the lap around the track. Craven heeded the advice, lit his tires up like John Force's champion NHRA dragster, and when he completed his run, he had knocked Hendrick Motorsports teammate Gordon from the pole.

Craven, as well as Gordon, was delighted with the fact that the Budweiser Chevrolet had claimed the Bud Pole and a place in the Bud Shootout in 1999. It marked Craven's second straight NASCAR Winston Cup pole at New Hampshire, and was the fifth of his career at the one-mile oval. Ricky's lap was almost a tenth of a second faster than Gordon's, and it pushed Jarrett and a strong-running Chad Little into the second row. Jeff Burton and Petty made up the third row ahead of Ernie Irvan and Darrell Waltrip, who had an excellent qualifying run in the Pennzoil Chevrolet. Rusty Wallace and Bobby Labonte claimed the fifth row ahead of Bradberry and Mike Skinner.

During the second round of qualifying, cooler temperatures prevailed, leading every team not already in the field to toss aside its first-round time and make another charge at the oval. Ken Schrader, who was fourth fastest during the first round but had his time disallowed when a piece of lead weight fell from his car during the lap, led the second round and turned the third-fastest lap of the two qualifying sessions. It was only

good for 26th place on the grid. Bobby Hamilton, Michael Waltrip, Johnny Benson, Steve Grissom, Robert Pressley and Geoff Bodine took provisionals to make the field, as did the LJ Racing Chevrolet. In practice, both Morgan Shepherd and Hillenburg drove the Monte Carlo, with Shepherd selected to qualify the car. Once the session was completed, Hillenburg was named as the starting driver for Sunday's race. Dave Marcis was the only driver who failed to make the race.

Early in the Jiffy Lube 300, it appeared that Gordon was ready to add another victory to his total. He immediately whipped the DuPont Chevrolet into the lead, and by the 50th lap, was well over a second clear of the battle behind him.

Then his challenger emerged.

Jeff Burton had spent the first 50 laps of the race learning that his Exide Ford would go anywhere he wanted it to go on the track, and would do it with great speed and precision. The Taurus was hooked up, and Burton carved his way past Jarrett into second place and set sail for Gordon. Lap after lap, he closed on the rainbow-hued machine, and by lap 80, he used the aero push of his car to loosen Gordon up enough to dive under the Monte Carlo driver.

Within two laps, he had pulled clear of Gordon by a second, only to see the margin disappear during the first round of green-flag pit stops. He regained the lead after the green-flag stops were completed, and for the remainder of the event, Burton's Ford was the car at which everyone would aim.

By the time the event concluded, Burton had turned in a dominant performance, leading nearly two-thirds of the race en route to his first victory of the season. He remarked after the event that the team members had put their collective heads together following the May California race, and he felt the corner had been turned. For five of the previous six races, the team had posted top-10 performances, and he credited much of the progress to crew chief Frank Stoddard, who received his initial NASCAR Winston Cup victory with Burton's Jiffy Lube 300 triumph.

Roush teammate Mark Martin came home second, more than seven seconds behind, while Gordon took third ahead of Rusty Wallace. Mike Skinner turned in an impressive performance, finishing fifth and underscoring the fact that car owner Richard Childress' decision to swap crew chiefs on the "3" and the "31" teams was bearing fruit. John Andretti beat Jarrett for sixth place, while Petty and Schrader finished eighth and ninth. Kenny Wallace claimed his fourth top-10 finish of the season, taking 10th ahead of Bobby Labonte, Jeff Green and Darrell Waltrip, the remaining cars on the lead lap at the conclusion of the race.

Ricky Craven (50) hugs the inside and jumps to an opening-lap lead over outside pole-winner Jeff Gordon. Craven led 13 of the first 14 laps before Gordon took over and led the next 66 circuits. Craven fell back with handling problems and finished 29th, five laps down. (Inset) Rick Mast backs the Remington Ford into the first-turn wall, bringing out the race's fourth caution on lap 116. Mast was able to continue in the race after repairs were made and managed to finish 32nd, nine laps down to the leaders.

Jeff Burton initiates mayhem at New Hampshire while celebrating his fourth career victory, deciding to shower everyone present in victory lane including his team owner, Jack Roush. Moments later, Roush wrestled the champagne away and returned the favor on Burton.

Jiffy Lube 300

[RACE #17 • NEW HAMPSHIRE INTERNATIONAL SPEEDWAY • JULY 12, 1998]

Fin. Pos.	Start Pos.	Car #	Driver	Team	Fin. Pos.	Start Pos.	Car #	Driver	Team
1	5	99	Jeff Burton	Exide Batteries Ford	23	34	22	Ward Burton	MBNA America Pontiac
2	15	6	Mark Martin	Valvoline/Cummins Ford	24	38	21	Michael Waltrip	CITGO Ford
3	2	24	Jeff Gordon	DuPont Automotive Finishes Chevrolet	25	23	23	Jimmy Spencer	Winston/No Bull Ford
4	9	2	Rusty Wallace	Miller Lite Ford	26	13	94	Bill Elliott	McDonald's Ford
5	12	31	Mike Skinner	Lowe's Chevrolet	27	22	13	Jerry Nadeau	FirstPlus Financial Ford
6	16	43	John Andretti	STP Pontiac	28	19	11	Brett Bodine	Paychex Ford
7	3	88	Dale Jarrett	Quality Care/Ford Credit Ford	29	1	50	Ricky Craven	Budweiser Chevrolet
8	6	44	Kyle Petty	Hot Wheels Pontiac	30	30	12	Jeremy Mayfield	Mobil 1 Ford
9	26	33	Ken Schrader	Skoal Bandit Chevrolet	31	43	91	Andy Hillenburg	Little Joe's Auto Chevrolet
10	17	81	Kenny Wallace	Square D Ford	32	18	75	Rick Mast	Remington Arms Ford
11	10	18	Bobby Labonte	Interstate Batteries Pontiac	33	25	28	Kenny Irwin	Texaco/Havoline Ford
12	28	46	Jeff Green	First Union Chevrolet	34	41	77	Robert Pressley	Jasper Engines Ford
13	8	1	Darrell Waltrip	Pennzoil Chevrolet	35	35	40	Sterling Marlin	Coors Light Chevrolet
14	32	5	Terry Labonte	Kellogg's Corn Flakes Chevrolet	36	21	42	Joe Nemechek	BellSouth Chevrolet
15	37	4	Bobby Hamilton	Kodak MAX Film Chevrolet	37	42	7	Geoff Bodine	Philips Consumer Comm. Ford
16	29	30	Derrike Cope	Gumout Pontiac	38	31	98	Rich Bickle	Thorn Apple Valley Ford
17	14	90	Dick Trickle	Heilig-Meyers Ford	39	27	16	Ted Musgrave	PRIMESTAR Ford
18	20	3	Dale Earnhardt	GM Goodwrench Service Plus Chevrolet	40	11	35	Gary Bradberry	Tabasco Pontiac
19	33	10	Ricky Rudd	Tide Ford	41	36	9	Lake Speed	Cartoon Network Ford
20	7	36	Ernie Irvan	Skittles Pontiac	42	24	96	Hut Stricklin	Caterpillar Chevrolet
21	39	26	Johnny Benson	Betty Crocker Ford	43	40	41	Steve Grissom	Kodiak Chevrolet
22	4	97	Chad Little	John Deere Ford					

Pennsylvania 500

Just five weeks earlier, Jeremy Mayfield left Pocono Raceway's 2.5-mile triangular superspeedway toting his first NASCAR Winston Cup race winner's trophy. He headed off into the sunset at the top of the point standings as the crews prepared to make the trip from Pennsylvania back to their shops to prepare for the Sears Point event.

How quickly things change.

Returning to Pocono, Mayfield found himself fourth in points, where he landed following the New Hampshire event. Jeremy and his Mobil 1 teammates now found themselves with considerable ground to make up. Jeff Gordon's victory at Sears Point and his third place at New Hampshire had vaulted him back to the top of the ladder, where he enjoyed a 52-point lead over Mark Martin. Dale Jarrett, third in the point standings, trailed Martin by 46 points, while Mayfield was 39 behind Jarrett and 137 behind Gordon. Mayfield and the Mobil 1 team had lost more than 175 points in the two races since his inaugural NASCAR Winston Cup victory.

Rusty Wallace held fifth in the points, 83 behind his teammate, while Bobby Labonte

(Right) *John Hunter Nemechek takes some time from his busy schedule to point out a few things to his father, Joe. Dad, usually strong at Pocono, is happy to oblige his son before starting the Pennsylvania 500 from fifth place on the grid.*

(Below) *Pole-winner Ward Burton rolls off the line to begin pacing the field for the start of the race. Burton would have a very strong run, staying among the leaders and in contention for the win, until he was involved in a multi-car accident on lap 172 that ended his day in the garage.*

Jeremy Mayfield discusses last-minute preparations with a crew member prior to the start of the race. Mayfield, returning to the site of his initial win just three races ago, was hoping to turn things around after falling from the point lead, but his bad luck continued with an accident that dropped him from second in the race to an 18th-place finish.

and older brother Terry were all but out of the point race this early in the season. Bobby trailed Gordon by 340, while Terry was another 32 behind, with New Hampshire winner Jeff Burton eighth ahead of Jimmy Spencer and Dale Earnhardt. Ken Schrader and Bill Elliott continued their battle for 11th place, with Bobby Hamilton, John Andretti and Michael Waltrip completing the top 15.

With Daytona's postponed Pepsi 400 inserted into the schedule's open date on October 17th, the Pennsylvania 500 became the first of 16 consecutive races that would determine the 1998 NASCAR Winston Cup champion. Clearly, the titlist would be determined by a combination of factors: on-track driving performance, crew work on pit road and in the garage area, a touch of luck — good or bad — and, perhaps most importantly in the stretch run, the organization and preparation of the team in the shop. With 16 consecutive races on every type of track — superspeedways, road courses and short tracks — the contenders and the pretenders would be sorted quickly.

In years past, teams had fought their way through 10 and 11 consecutive race strings in the torrid stretch run that ultimately determines the champion. But a 16-race battle was one that had not been faced before.

The pressure of running well at the NASCAR Winston Cup level continued to show its face within teams in the garage area. By the time the crew members were ready for the first practice session at Pocono, Lake Speed had resigned from Harry Melling's Cartoon Network Ford team. He had suffered rib and chest injuries in a practice accident at Sears Point, and further aggravated those injuries with another crash at New Hampshire and yet again during a testing mishap at Indianapolis.

Ward Burton (22) and Dale Earnhardt (3) engage in battle at the front of the pack after a restart on lap 120. The two drivers swapped the lead several times before Burton pulled away, leaving Earnhardt to fight with Gordon for second place.

Feeling as though he could not properly uphold his end of the bargain as a driver, and needing time to rest and rehabilitate, Lake resigned from the seat of the "9" car.

Jerry Nadeau, second to Kenny Irwin in the rookie point standings, was released from the FirstPlus Financial Ford team of Bill Elliott and Dan Marino. Wally Dallenbach would replace him for the Pocono and Indianapolis events, and Nadeau wound up behind the controls of the Taurus vacated by Lake

ing it from Darrell, and had spent several months preparing for the team to return to the sport. Jimmy Horton, a Pennsylvania favorite, had been hired to drive the Tabasco Pontiac for the Pocono event, but ultimately would not make the field.

For the longest time during Bud Pole qualifying, it looked like Gordon would add another award to the five he had al-

Rounding the third turn, Jeff Gordon prepares to take the green flag for a restart with Darrell Waltrip crowding him on the inside, ready to get a jump on the leader and make up a lap lost earlier in the race. Waltrip was able to regain his lap and pull around to a 13th-place finish in his last race driving the Pennzoil Chevrolet.

Speed at Pocono. Morgan Shepherd was in the LJ Racing Chevrolet for the weekend, while Hut Stricklin was announced as the Caterpillar Chevrolet driver for the remainder of the season after being released by the Stavola Brothers back in May. The Stavolas had announced they would team with NASCAR Busch Series star Buckshot Jones for at least nine of the season's remaining races.

The Pennsylvania 500 would be the final race for Darrell Waltrip in a Pennzoil uniform. With Steve Park ready to return to the wheel of the Pennzoil Chevrolet, Waltrip prepared to say farewell to Dale Earnhardt's team, where he had several outstanding runs that rejuvenated his morale and his career. Darrell would move back to Tim Beverly's cars. Beverly had temporarily closed the doors at his team's shop after purchas-

ready won during the season. He knocked Rusty Wallace from the top of the leader board, and with the session winding down, just two drivers remained with the opportunity to beat Gordon's time. Ward Burton, who had the fastest time at Charlotte until Gordon ran late in the session and claimed the pole, had his opportunity at Pocono. He did exactly what he needed to do, and whistled the silver MBNA Pontiac to a lap more than a tenth of a second faster than Gordon's time to win his second Bud Pole of the season.

Wallace and Bobby Labonte shared the second row, with Joe Nemechek and Mark Martin right behind. Shepherd had a solid qualifying run in the LJ Racing Chevrolet to claim the seventh-fastest lap, while Kenny Wallace, Earnhardt and Michael Waltrip made up the remainder of the top 10, just acing Jarrett and Ted Musgrave.

(Above) *Crew members work frantically during a caution to repair an apparent oil leak while a NASCAR official inspects the underside of the Quality Care Ford. The crew was able to send Dale Jarrett back to the action without losing a lap, helping Jarrett post a top-five finish in the race.*

(Right) *Mike Skinner limps toward pit road in the Lowe's Chevrolet after slapping the third-turn wall on lap 143. The resulting caution allowed Gordon's crew to give him a lead that he would keep for the rest of the race.*

Dick Trickle was the fastest of the drivers who ran in the second qualifying session, while Bobby Hamilton, Brett Bodine, Robert Pressley, Geoff Bodine, Derrike Cope, Dallenbach and Rich Bickle were the provisional starters. In addition to Horton, Gary Bradberry and Randy MacDonald failed to make the field.

At New Hampshire the previous weekend, Jeff Burton dominated the action. At Pocono, it was Gordon's turn. Other than one portion of the race — some 20 laps when Ward Burton and Dale Earnhardt gave Gordon all he could handle — the defending Series champion was easily the class of the field. He led three times for 164 of the event's 200 laps, but it was the 20 laps when he fought with Earnhardt and Ward Burton that electrified the crowd.

Earnhardt was on form, and he and Gordon simply fought tooth and nail for position. Burton was the race leader after a caution flag, with Gordon tucked in behind and Earnhardt right on Jeff's rear bumper. Within two laps, Earnhardt had dispatched both Gordon and Burton, but Burton eventually regained the point after fighting with Gordon for 14 laps for second place. That put Dale and Jeff into a brilliant duel, and for eight laps the two battled until Mike Skinner hit the wall, bringing out another yellow flag. The Rainbow Warriors put Gordon in the lead after the pit stops, and for the remainder of the race Jeff was never again challenged.

Mark Martin and Jeff Burton were left to battle for the scraps, with Martin beating his Roush teammate for second place. Bobby Labonte came home in fourth place ahead of Jarrett, while Rusty Wallace claimed the sixth spot just ahead of Earnhardt. Ken Schrader, Ernie Irvan and Michael Waltrip took eighth, ninth and 10th in the 200-lap race, with Waltrip posting the best finish for the CITGO Ford since a ninth place in April at Texas Motor Speedway. It was Irvan's first top 10 since the May Dover event.

For Earnhardt and the Goodwrench crew, the Pocono finish was vastly encouraging. He had led the event, and had battled with Gordon to the delight of the immense crowd on hand for the race. He was in the battle for the victory throughout the race until the nose of his Monte Carlo was banged up during a restart, taking the needed aerodynamic edge off the black Chevrolet. He knew he had a car good enough for at least the runner-up position, but his seventh place helped him move to ninth in the overall NASCAR Winston Cup point standings.

Jeff Gordon (24) sails into the first turn ahead of (in order) Rusty Wallace, Bobby Labonte, Mark Martin and Ward Burton, after taking the lead from Wallace in the opening laps of the race. Gordon had by far the dominant car in the race, leading the most laps during the day including the final 55 to become the first five-time winner of the season.

Pennsylvania 500

[*RACE #18 • POCONO RACEWAY • JULY 26, 1998*]

Fin. Pos.	Start Pos.	Car #	Driver	Team		Fin. Pos.	Start Pos.	Car #	Driver	Team
1	2	24	Jeff Gordon	DuPont Automotive Finishes Chevrolet		23	41	30	Derrike Cope	Gumout Pontiac
2	6	6	Mark Martin	Valvoline/Cummins Ford		24	15	46	Jeff Green	First Union Chevrolet
3	19	99	Jeff Burton	Exide Batteries Ford		25	42	13	Wally Dallenbach	FirstPlus Financial Ford
4	4	18	Bobby Labonte	Interstate Batteries Pontiac		26	34	9	Jerry Nadeau	Cartoon Network Ford
5	11	88	Dale Jarrett	Quality Care/Ford Credit Ford		27	32	96	Hut Stricklin	Caterpillar Chevrolet
6	3	2	Rusty Wallace	Miller Lite Ford		28	43	98	Rich Bickle	Thorn Apple Valley Ford
7	9	3	Dale Earnhardt	GM Goodwrench Service Plus Chevrolet		29	26	90	Dick Trickle	Heilig-Meyers Ford
8	17	33	Ken Schrader	Skoal Bandit Chevrolet		30	28	31	Mike Skinner	Lowe's Chevrolet
9	16	36	Ernie Irvan	Skittles Pontiac		31	22	5	Terry Labonte	Kellogg's Corn Flakes Chevrolet
10	10	21	Michael Waltrip	CITGO Ford		32	39	77	Robert Pressley	Jasper Engines Ford
11	31	40	Sterling Marlin	Coors Light Chevrolet		33	36	26	Johnny Benson	Cheerios Ford
12	18	43	John Andretti	STP Pontiac		34	1	22	Ward Burton	MBNA America Pontiac
13	27	1	Darrell Waltrip	Pennzoil Chevrolet		35	8	81	Kenny Wallace	Square D Ford
14	40	7	Geoff Bodine	Philips Consumer Comm. Ford		36	33	94	Bill Elliott	McDonald's Ford
15	12	16	Ted Musgrave	PRIMESTAR Ford		37	30	75	Rick Mast	Remington Arms Ford
16	23	97	Chad Little	John Deere Ford		38	38	11	Brett Bodine	Paychex Ford
17	5	42	Joe Nemechek	BellSouth Chevrolet		39	20	41	Steve Grissom	Kodiak Chevrolet
18	29	12	Jeremy Mayfield	Mobil 1 Ford		40	7	91	Morgan Shepherd	Little Joe's Auto Chevrolet
19	21	23	Jimmy Spencer	Winston/No Bull Ford		41	24	50	Ricky Craven	Budweiser Chevrolet
20	37	4	Bobby Hamilton	Kodak MAX Film Chevrolet		42	13	10	Ricky Rudd	Tide Ford
21	35	44	Kyle Petty	Hot Wheels Pontiac		43	25	71	Dave Marcis	Realtree Camouflage Chevrolet
22	14	28	Kenny Irwin	Texaco/Havoline Ford						

August 1, 1998

Brickyard 400

Despite the fact that he had a 62-point lead over Mark Martin and was 128 markers clear of third-place Dale Jarrett, Jeff Gordon knew he had little breathing room as teams arrived at Indianapolis Motor Speedway.

The Brickyard 400 held its own special place in the mind of every competitor. The four drivers who had won the race in the past — Jeff Gordon, Dale Earnhardt, Dale Jarrett and defending Brickyard 400 champion Ricky Rudd — knew first hand the thrill of standing in the famed winner's circle at Indy, accepting the silver brick trophy emblematic of triumph in one of the most prestigious events on the entire schedule. For the others who had tried, but had yet to experience that thrill, there was added importance to the fifth Brickyard 400. For drivers, it was a special place to compete and win, and in the five years the race had been held, the mystique of The Brickyard had not faded one iota. For team sponsors, the event's high visibility made it a special race for hospitality and entertainment purposes.

Because of the importance of the event, teams would bring the very best equipment

(Right) *With the Indianapolis skyline as a backdrop, Jeff Gordon tracks down Dale Earnhardt off the third turn, vying for the lead at the three-quarter mark in the race. Gordon finally slipped past the black Chevrolet on lap 127, and led the rest of the way to score the huge Brickyard payday.*

(Below) *The front row of Ernie Irvan and Dale Jarrett lead the starting field across the start/finish line and under the green flag to begin the fifth running of the Brickyard 400. Irvan was the fastest qualifier for the second straight year, this time notching the first pole for the MB2 Skittles team.*

The Quality Care crew pushes Dale Jarrett's car, out of gas just past the midway point in the race. Jarrett, after coasting for nearly an entire lap, had come to a rest at the pit entrance, forcing the team to run the length of pit road to retrieve the car, then push it all the way back to their pit stall. The entire crew was exhausted after the run and subsequent pit stop, including jackman Mike Ford (below) who catches his breath while resting on the pit wall.

in their shops, and most of them had already spent several days testing at the 2.5-mile oval, fine-tuning chassis and suspension settings. Anything could happen at The Brickyard and Gordon knew it. His point lead could evaporate in a single instant on the track.

For Gordon, Jarrett, Martin, Rusty Wallace and Bobby Labonte, the Brickyard 400 held even more importance. They had finished in the top five positions in the Coca-Cola 600 at Charlotte in May, and thus were eligible for Winston's No Bull 5 $1-million bonus at stake at Indianapolis. If any of the five eligible drivers won the Brickyard 400, they would also pocket a cool $1 million from Winston.

From Winston's standpoint, this No Bull 5 race couldn't have come at a better time. Not only was the battle for the NASCAR Winston Cup championship heating up in the stretch run for the title, but the drivers in contention for the Brickyard bonus were also atop the point standings. Behind Gordon, Martin and Jarrett, Jeremy Mayfield was the only interloper. He was fourth in the standings, but was continuing to fall away from the battle. After finishing 18th at Pocono, he had now slid to 213 points behind

Gordon. Penske teammate Wallace, however, was 37 points behind Mayfield, and Bobby Labonte continued his move toward the front, trailing Rusty by 97 points. To have the No Bull 5 decided by five of the top six drivers in the point standings was an added promotional plus for Series sponsor Winston.

Jeff Burton and Terry Labonte held seventh and eighth in the standings entering The Brickyard, while Earnhardt had moved to ninth after his strong performance at Pocono. Jimmy Spencer held 10th by just eight points from Ken Schrader, while Bill Elliott and Bobby Hamilton were locked in a battle for 12th, just three points apart. The struggle for 14th place was even tighter, with John Andretti holding a two-point margin over Michael Waltrip.

Steve Park, recovered from his Atlanta injuries, was back behind the wheel of the Pennzoil Chevrolet from Dale Earnhardt's shop, while Darrell Waltrip moved to the seat of the Tyler Jet team in its first outing since Darrell sold the team earlier in the season. That in itself was a story, with Tim Beverly, who had purchased Darrell's team, also purchasing part of the ISM effort

(Above) *The STP crew rushes to repair John Andretti's STP Pontiac, which sits on pit road after picking up some debris on the track. Andretti, who qualified ninth and had a competitive run to this point, managed to stay on the lead lap and pull out a seventh-place finish.*

(Right) *For defending Brickyard 400 champion Ricky Rudd, an already tough day came to an abrupt end just two laps from the finish when his Tide Ford was involved in an accident that also included Kyle Petty, Jeff Green and Robert Pressley.*

(Below) *Veteran car owners Bud Moore (left) and Junie Donlavey talk in the garage along Gasoline Alley. Moore had returned to NASCAR Winston Cup racing with a Ford for driver Loy Allen, but the car failed to qualify for the race.*

that had fielded the Tabasco-sponsored Pontiacs during the year. The purchase and subsequent merger of the two teams resulted in a Tabasco-sponsored Chevrolet for Waltrip to drive at Indy, and prompted folks at the McIlhenny Company, the makers of Tabasco, to rethink their sponsorship program. It was the beginning of a story that would continue through much of the remaining season.

Martin had a new paint scheme on his Valvoline Ford for the Brickyard race, and Buckshot Jones was on hand with the Stavola Brothers, with sponsorship from Realtree camouflage. Bud Moore's team, which had not competed in more than a year, had Loy Allen behind the wheel with Rescue Oil sponsorship. The First Union folks had changed brands on the "46" car, with Jeff Green set to drive for the rest of the season, now behind the wheel of the Money Store Chevrolet.

In encouraging news, Paychex announced it would continue its sponsorship of Brett Bodine's team for the 1999 season. Kyle Petty had also disclosed that his team would be moving to Level Cross at the conclusion of the season, taking up residence at Petty Enterprises so both pe2 and Petty Enterprises could campaign as a real two-car team in 1999. Kyle said his Hot Wheels sponsorship was set for the '99 season and that discussions were ongoing with STP regarding the continuation of their sponsorship on John Andretti's Pontiac.

One look at the weather forecast underscored the importance of first-round qualifying. Rain delayed the start of the session for some four hours, but when the surface was dry enough to begin, the track was cool, providing extra grip and traction. The weather forecast for the following day was for increased temperatures, meaning the surface would heat up, providing less grip and adhesion. It would be important for every driver to get his best lap in on the first day if he wanted to ensure himself of a spot on the grid for the Brickyard 400.

When the session was finally completed, Ernie Irvan's No. 36 shown atop the scoring pylon. He had claimed his second straight Brickyard 400 pole after starting on the inside of the front row last year in Robert Yates' Texaco Ford. This time it came with the Skittles Pontiac, giving crew chief Ryan Pemberton and the MB2 Motorsports team their first Bud Pole Award, Dale Jarrett, who was just the tiniest bit off line through the first corner, had to settle for the outside of the front row, while Gordon was third fastest, just a tick better than Kenny Irwin. The third row was comprised of surprisingly fast Jeff Green, with Ricky Craven on his right, while Martin and Terry Labonte were seventh and eighth fastest in the session. John Andretti and Bobby Labonte put their Pontiacs in the fifth row, making three Tin Indians in the top 10 qualifiers.

(Left) Mark Martin (6) muscles his way inside Rich Bickle while working toward the front of the field. Martin's car was very strong, particularly in the late going, but a miscue on a pit stop dropped him out of the top 10 and forced him to fight through traffic in his pursuit of Gordon.

(Below) Jeff Gordon (24) leads on a restart in the closing laps with Mark Martin following in second place and Ken Schrader (33), a lap down, on the inside followed by Dale Jarrett. Schrader and Jarrett were able to maintain the inside and squeeze past Gordon, allowing both drivers to finish on the lead lap, but Martin would not be able to catch the DuPont Chevrolet before the final yellow that ended the race under caution.

Steve Park was the final first-day qualifier, and with temperatures increased some 50 degrees on the track surface for the second round, drivers and teams were faced with the difficult decision to either run again or stand on their first-round times. Only seven drivers ran, and none of them were able to race their way into the field. Derrike Cope, the fastest of those who ran, bumped the third-turn wall and finished 43rd on the time sheet, costing him a chance to make the race.

Provisionals went to Bill Elliott, Ted Musgrave, Johnny Benson, Brett Bodine, Jerry Nadeau, Rick Mast and Darrell Waltrip, while Hut Stricklin, Robby Gordon, Gary Bradberry, Randy MacDonald and Loy Allen joined Cope on the sidelines.

At times, things seem to be preordained. That might be the simplest explanation of this year's running of the Brickyard 400. On a day when many challengers had problems, Gordon simply maintained. Rusty Wallace had a flat tire early, taking him from contention. Steve Park crashed with a cut tire, Irvan struggled with a balky chassis, Mayfield cut a tire while running in second place, and Jarrett ran out of fuel on pit road, needing to be pushed to his pit.

For Gordon, the event came down to the final 40 laps, when the Rainbow Warriors sent him back onto the track with four new tires during the sixth caution period. He was fourth in line and needed just four laps to pass the three drivers — Earnhardt, Mike Skinner and

Sterling Marlin — who had taken just two tires during the stop. Behind him, Martin, who was making up for a poor pit stop that left him 11th on the restart, was charging through the field and eventually moved into second place with just 16 laps left in the race. Mark was 2.5 seconds behind, and Gordon's win looked assured.

Three yellow flags in the final 10 laps, including the last one with two laps remaining that brought the event to a close under caution, kept Martin from mounting a frantic assault on the DuPont Chevrolet. Mark had to settle for second place, dawdling around the track behind the pace car and Gordon's Monte Carlo.

Gordon's win etched his name in the record book as the first driver to win two Brickyard 400s. By also claiming the No Bull 5 $1-million bonus from Winston, his take from the event totaled more than $1.6 million — the richest total for a race winner in the history of the sport.

Bobby Labonte claimed third place ahead of Skinner and Earnhardt, while Irvan was sixth and Andretti seventh. Rusty Wallace came home eighth ahead of Terry Labonte, with Schrader rounding out the top 10.

A triumphant Jeff Gordon claims his second silver brick in Indy's Victory Circle, with an enthusiastic crowd cheering from the nearby grandstands. Gordon, who became the first two-time winner of the event, was raised in nearby Pittsboro, Indiana, making his victory that much more popular among the fans.

Brickyard 400

[*RACE #19 • INDIANAPOLIS MOTOR SPEEDWAY • AUGUST 1, 1998*]

Fin. Pos.	Start Pos.	Car #	Driver	Team	Fin. Pos.	Start Pos.	Car #	Driver	Team
1	3	24	Jeff Gordon	DuPont Automotive Finishes Chevrolet	23	26	41	Steve Grissom	Kodiak Chevrolet
2	7	6	Mark Martin	Valvoline/Cummins Ford	24	17	42	Joe Nemechek	BellSouth Chevrolet
3	10	18	Bobby Labonte	Interstate Batteries Pontiac	25	39	26	Johnny Benson	Cheerios Ford
4	16	31	Mike Skinner	Lowe's Chevrolet	26	41	9	Jerry Nadeau	Cartoon Network Ford
5	28	3	Dale Earnhardt	GM Goodwrench Service Plus Chevrolet	27	15	00	Buckshot Jones	Realtree Extra Chevrolet
6	1	36	Ernie Irvan	Skittles Pontiac	28	35	97	Chad Little	John Deere Ford
7	9	43	John Andretti	STP Pontiac	29	20	77	Robert Pressley	Jasper Engines Ford
8	14	2	Rusty Wallace	Miller Lite Ford	30	5	46	Jeff Green	The Money Store Chevrolet
9	8	5	Terry Labonte	Kellogg's Corn Flakes Chevrolet	31	27	10	Ricky Rudd	Tide Ford
10	19	33	Ken Schrader	Skoal Bandit Chevrolet	32	21	23	Jimmy Spencer	Winston/No Bull Ford
11	11	40	Sterling Marlin	Coors Light Chevrolet	33	40	11	Brett Bodine	Paychex Ford
12	37	94	Bill Elliott	McDonald's Ford	34	30	22	Ward Burton	MBNA America Pontiac
13	43	35	Darrell Waltrip	Tabasco Chevrolet	35	25	1	Steve Park	Pennzoil Chevrolet
14	33	44	Kyle Petty	Hot Wheels Pontiac	36	34	99	Jeff Burton	Exide Batteries Ford
15	36	91	Morgan Shepherd	Little Joe's Auto Chevrolet	37	13	7	Geoff Bodine	Philips Consumer Comm. Ford
16	2	88	Dale Jarrett	Quality Care/Ford Credit Ford	38	4	28	Kenny Irwin	Texaco Havoline Ford
17	6	50	Ricky Craven	Budweiser Chevrolet	39	31	98	Rich Bickle	Thorn Apple Valley Ford
18	18	90	Dick Trickle	Heilig-Meyers Ford	40	22	13	Wally Dallenbach	FirstPlus Financial Ford
19	38	16	Ted Musgrave	PRIMESTAR Ford	41	32	71	Dave Marcis	Realtree Camouflage Chevrolet
20	24	4	Bobby Hamilton	Kodak MAX Film Chevrolet	42	12	12	Jeremy Mayfield	Mobil 1 Ford
21	29	21	Michael Waltrip	CITGO Ford	43	23	81	Kenny Wallace	Square D Ford
22	42	75	Rick Mast	Remington Arms Ford					

The Bud at the Glen

With three victories in the last four races, including successive wins at Pocono and The Brickyard, Jeff Gordon's trip to Upstate New York's lovely Finger Lakes region was a pleasant one. His margin in the standings had expanded to 72 points after his rich, $1.6-million victory at Indianapolis, and his DuPont Chevrolet team had high hopes of sweeping both road-course events on the schedule.

Gordon claimed his first career road-course win here at The Glen last August and now had the chance to win three consecutive events on the winding tracks that provided additional challenges to the teams. The Monte Carlo that Jeff wheeled to victory in Sonoma in May had been relegated to the role of a "spare" after the team had taken all it had learned at Sears Point and incorporated it into a new chassis for The Glen. As far as Gordon was concerned, the new car had just as good a chance to win as the old one.

Martin clearly remained in the hunt for the NASCAR Winston Cup championship. His Valvoline team continued to provide him with sturdy Ford Tauruses at every event, and Mark was driving with brio and panache. His skills behind the wheel had brought

(Right) *Jeff Gordon celebrates a day of threes at Watkins Glen: It was his third consecutive win on a road course dating back to this event one year ago, and was also his third straight win following victories at Pocono and Indianapolis during the previous two weekends.*

(Below) *Jeff Gordon leads the field, already sorted into single file, through the esses in the opening laps. After winning his sixth pole of the season, Gordon led the first 28 laps in his early domination of the event.*

him a record fourth career and third consecutive IROC championship the previous weekend at Indianapolis, and he was grimly chasing Gordon for the Cup title he had yet to win in his career.

Unlike Gordon and Martin, Indianapolis had not treated Dale Jarrett, Rusty Wallace and Jeremy Mayfield kindly. Jarrett finished 16th and now found himself 121 points behind Martin and 193 behind Gordon in the quest for the Cup. Wallace finished eighth and moved to fourth in the standings,

but now was nearly 300 points behind Gordon. Mayfield's slide continued at Indy, where he finished 42nd after a cut tire cost him the second place he was holding at the time. He slipped to fifth in the points and now sat 361 behind Gordon.

Bobby Labonte found himself just six points behind Mayfield, while older brother Terry was now in seventh place in the standings, but 151 behind his sibling. Jeff Burton, after finishing 36th at Indianapolis, slipped to eighth place, 20 behind Terry and just 87 ahead of Dale Earnhardt. Ken Schrader, 72 points behind Earnhardt, moved into the top 10, displacing Jimmy Spencer, while John Andretti moved to 12th place in the standings, three points ahead of Bill Elliott, 30 points ahead of Bobby Hamilton and 48 points ahead of Ernie Irvan.

While a smiling Gordon arrived at The Glen with bulging pockets from the richest single-event payoff in the history of the sport, the dregs of the controversial finish at Indianapolis were still swirling around the garage area. At Richmond earlier in the season, the event was red-flagged to clean up debris, creating a green-flag dash to victory in the final laps. At Indianapolis, the race finished under caution, keeping Martin from mounting a final charge at the victory. NASCAR officials

(Left) *NASCAR President Bill France takes the opportunity to join Jeff Gordon on the parade lap during driver introductions, experiencing first hand the fans' "enthusiasm" for the defending champion.* (Below Left) *Veteran road racer and NASCAR Craftsman Truck Series competitor Boris Said stands ready to take the wheel of the Winston Ford for the ailing Jimmy Spencer. Said qualified the car for Spencer, posting the fifth-fastest lap, then took over at the race's first caution and drove to a 20th-place finish on the lead lap.* (Below) *Ron Fellows (left) was named to drive the Caterpillar Chevrolet at The Glen, and rewarded car owner Buzz McCall (right) by qualifying on the outside pole, the highest starting spot ever for the team. Unfortunately, the car suffered rear-end problems in the race while running second to Gordon, dropping Fellows to a disappointing 42nd-place finish.*

Terry Labonte's Kellogg's Chevrolet is equipped to funnel extra air inside the car, routed through this intricate system to provide cooling for the rear end and brakes — essential to performing well on the road course.

Ted Musgrave was in the awkward position of trying to make his last outing with the Roush Racing PRIMESTAR team a successful one. Although he would remain under contract to Jack Roush for the remainder of the season, Musgrave had been cut loose by the organization and would be replaced by Kevin Lepage after The Bud at the Glen.

explained the differences between the final laps of the two events, and reiterated that the individual circumstances of each event would continue to determine the calls from the tower.

Spencer found himself struggling from injuries suffered in his late-race collision with the concrete wall at Indianapolis, prompting car owner Travis Carter to enroll the services of road racer and NASCAR Craftsman Truck Series competitor Boris Said to assist Spencer at The Glen. Said wasn't the only specialist employed for the road-course event, with Ron Fellows named to drive the Caterpillar Chevrolet and Tom Hulbert slotted into the FirstPlus Financial Ford. Tom Kendall was in The Money Store Chevrolet for car owner Felix Sabates, and Ted Christopher took over for Dick Trickle in the Heilig-Meyers Ford.

Bobby Hamilton found himself working with a new crew chief at The Glen, with Charley Pressley joining the Kodak effort after leaving Larry Hedrick's Kodiak team. Tim Brewer was named as the new crew chief for the "41" car, where Steve Grissom was still trying to get untracked.

Steve Park (1) chases Mike Skinner through the esses at Watkins Glen. Using a brilliant fuel strategy engineered by Larry McReynolds, Skinner took over the point with 20 laps left in the race when the leaders pitted under green, but couldn't fend off the charges of Gordon and Martin, finishing a career-best third.

One of the drivers expected to challenge strongly during the first round of qualifying was Bill Elliott, who was listed second fastest during practice. But he hit a curb at the far end of the course, went off the track and did not complete his lap. That left the pole wide open, and Gordon wasted no time in grabbing his sixth Bud Pole of the season. His biggest competition came from Fellows, who had the CAT Chevrolet cooking, but in the end, Gordon had claimed the inside front-row starting position by just over two-tenths of a second.

Ricky Rudd and Jeff Burton took care of the second row, and Said clipped off an excellent lap in the Winston Ford to claim the inside of the third row, where he found Rusty Wallace alongside for the start of the race. Spencer would start the car, but Said would get into it at the first opportunity during the race. Martin was right in the hunt, claiming the inside of the fourth row, while Jerry Nadeau continued to turn in sparkling qualifying performances in the Cartoon Network Ford for Harry Melling's team, claiming the eighth starting

Gordon threatened to make a mockery of the race in the first half, leading handily with no one apparently able to challenge the newest road-racing edition of the DuPont Monte Carlo. But after the field made its final round of green-flag stops, Gordon found himself trailing Mark Martin and Rusty Wallace in the middle of the field. Mike Skinner, who had made his final stop under caution and hoped to stretch the fuel mileage into his first career NASCAR Winston Cup victory, was at the point with 20 to go.

Kenny Wallace's Square D crew provides new tires and fuel under green. Watkins Glen offers a special challenge to pit crews as the only track on the tour where the cars pit with the right side toward the wall.

spot. Irvan and Dale Jarrett made up the fifth row, just beating Geoff Bodine and Terry Labonte for the final top-10 positions. Bobby Labonte, Chad Little, Dick Trickle, Steve Grissom, Morgan Shepherd, Derrike Cope and Darrell Waltrip were the provisional starters, while Dave Marcis, Brian Cunningham and Larry Gunselman failed to make the field.

Sunday, under brilliant blue skies, an enormous throng of spectators had the opportunity to answer a multiple-choice question:

"Choose the answer that best describes Jeff Gordon's drive in the final 20 laps of The Bud at the Glen:

A. Spectacular
B. Scintillating
C. Incredible
D. All of the above"

It looked easy enough. Skinner, with sufficient fuel to run to the victory, was more than 15 seconds ahead, with Martin, Wallace and Gordon eighth, ninth and 10th, respectively, after flailing their way through some slower cars following their green-flag stops.

The three continued their torrid pace, running a second to 1.5 seconds faster than Skinner. With 11 to go, Wallace moved past Martin and led the trio of challengers to third, fourth and fifth places.

Headed down the backstretch, the three dispatched Kyle Petty, then Gordon saw an opportunity and made a daring move to pass Martin entering the "Inner Loop" and emerge third behind Wallace. Skinner was still eight seconds clear of the furious charge with nine laps to go, and Gordon made another gutsy move, shouldering Wallace from second as the two

drivers entered the next-to-last turn on the track. He was now second, and had Skinner in his sights.

The Lowe's Chevrolet driver looked in the mirror, saw Gordon in second place and began to lose his rhythm on the track, trying to win his first race. And as he did, Jeff reeled him in, lap after lap, second by second. With four laps to go, Gordon sailed past Skinner heading down the backstretch and rolled into the lead, immediately stretching it from car-lengths into seconds. Martin found his way past Wallace to move to third place at almost the same moment that Gordon took the lead, and on the final lap, Mark dove inside Skinner to claim second place.

They ended that way, with Gordon winning his third on the trot, and his third straight road-course event. Martin finished second for the fourth straight race, while Skinner scored the best finish of his Cup career with his third place. Wallace was fourth, barely ahead of Dale Jarrett, while Petty finished sixth ahead of Sterling Marlin, Andretti, Johnny Benson and Bobby Labonte.

Mark Martin (6) and Rusty Wallace (2) battle furiously in the waning laps of the race. Wallace worked past Martin in their charge toward the front, but Mark got the position back in the final laps to finish second for the fourth straight time. Wallace did not have time to overtake Skinner and wound up fourth in the race.

The Bud at the Glen

[*RACE #20 • WATKINS GLEN INTERNATIONAL • AUGUST 9, 1998*]

Fin. Pos.	Start Pos.	Car #	Driver	Team	Fin. Pos.	Start Pos.	Car #	Driver	Team
1	1	24	Jeff Gordon	DuPont Automotive Finishes Chevrolet	23	4	99	Jeff Burton	Exide Batteries Ford
2	7	6	Mark Martin	Valvoline/Cummins Ford	24	16	33	Ken Schrader	Skoal Bandit Chevrolet
3	23	31	Mike Skinner	Lowe's Chevrolet	25	43	35	Darrell Waltrip	Tabasco Chevrolet
4	6	2	Rusty Wallace	Miller Lite Ford	26	19	81	Kenny Wallace	Square D Ford
5	10	88	Dale Jarrett	Quality Care/Ford Credit Ford	27	27	94	Bill Elliott	McDonald's Ford
6	33	44	Kyle Petty	Hot Wheels Pontiac	28	28	21	Michael Waltrip	CITGO Ford
7	13	40	Sterling Marlin	Coors Light Chevrolet	29	24	77	Robert Pressley	Jasper Engines Ford
8	17	43	John Andretti	STP Pontiac	30	35	75	Rick Mast	Remington Arms Ford
9	21	26	Johnny Benson	Cheerios Ford	31	31	12	Jeremy Mayfield	Mobil 1 Ford
10	37	18	Bobby Labonte	Interstate Batteries Pontiac	32	11	7	Geoff Bodine	Philips Consumer Comm. Ford
11	22	3	Dale Earnhardt	GM Goodwrench Service Plus Chevrolet	33	9	36	Ernie Irvan	Skittles Pontiac
12	26	42	Joe Nemechek	BellSouth Chevrolet	34	36	11	Brett Bodine	Paychex Ford
13	14	4	Bobby Hamilton	Kodak MAX Film Chevrolet	35	32	50	Ricky Craven	Budweiser Chevrolet
14	3	10	Ricky Rudd	Tide Ford	36	20	13	Tom Hubert	First Plus Financial Ford
15	8	9	Jerry Nadeau	Cartoon Network Ford	37	18	28	Kenny Irwin	Texaco/Havoline Ford
16	38	97	Chad Little	John Deere Ford	38	40	41	Steve Grissom	Kodiak Chevrolet
17	30	46	Tommy Kendall	The Money Store Chevrolet	39	42	30	Derrike Cope	Gumout Pontiac
18	34	1	Steve Park	Pennzoil Chevrolet	40	12	5	Terry Labonte	Kellogg's Corn Flakes Chevrolet
19	15	16	Ted Musgrave	PRIMESTAR Ford	41	39	90	Dick Trickle	Heilig-Meyers Ford
20	5	23	Jimmy Spencer	Winston/No Bull Ford	42	2	96	Ron Fellows	Caterpillar Chevrolet
21	25	22	Ward Burton	MBNA America Pontiac	43	41	91	Morgan Shepherd	Little Joe's Auto Chevrolet
22	29	98	Rich Bickle	Thorn Apply Valley Ford					

Pepsi 400 Presented by DeVilbiss

Mark Martin slid through the window of his Valvoline Ford at The Glen after finishing second for the fourth straight race. He was worn from the grind at The Glen, from pouring every iota of himself into the unsuccessful chase of Jeff Gordon in the event. He was pleased with the second place but frustrated with finishing in the runner-up slot for the fourth straight race and losing another 10 points in his battle with Gordon for the NASCAR Winston Cup championship.

He exited the track and headed home to Florida in his jet, arriving at his fly-in community near Daytona Beach. Within minutes of his arrival, the chase, the second place, the battle for victory, the quest for the championship, the accolades and the weariness all meant nothing.

He was told that his father, Julian, his stepmother, Shelley, and his stepsister, Sarah, 11, all had perished when his father's private plane crashed in Nevada, where the family had been visiting friends. The news was devastating to Mark, who had learned to drive while sitting on his dad's lap, steering the car while his dad worked the pedals long be-

(Right) *Ernie Irvan, accompanied by daughter Jordan and wife Kim, wears a bright smile after capturing the first Michigan pole of his career. The pole was his second in the last three events, and came at the track that has seen the highs and lows of his racing career.*

(Below) *Bill Elliott (94), John Andretti (43) and Jeff Burton (99) use up Michigan's roomy frontstretch to race three wide in front of the huge crowd on hand in the Irish Hills. Elliott, usually strong at Michigan, suffered a blown engine in the race, while Andretti continued his recent string of good runs by finishing ninth.*

(Above) *Ted Musgrave discusses the setup on Bud Moore's Ford with veteran crew chief Joey Knuckles. Musgrave took the wheel for the one-off effort in his first race since being released from Jack Roush's PRIMESTAR team.*

(Below) *Bobby Labonte, with a pole and two career wins at Michigan, prepares to start outside of pole-winner Ernie Irvan, giving Pontiac a front-row sweep for the second time this season. Bobby stayed among the leaders for most of the day to finish right where he started, in second.*

fore Mark's legs would reach the floorboard. Throughout Mark's career, Julian Martin had been there, helping build the first dirt-track car mark drove at age 13 until he graduated to the NASCAR Winston Cup level with Jack Roush's team. Now Julian, Shelly and Sarah were gone.

After flying to Arkansas to attend to the details, Mark arrived at Michigan emotionally drained. He knew that his dad would have wanted him to compete at Michigan, and Mark was hopeful he would be able pay tribute to his father and his family by making a trip to victory lane at the conclusion of the 400-mile event.

Gordon, one of Martin's good friends away from the track, found himself in the position to score a fourth straight victory. If he could accomplish that with the DuPont Chevrolet, he would tie a modern-day record first set by Cale Yarborough in 1976, and then matched by Darrell Waltrip in 1981, Dale Earnhardt in 1987, Harry Gant in 1991, Bill Elliott in 1992 and Martin in 1993. Although he hoped to tie the mark, he also clearly understood Mark's motivation for winning in the Irish Hills.

With Gordon leading the most laps at The Glen, Martin now found himself 82 points behind, while Dale Jarrett's fighting fifth place at The Glen kept his title hopes alive. He was 141 behind Martin, while Rusty Wallace now trailed Jarrett by 90 markers. Bobby Labonte edged past the slumping Jeremy Mayfield into fifth place on the point ladder, while Jeff Burton and Terry Labonte swapped spots after The Glen with Burton moving to seventh. Dale Earnhardt was now just 20 points behind Terry, while Ken Schrader remained in 10th place, 42 ahead of Jimmy Spencer. John Andretti was 26 behind Spencer and 48 ahead of Bobby Hamilton, while Bill Elliott was 48 points ahead of Michael Waltrip in their battle for the 14th position.

Spencer, after driving just eight laps at The Glen before turning the Winston Ford over to Boris Said, talked with car owner Travis Carter immediately after the event. He took himself out of the Winston Ford for the Michigan and Bristol races, giving his injuries

(Above) *Jeff Burton and crew chief Frank Stoddard find a quiet place along pit road to discuss their strategy for the Michigan event. Burton barely made the field during first-round qualifying by turning the 25th-fastest lap, but with the help of fine work by his crew on pit road, worked his way to a fifth-place finish.*

time to heal properly, and Travis asked ARCA star Frank Kimmel to drive the red-and-white Ford at Michigan.

The Michigan race marked the debut of Kevin Lepage behind the wheel of the PRIMESTAR Ford from the Roush stable, and Ted Musgrave was enlisted to drive Bud Moore's Rescue Oil Taurus at Michigan. Ricky Craven, after a discussion with John Hendrick, resigned from the Budweiser Chevrolet after three races back in the car following his recovery from injuries earlier in the year. Craven said he hoped to land another ride, and was replaced for the rest of the season by Wally Dallenbach. In the FirstPlus Financial camp, Dennis Setzer was the choice for the Michigan race as team owners Bill Elliott and Dan Marino continued to work toward finding a permanent driver for the 1999 season.

Jeff Gordon comes to a smoking halt on pit road as his Rainbow Warriors fly over pit wall to service the Chevrolet. A crucial pit stop under caution in the late going allowed the team to make a final adjustment on the car, giving Gordon what he needed to take the lead for the first time in the race with just eight laps remaining.

As if media members did not have enough to choose from for their weekend stories, Ernie Irvan decided to add a delicious dollop to the mix when he ripped around Gene Haskett's two-mile oval to plant the Skittles Pontiac on the pole for the second time in the last three races. Irvan's well-chronicled return to prominence in the sport, including his superiority at the track where he nearly lost his life, provided even more grist for the hungry reporters.

Irvan's run provided the first Michigan pole of his career, and he needed every tick of the stopwatch to claim it. Fellow Pontiac driver Bobby Labonte whistled to the outside of the front row, giving the Tin Indian forces their second front row of the season, matching the March Atlanta race, where John Andretti and Todd Bodine accomplished the same feat.

Gordon claimed the third-fastest lap, barely beating Dale Jarrett's run, while Martin and Joe Nemechek grabbed the third row. Dallenbach, who returned from a bird-hunting trip in Bolivia to learn on ESPN's sports ticker that he would be driving the Budweiser car (courtesy of a deal negotiated by his wife Robin), was seventh fastest ahead of Mayfield.

Ward Burton and Ken Schrader made up the fifth row for the start of the race ahead of Rusty Wallace and Rich Bickle. Dale Earnhardt, Johnny Benson, Kevin Lepage, Chad Little, Brett Bodine, Steve Grissom and Darrell Waltrip used provisionals, while Dave Marcis and Gary Bradberry failed to make the field. They weren't alone. Hut Stricklin, back in the

Caterpillar Chevrolet for Michigan, and Kenny Wallace also failed to make the field.

The Pepsi 400 at Michigan began as a two-car battle between Irvan and Martin, with both showing they had the horses for the courses this day. The two fought at the front of the field, with the Valvoline Ford and the Skittles Pontiac trading the lead back and forth throughout the first 55 laps. After being forced to pit road for fuel, they returned to the track and picked up right where they left off, and were soon joined by Jarrett in his Robert Yates Ford. The torrid battle continued.

Martin finally returned to the point, leading until another set of green-flag stops. During Martin's stop, the Valvoline team slapped four sticker Goodyear Eagles on the Ford, and although he returned to the track five seconds behind Irvan, he was able to roll up behind the Pontiac. Ernie had gambled with just two tires during his stop, and once Mark caught him and put him away, the red-white-and-blue Ford began to open the distance.

Martin built his lead, and with just over 20 laps left in the race, Mark was nearly two seconds clear of the field. He appeared headed for the victory, and with Gordon struggling in sixth place, Martin also looked ready to close the point gap.

Then the engine let go in Ward Burton's Pontiac, bringing out the third caution of the race and erasing Martin's lead. On pit road, the Rainbow Warriors were waiting in hopes of tightening up the loose DuPont Chevrolet. They ripped off the right-side tires, took a spring rubber out of the right rear and slapped two new Goodyears on the car, sending Gordon back to the track after a nine-second stop, third in line for the restart behind Martin and Jarrett. Suddenly, the rainbow-hued Chevrolet came to life.

With 11 laps remaining, Gordon sliced past Jarrett to take second, and began to stalk Martin. Two laps later, he challenged Mark for the lead, with Martin blocking his every move. Gordon finally found a way past the Taurus driver in fourth turn and began to pull away, leaving Martin to battle with Jarrett and Bobby Labonte for second place. Labonte prevailed to finish in the runner-up slot, while Jarrett came home third, dropping Martin to fourth place.

Jeff Burton, who was penalized on his final pit stop for loose lug nuts and running over the air hose, finished fifth ahead of Irvan, while Mayfield stopped his string of poor finishes with a seventh place. Dallenbach was eighth with a solid run in the Budweiser Chevrolet ahead of John Andretti and Chad Little.

Derrike Cope tries to guide the damaged Gumout Pontiac toward pit road after he and Morgan Shepherd got together in the fourth turn following a restart on lap seven. Buckshot Jones (00), making his third start of the season, whips past on the track.

With four straight victories, Gordon had tied the modern-era record, while Martin, spent after his effort, was forced to wait for another chance to win one in honor of his dad and family.

Pepsi 400 Presented by DeVilbiss

[*RACE #21 • MICHIGAN SPEEDWAY • AUGUST 16, 1998*]

Fin. Pos.	Start Pos.	Car #	Driver	Team	Fin. Pos.	Start Pos.	Car #	Driver	Team
1	3	24	Jeff Gordon	DuPont Automotive Finishes Chevrolet	23	11	2	Rusty Wallace	Miller Lite Ford
2	2	18	Bobby Labonte	Interstate Batteries Pontiac	24	33	77	Robert Pressley	Jasper Engines Ford
3	4	88	Dale Jarrett	Quality Care/Ford Credit Ford	25	43	35	Darrell Waltrip	Tabasco Pontiac
4	5	6	Mark Martin	Valvoline/Cummins Ford	26	31	75	Rick Mast	Remington Arms Ford
5	25	99	Jeff Burton	Exide Batteries Ford	27	34	00	Buckshot Jones	Realtree Chevrolet
6	1	36	Ernie Irvan	Skittles Pontiac	28	12	98	Rich Bickle	Thorn Apple Valley Ford
7	8	12	Jeremy Mayfield	Mobil 1 Ford	29	27	44	Kyle Petty	Hot Wheels Pontiac
8	7	50	Wally Dallenbach	Budweiser Chevrolet	30	22	9	Jerry Nadeau	Cartoon Network Ford
9	15	43	John Andretti	STP Pontiac	31	36	23	Frank Kimmel	Winston/No Bull Ford
10	40	97	Chad Little	John Deere Ford	32	41	11	Brett Bodine	Paychex Ford
11	21	1	Steve Park	Pennzoil Chevrolet	33	42	41	Steve Grissom	Kodiak Chevrolet
12	6	42	Joe Nemechek	BellSouth Chevrolet	34	38	26	Johnny Benson	Cheerios Ford
13	19	10	Ricky Rudd	Tide Ford	35	28	13	Dennis Setzer	FirstPlus Financial Ford
14	10	33	Ken Schrader	Skoal Bandit Chevrolet	36	13	5	Terry Labonte	Kellogg's Corn Flakes Chevrolet
15	20	40	Sterling Marlin	Coors Light Chevrolet	37	9	22	Ward Burton	MBNA America Pontiac
16	18	28	Kenny Irwin	Texaco/Havoline Ford	38	29	90	Dick Trickle	Heilig-Meyers Ford
17	39	16	Kevin Lepage	PRIMESTAR Ford	39	32	15	Ted Musgrave	Rescue Engine Formula Ford
18	37	3	Dale Earnhardt	GM Goodwrench Service Plus Chevrolet	40	17	94	Bill Elliott	McDonald's Ford
19	26	31	Mike Skinner	Lowe's Chevrolet	41	35	46	Jeff Green	The Money Store Chevrolet
20	24	4	Bobby Hamilton	Kodak MAX Film Chevrolet	42	16	91	Morgan Shepherd	Little Joe's Auto Chevrolet
21	23	7	Geoff Bodine	Philips Consumer Comm. Ford	43	14	30	Derrike Cope	Gumout Pontiac
22	30	21	Michael Waltrip	CITGO Ford					

Goody's Headache Powder 500

Jeff Gordon's record-tying, come-from-behind victory at Michigan set tongues wagging in the garage area following the 200-lapper in the Irish Hills. Four in a row, including the high-dollar Indianapolis victory, put him in very classy company. But it was the manner in which the victory came that startled many.

Gordon had been well beaten on the track, not a factor in the race until the final pit stop, when his car took off like a rocket ship. It was a totally different type of victory than the one at The Glen, for example, when he drove a brilliant race and took a couple of exceedingly calculated moves in his passes of Mark Martin and Rusty Wallace that eventually put him in position for the win.

Instead, at Michigan, his crew on pit road provided the work when the chips needed to be cashed, and Gordon rolled on to the victory.

Now, he was in a position to put his name on a clean sheet of paper in the NASCAR Winston Cup record book. If he could win the Goody's Headache Powder 500 at Bristol, he would be the first driver in the sport's modern era to win five consecutive races. The

(Right) *Physically and emotionally drained, Mark Martin sits in his car after rolling into Bristol's victory lane to celebrate his fifth win of the season. Kneeling beside the car is Max Helton of Motor Racing Outreach, who had been helping Mark through his recent personal tragedy.*

(Below) *The cars of Rusty Wallace (2), Ted Musgrave (filling in for Jimmy Spencer) and Jeff Gordon (24) are dwarfed in front of Bristol's main grandstand. An enthusiastic crowd in excess of 130,000 encircled the half-mile oval to witness perhaps the most exciting event on the schedule each year.*

heat was on, and Gordon knew that his chances were not the best. He had been good at Bristol in the past — in fact, he had won the last four consecutive spring races at the half-mile oval. Despite those four triumphs, Gordon also knew that winning at Bristol is exceedingly difficult. The high banks and high speeds leave no margin for error, and it is very easy for a driver to either make a mistake or be collected in another driver's error. Winning the fifth straight would not be an easy task at any track, but having the venue be Bristol made it exponentially more difficult.

Mark Martin's fourth place at Michigan increased Gordon's margin over the Valvoline Ford driver, and Mark now found himself 97 points behind. Dale Jarrett remained third in the standings, 136 behind Martin and 166 ahead of Rusty Wallace, while Bobby Labonte continued his march toward the upper rungs of the ladder, now just 24 points behind Wallace. Jeremy Mayfield found himself 87 behind Bobby and 144 clear of Jeff Burton. The Michigan results enabled Dale Earnhardt to move ahead of Terry Labonte into eighth place in the standings, where Earnhardt trailed Burton by 92 points. Ken Schrader maintained 10th place in the standings, 70 behind Labonte and 51 ahead of a charging John Andretti, who climbed a notch to 11th place at Michigan. Bobby Hamilton and Ernie Irvan moved ahead of the idled Jimmy Spencer, while Sterling Marlin moved past his good friend Michael Waltrip to take over 15th place.

Race-leader Jeremy Mayfield (12) leads Mark Martin (6) toward the green flag for a restart with Johnny Benson (26) leading the lap-down cars. Mayfield led three times during the race, but it was Martin who took over the event, leading the final 180 laps on the way to victory.

NASCAR Busch Series regular Elliott Sadler (92), driving for the Diamond Ridge team in his second start of the season, chases Sterling Marlin down the straightaway. Sadler, who hopes to move up to Cup full time next season, did a very respectable job, staying out of trouble to finish 24th in the race.

kept the crowd on the edge of their seats. Earnhardt bumped, ground, pushed and fought his way toward the front, and in the end, was challenging Jarrett for fifth place. The run through the field reminded many of his halcyon years as the premier short-track driver in the sport, and it gave the fathers in the stands and in their living rooms the opportunity to point and show their sons and daughters saying, "See? Isn't he the best? And you said he couldn't drive that way anymore. That's why I'm an Earnhardt fan!"

For Gordon, his hopes for a fifth straight victory ended with a Monte Carlo that clearly didn't have the right stuff for this Saturday night. Jeff failed to lead a lap, but still brought home a fifth-place finish.

When it was over, Mark Martin was climbing through the window of his car, raising his arms to the crowd and his face

to the skies. It was a week late, but he had won handily and claimed the victory he wanted to dedicate to his father, stepmother and stepsister. He had hoped to do it at Michigan, but instead, the dedication came after a dominating performance in Thunder Valley.

It seemed appropriate to many in the audience. Martin is — sinews, muscles, bones and chromosomes — a racer. He is one of the most intense and dedicated people in the sport, a man who thinks of nothing but racing and how to improve himself, his team and his cars. The Bristol victory, in front of an audience that is one of the sport's most dedicated and appreciative, was a perfect ending to Mark's night of triumph.

Goody's Headache Powder 500

[RACE #22 • BRISTOL MOTOR SPEEDWAY • AUGUST 22, 1998]

Fin. Pos.	Start Pos.	Car #	Driver	Team	Fin. Pos.	Start Pos.	Car #	Driver	Team
1	4	6	Mark Martin	Valvoline/Cummins Ford	23	35	97	Chad Little	John Deere Ford
2	19	99	Jeff Burton	Exide Batteries Ford	24	32	92	Elliott Sadler	Phillips 66/Trop Artic Chevrolet
3	1	2	Rusty Wallace	Miller Lite Ford	25	10	18	Bobby Labonte	Interstate Batteries Pontiac
4	9	88	Dale Jarrett	Quality Care/Ford Credit Ford	26	16	11	Brett Bodine	Paychex Ford
5	7	24	Jeff Gordon	DuPont Automotive Finishes Chevrolet	27	43	35	Darrell Waltrip	Tabasco Pontiac
6	30	3	Dale Earnhardt	GM Goodwrench Service Plus Chevrolet	28	38	50	Wally Dallenbach	Budweiser Chevrolet
7	2	31	Mike Skinner	Lowe's Chevrolet	29	40	91	Morgan Shepherd	Little Joe's Auto Chevrolet
8	5	12	Jeremy Mayfield	Mobil 1 Ford	30	11	7	Geoff Bodine	Philips Consumer Comm. Ford
9	3	10	Ricky Rudd	Tide Ford	31	22	42	Joe Nemechek	BellSouth Chevrolet
10	24	16	Kevin Lepage	PRIMESTAR Ford	32	18	9	Jerry Nadeau	Cartoon Network Ford
11	33	4	Bobby Hamilton	Kodak MAX Film Chevrolet	33	23	26	Johnny Benson	The Kids Car Ford
12	21	44	Kyle Petty	Hot Wheels Pontiac	34	36	1	Steve Park	Pennzoil Chevrolet
13	15	5	Terry Labonte	Kellogg's Corn Flakes Chevrolet	35	26	75	Rick Mast	Remington Arms Ford
14	13	33	Ken Schrader	Skoal Bandit Chevrolet	36	20	30	Derrike Cope	Gumout Pontiac
15	34	28	Kenny Irwin	Texaco/Havoline Ford	37	8	22	Ward Burton	MBNA America Pontiac
16	12	21	Michael Waltrip	CITGO Ford	38	28	43	John Andretti	STP Pontiac
17	14	46	Jeff Green	The Money Store Chevrolet	39	41	13	Dennis Setzer	FirstPlus Financial Ford
18	17	98	Rich Bickle	Thorn Apple Valley Ford	40	25	77	Robert Pressley	Jasper Engines Ford
19	27	94	Bill Elliott	McDonald's Ford	41	42	96	Hut Stricklin	Caterpillar Chevrolet
20	6	23	Ted Musgrave	Winston/No Bull Ford	42	31	81	Kenny Wallace	Square D Ford
21	29	40	Sterling Marlin	Coors Light Chevrolet	43	39	90	Dick Trickle	Heilig-Meyers Ford
22	37	36	Ernie Irvan	Skittles Pontiac					

Farm Aid on CMT 300

Mark Martin's emotional Bristol victory combined with a well-beaten Jeff Gordon in Thunder Valley breathed new life into the NASCAR Winston Cup championship battle by the time the teams arrived at the Bahre family's one-mile oval in lovely New Hampshire.

The combination of finishes at Bristol helped Mark move to within 67 points of the defending NASCAR Winston Cup champion, and the Valvoline Ford driver arrived at the track focused on the task at hand. Because of the circumstances surrounding the death of his father, stepmother and stepsister, he knew he had not been 100 percent at the race track. But his team, led by crew chief Jimmy Fennig, had picked up the slack, giving Mark outstanding Tauruses to drive.

The Bristol victory was extremely meaningful to Martin and the entire team. Now, in the middle of the stretch run, Martin felt he could put the recent tragic events behind him and make a charge at the championship. Winning the title was something his father had hoped to see come to fruition for Mark, and in the weeks before his death,

(Right) *There's plenty of action on pit road as crews compete head to head to gain track position for their drivers under caution. Gordon's DuPont crew works from the first pit stall, taken by virtue of Jeff winning his seventh pole of the year.*

(Below) *Mark Martin, refocused on his quest for the championship after his convincing win at Bristol, prepares to compete at New Hampshire, hoping to close the gap on point leader Jeff Gordon.*

(Left) *Brothers Charlie (left) and Robert Pressley find a few minutes to talk in the garage area. Charlie recently had turned in his green-and-white Kodiak uniform and made the move to the yellow-and-black colors of the Kodak team to work with driver Bobby Hamilton.*

(Below) *Hamilton feels the presence of Dale Earnhardt on his right and the pressure of Rusty Wallace at the rear. Wallace and Earnhardt found their way past Hamilton and finished together, with Rusty taking eighth place in front of Earnhardt in ninth.*

he had remarked to an employee that if anything should happen to him, to be sure to tell Mark to continue on and win the title. Mark was ready to do just that, fulfilling not only his own career goal, but also his father's request.

The battle for the championship was quickly becoming a two-driver affair. Dale Jarrett was solidly in third place in the standings, but was well over 200 points behind. Rusty Wallace, fourth in the standings, was more than 350 points out of the title hunt, while fifth-place Bobby Labonte was another 101 behind Wallace. Jeremy Mayfield, now 33 points behind Bobby, was 121 clear of Jeff Burton, while Dale Earnhardt held eighth place in the point standings, but was 117 behind

Burton. Terry Labonte's struggles continued, and the two-time champion was now 65 points behind Earnhardt and just 73 ahead of Ken Schrader.

The New Hampshire weekend was a difficult one for Waltrip and the Wood Brothers. Saturday the team was informed that Ed Mattei, the advertising and sales promotion development manager for CITGO, responsible for the team's sponsorship program, had died of heart problems. He was a good friend of the team, Michael and the sport, and all were deeply saddened by his passing.

With the Jasper Motorsports and Cale Yarborough-owned teams making crew chief changes centered on the New

After starting third on a track where he traditionally runs well, Ken Schrader finds the fourth-turn wall, bringing out the second of four cautions in the race. Joe Nemechek (42) gets by safely on the inside and went on to finish on the lead lap.

Hampshire weekend, "Silly Season" continued. Kenny Wallace, in the middle of a four-year agreement, came to terms with car owner Filbert Martocci to leave the "81" team at the end of the season. It left him free to sign a contract with Andy Petree to drive for a second team that Petree would field in 1999. In the meantime, Kenny and his FILMAR teammates were determined to finish the season on a high note, and arrived at New Hampshire with Robert Yates engines in their Square D Taurus.

Geoff Bodine took a break from talking with other teams about driving their cars for the 1999 season to throw out the ceremonial first pitch at Yankee Stadium in the days prior to the race at New Hampshire. It was a huge thrill for the Upstate New York native who grew up a Yankee fan. He was still brimming with excitement about his day at the Stadium when he arrived at the one-mile oval.

Three days before the teams arrived, the track's owners had the racing surface sealed in hopes of promoting a second groove on the oval. The sealer failed miserably, making the surface slick. During practice and qualifying, teams watched car after car collide with the concrete wall after drivers lost adhesion on the track. Among those forced to resort to backup cars were Earnhardt, Jeff Burton, Ernie Irvan and the Caterpillar team with Ron Fellows behind the wheel. By the time the field prepared to take the green flag, Fellows had damaged the team's second car during the final qualifying session, forcing them to prepare a third car that was trucked in overnight on Saturday from the North Carolina shop.

With the track as treacherous as it was, drivers realized that they needed to be conservative during first-round qualifying,

Kenny Wallace takes an early-race lead in front of his future teammate, Ken Schrader. Wallace took the point from Schrader on the fourth lap of the race, led the next 30 circuits and finished sixth in the event to score his fifth top-10 finish of the season.

Michael Waltrip (21) and Dale Jarrett chase the Valvoline Ford of Mark Martin, who was dominating the event and appeared unbeatable. But a caution on lap 233 when Martin got into the Ford of Rich Bickle, handed the lead to Gordon, forcing car owner Jack Roush (below) to watch, bewildered, as Martin finished second to Gordon for the fourth time in the last six events.

but easing back to save the car when he had enough in hand over the field to justify slowing a tenth or two a lap.

The race, however, turned on a caution flag that appeared on lap 233. Martin, leading easily, inadvertently sent Rick Bickle's lapped Ford into the wall, bringing out the final yellow of the afternoon. Gordon, running fifth at the time, headed for pit road.

The Rainbow Warriors gambled on a two-tire stop, giving Jeff right sides and sending him back into the fray at the point. Behind him, drivers received four fresh tires for the 60-plus lap sprint to the finish.

and the one who tiptoed the fastest around the oval was Gordon. It was his seventh Bud Pole of the season, but in some ways, he would have been just as pleased if Bobby Labonte, who turned the second-fastest lap, had been a tick faster than the DuPont Chevrolet. Why? No driver has won from the pole at New Hampshire.

Ken Schrader turned in his best qualifying lap of the year to gain the inside of the second row, with Kenny Wallace alongside, destined to become Schrader's new teammate at Petree's team next season. Martin and Mayfield made up the third row, while Jarrett and Rick Mast were seventh and eighth fastest after the first qualifying session. Andretti and Hamilton beat the times posted by Kenny Irwin and Mike Skinner to grab the final top-10 starting positions.

Jimmy Spencer returned to the seat of the Winston Ford and qualified 17th, and Dennis Setzer found himself in the FirstPlus Financial Ford, taking 34th place on the grid. Sterling Marlin, Johnny Benson, Steve Park, Rich Bickle, Ron Fellows, Dave Marcis and Darrell Waltrip used provisionals to make the field, leaving Derrike Cope, Buckshot Jones and Dan Pardus standing on the sidelines.

After leading the first lap of the race, it appeared that the pole-sitter jinx at New Hampshire would once again come into play. Gordon drifted backward in the field and was never a factor in the first two thirds of the race. Martin flashed to the front and began to put together another dominating display with his red-white-and-blue Taurus. He led handily, stretching the lead when he needed to,

Consistently through the years, four new tires have been better than just two over a long haul, and the choice seemed logical. In the stands, fans prepared to see the likes of Martin, Jarrett or Rusty Wallace dust off Gordon in the final run to the checkers.

Gordon, however, had other thoughts, and when the green fell for the last time, the rainbow-hued Monte Carlo became the car to beat.

No one could. Jarrett and Wallace faded in the stretch run, and Martin was unable to find a way to make his four new tires perform better than Gordon's two. In fact, Mark was trying so hard that he ended up slapping the wall twice as he put the Taurus slightly over the edge of control.

Gordon moseyed on to a six car-length victory, with Andretti coming home third ahead of Jarrett, Jeff Burton, Kenny Wallace and Bobby Labonte. Rusty was eighth, Earnhardt ninth and Ricky Rudd 10th at the conclusion of the 300-lapper.

Gordon was astounded to win his ninth race of the season. For the second time in three races, the two-tire decision at the end of the event had provided him with the tools for victory. In the media center after the race, Gordon answered questions regarding the win and the team's strategy, while on the other side of the door, NASCAR inspectors were giving the DuPont Chevrolet — and its tires — the third degree.

Emerging from his car in the winner's circle for the ninth time this season, Jeff Gordon must have felt he was living a charmed life. After struggling with his car for three-quarters of the race, a two-tire stop under caution put him out front for good.

Farm Aid on CMT 300

[RACE #23 • NEW HAMPSHIRE INTERNATIONAL SPEEDWAY • AUGUST 30, 1998]

Fin. Pos.	Start Pos.	Car #	Driver	Team	Fin. Pos.	Start Pos.	Car #	Driver	Team
1	1	24	Jeff Gordon	DuPont Automotive Finishes Chevrolet	23	31	7	Geoff Bodine	Philips Consumer Comm. Ford
2	5	6	Mark Martin	Valvoline/Cummins Ford	24	34	13	Dennis Setzer	FirstPlus Financial Ford
3	9	43	John Andretti	STP Pontiac	25	15	41	Steve Grissom	Kodiak Chevrolet
4	7	88	Dale Jarrett	Quality Care/Ford Credit Ford	26	30	91	Morgan Shepherd	Little Joe's Auto Chevrolet
5	25	99	Jeff Burton	Exide Batteries Ford	27	29	21	Michael Waltrip	CITGO Ford
6	4	81	Kenny Wallace	Square D Ford	28	19	36	Ernie Irvan	Skittles Pontiac
7	2	18	Bobby Labonte	Interstate Batteries Pontiac	29	26	9	Jerry Nadeau	Cartoon Network Ford
8	14	2	Rusty Wallace	Miller Lite Ford	30	16	11	Brett Bodine	Paychex Ford
9	18	3	Dale Earnhardt	GM Goodwrench Service Plus Chevrolet	31	20	22	Ward Burton	MBNA America Pontiac
10	35	10	Ricky Rudd	Tide Ford	32	43	35	Darrell Waltrip	Tabasco Pontiac
11	11	28	Kenny Irwin	Texaco/Havoline Ford	33	23	44	Kyle Petty	Hot Wheels Pontiac
12	24	77	Robert Pressley	Jasper Engines Ford	34	10	4	Bobby Hamilton	Kodak MAX Film Chevrolet
13	17	23	Jimmy Spencer	Winston/No Bull Ford	35	42	71	Dave Marcis	Realtree Camouflage Chevrolet
14	27	97	Chad Little	John Deere Ford	36	41	96	Ron Fellows	Caterpillar Chevrolet
15	12	31	Mike Skinner	Lowe's Chevrolet	37	22	94	Bill Elliott	McDonald's Ford
16	33	16	Kevin Lepage	PRIMESTAR Ford	38	21	46	Jeff Green	The Money Store Chevrolet
17	37	40	Sterling Marlin	Coors Light Chevrolet	39	13	5	Terry Labonte	Kellogg's Corn Flakes Chevrolet
18	32	42	Joe Nemechek	BellSouth Chevrolet	40	40	98	Rich Bickle	Thorn Apple Valley Ford
19	28	90	Dick Trickle	Heilig-Meyers Ford	41	39	1	Steve Park	Pennzoil Chevrolet
20	6	12	Jeremy Mayfield	Mobil 1 Ford	42	3	33	Ken Schrader	Skoal Bandit Chevrolet
21	38	26	Johnny Benson	Cheerios Ford	43	36	50	Wally Dallenbach	Budweiser Chevrolet
22	8	75	Rick Mast	Remington Arms Ford					

Pepsi Southern 500

After leading the most laps at New Hampshire, but watching his dominant performance wasted with the miraculous recovery of Jeff Gordon that resulted in the DuPont driver rolling into the winner's circle, Mark Martin remained 67 points behind Gordon in the standings.

The days between the New Hampshire event and the Pepsi Southern 500 at Darlington were filled with controversy that followed the conclusion of the Loudon event. Jack Roush had received a letter and a sample of "undetectable" tire softener from the president of the company that manufactures the chemical agent, and had turned the letter over to NASCAR officials. It stated that some teams were using the softener, and Roush asked that NASCAR scrutinize the tire situation, after having seen Gordon come from behind to win two of the last three races.

Gordon and his team were furious that anyone would feel they were cheating in any way, and welcomed any inspections or analysis of the tires used on the DuPont Chevrolet. NASCAR officials instituted several steps at Darlington to assist in making

(Right) *For the second straight year, Jeff Gordon and Ray Evernham collect a million-dollar check from Winston in Darlington's victory lane. Gordon also entered his name in the record book as the only driver to win the prestigious Labor Day classic four consecutive years.*

(Below) *From left, Dale Jarrett, Jeff Burton, Dale Earnhardt, Jeff Gordon and Jeremy Mayfield, the No Bull 5 at Darlington, look very serious about staking their claim to Winston's $1-million bonus that was on the line in the Pepsi Southern 500.*

sure there was no tampering with the Goodyear Eagles, and sent tires used by Gordon, Martin and others at New Hampshire to an independent laboratory for a series of testing procedures.

The battle for the title had truly come down to two drivers by the time the teams assembled at venerable Darlington for one of the most sought-after victories on the tour. A win in the Southern 500 remains at the top of almost every driver's wish list, because of the difficulty of the track and the challenge it presents to driver and team. It also is the fourth race in Winston's No Bull 5 program, with the top five finishers from the Brickyard 400 eligible to win a $1-million bonus.

(Above) *Derrike Cope (30) spins after being tagged from behind on a restart, causing Ward Burton to take evasive action on the inside in his MBNA Pontiac. Cope recovered and the race continued, limiting the number of cautions during the day to an unusually low two.*

(Top Left) *Darrell Waltrip and team owner Tim Beverley (left) had more than a race to run at Darlington. They also were in the midst of trying to secure the lucrative Tabasco sponsorship for their team, a situation that had become shaky as of late.*

(Middle Left) *Kenny Irwin talks with chassis specialist Raymond Fox about the setup on the Texaco Ford for tricky, old Darlington. Irwin, who had to take a provisional to make the field, had an oil pump go bad in the race causing him to fall to a 41st-place finish.*

(Left) *Crew chief Robbie Loomis and driver John Andretti review their notes in Darlington's garage. Andretti, coming off a third place at New Hampshire, continued to run well, qualifying fourth for the Southern 500.*

Gordon's Brickyard victory, along with three straight Pepsi Southern 500 victories made him the favorite to claim a second $1-million bonus from Winston at Darlington. At the same time, he knew that Jeff Burton, Dale Earnhardt, Dale Jarrett and Jeremy Mayfield, the other four drivers eligible for the Winston No Bull 5 million at Darlington, would bring the very best cars in their stables in an effort to win both the Southern 500 and the $1-million bonus.

Several announcements had been made by the Darlington weekend, including Kenny Wallace and Square D's decisions to join Andy Petree with a second team for 1999 and beyond. The Wood Brothers surprised many by naming NASCAR

the success of the entire effort.

While the garage buzzed about all the activities of the week, Jarrett and Rusty Wallace knew they were faced with a do-or-die situation regarding to the point chase. They were third and fourth on the point ladder, but unless they turned their seasons around at Darlington, the chase would be over for them. Jarrett trailed by more than 250 points, and Wallace was 184 further back. Bobby Labonte was solidly in fifth place, 81 ahead of Mayfield, with Jeff Burton 69 points behind the Mobil 1 driver. Earnhardt held eighth place, 152 ahead of Terry Labonte, while John Andretti's third place at New Hampshire pulled him into a tie for 10th place with Ken Schrader.

Busch Series standout Elliott Sadler to drive the CITGO Ford in 1999, while Heilig-Meyers made public its decision to end sponsorship of Junie Donlavey's team at the conclusion of the 1998 season. Joe Gibbs and The Home Depot unveiled their orange number 20 for Tony Stewart for the 1999 season, and crew chief Newt Moore left FILMAR to become the new crew chief at the Jasper team with driver Robert Pressley.

The Tabasco situation heated up, with The McIlhenny Company filing suit against ISM Racing in an effort to bring that situation to a head, while driver Darrell Waltrip and owner Tim Beverley worked behind the scenes to salvage the Tabasco sponsorship for 1999. And in one of the biggest shockers of the year, Roush released Steve Hmiel, team manager for Jack Roush's two-car effort from Liberty, N.C., and crew chief for Johnny Benson's Cheerios Ford, from his duties. Hmiel was one of the blocks the Roush team had been built on since its inception in late 1987 and had been instrumental in

After a couple of mock qualifying runs during practice, Jarrett knew that if he did everything right, his Quality Care Ford was capable of notching his second Bud Pole of the season. But when Ward Burton ripped a lap at 168.677 miles per hour, Jarrett wasn't sure that what he had in his car would be enough. With what he called "the best Robert Yates engine I've ever had" stuffed in the front of his red-white-and-blue Taurus, Jarrett put it all together, clicking off a lap just good enough to beat Burton's.

Wallace, showing that he was ready to rumble, claimed the third-fastest lap, while Andretti rode his New Hampshire high to the outside of the second row. Gordon and Schrader had the fastest Chevrolets in the third row, with Bill Elliott and Sterling Marlin right behind them. Jerry Nadeau turned in yet another outstanding qualifying lap to put the Cartoon Network Ford on the inside of the fifth row, with Martin's Valvoline Ford alongside. Benson and Jeff Burton just missed the top 10.

With Terry Labonte and Brett Bodine claiming the final positions in the field based on timed laps, provisionals went to Kenny Irwin, Steve Grissom, Kenny Wallace, Rich Bickle, Jeff Green, Dennis Setzer and Darrell Waltrip. Dave Marcis and Hut Stricklin in the Caterpillar Chevrolet failed to make the field, while the LJ Racing Chevrolet driven by Morgan Shepherd was withdrawn from the event.

Gordon may have been the favorite to pocket another $1 million from Winston, but for the majority of the race, it looked like the big bucks would end up in the pocket of Jeff Burton, the Exide Ford driver. Burton was simply outstanding, and he dominated the Pepsi Southern 500, leading great chunks of the event and seeming invincible. But Burton was suffering from the lingering effects of a flu bug, and his stamina simply wore down in the final portions of the race.

And who was there to capitalize? None other than the Money Man.

After winning the Winston Million last Labor Day weekend at Darlington, Gordon had claimed another $1 million at The Brickyard. Running a determined second behind Burton at Darlington this day, Gordon seized the opportunity, found a way to work past the wilting Burton on lap 341, and then cruised to his 10th victory of the season and his fourth straight Pepsi Southern 500 triumph, etching his name on yet another page in the record book.

There were other pages he wrote this Sunday afternoon, as well. He became the first driver to record double-digit victories in three successive seasons, and the win marked the seventh for him and his Rainbow Warriors in the last nine events.

More importantly, perhaps, was the fact that Martin lost a cylinder in his Ford and then was forced to retire with a blown engine, finishing 40th in the final rundown. Jarrett finished third with a strong run, and Earnhardt came home in fourth place.

Mayfield, a lap behind, finished fifth and qualified for the final Winston No Bull 5 event of the season, Talladega's Winston 500. Irvan was sixth, Rusty Wallace finished seventh and Sterling Marlin beat Geoff Bodine for eighth place. Kenny Wallace, three laps behind, beat Elliott for the final top-10 position.

(Top) *Jeff Burton (99) tears away from his pit, beating Jeff Gordon (24) off pit road to continue his run at the front of the field. In the end, however, Burton would yield to the DuPont driver and finish second in a repeat of last year's results.* **(Middle)** *The Valvoline team diagnoses their motor in the garage area, determining the problem that took Mark Martin out of the race was indeed terminal. Martin's resulting 40th-place finish proved to be devastating in the point standings, as Jeff Gordon was able to stretch his lead by a whopping 132 points.* **(Left)** *Gary Bradberry (78), making his eighth start of the year in the Pilot Travel Centers Ford, races the Kodiak Chevrolet of Steve Grissom along Darlington's frontstretch.*

With the grandstands packed along Darlington's new front straight, pit road begins to clear as the drivers prepare to roll off the line to begin warm-up laps. ESPN, televising the event again this year, mounted a camera on a long boom to give viewers a new angle of the action in the pits.

Pepsi Southern 500

[*Race #24 • Darlington Raceway • September 6, 1998*]

Fin. Pos.	Start Pos.	Car #	Driver	Team	Fin. Pos.	Start Pos.	Car #	Driver	Team
1	5	24	Jeff Gordon	DuPont Automotive Finishes Chevrolet	23	23	4	Bobby Hamilton	Kodak MAX Film Chevrolet
2	12	99	Jeff Burton	Exide Batteries Ford	24	31	1	Steve Park	Pennzoil Chevrolet
3	1	88	Dale Jarrett	Quality Care/Ford Credit Ford	25	35	5	Terry Labonte	Kellogg's Corn Flakes Chevrolet
4	18	3	Dale Earnhardt	GM Goodwrench Service Plus Chevrolet	26	13	31	Mike Skinner	Lowe's Chevrolet
5	27	12	Jeremy Mayfield	Mobil 1 Ford	27	22	30	Derrike Cope	Gumout Pontiac
6	26	36	Ernie Irvan	Skittles Pontiac	28	28	44	Kyle Petty	Hot Wheels Pontiac
7	3	2	Rusty Wallace	Miller Lite Ford	29	42	13	Dennis Setzer	FirstPlus Financial Ford
8	8	40	Sterling Marlin	Coors Light Chevrolet	30	21	77	Robert Pressley	Jasper Engines Ford
9	15	7	Geoff Bodine	Philips Consumer Comm. Ford	31	34	50	Wally Dallenbach	Budweiser Chevrolet
10	39	81	Kenny Wallace	Square D Ford	32	9	9	Jerry Nadeau	Cartoon Network Ford
11	7	94	Bill Elliott	McDonald's Ford	33	19	90	Dick Trickle	Heilig-Meyers Ford
12	2	22	Ward Burton	MBNA America Pontiac	34	29	23	Jimmy Spencer	Winston/No Bull Ford
13	6	33	Ken Schrader	Skoal Bandit Chevrolet	35	30	42	Joe Nemechek	BellSouth Chevrolet
14	4	43	John Andretti	STP Pontiac	36	25	75	Rick Mast	Remington Arms Ford
15	24	18	Bobby Labonte	Interstate Batteries Pontiac	37	33	78	Gary Bradberry	Pilot Travel Centers Ford
16	41	46	Jeff Green	The Money Store Chevrolet	38	43	35	Darrell Waltrip	Tabasco Pontiac
17	20	21	Michael Waltrip	CITGO Ford	39	16	16	Kevin Lepage	PRIMESTAR Ford
18	17	97	Chad Little	John Deere Ford	40	10	6	Mark Martin	Valvoline/Cummins Ford
19	40	98	Rich Bickle	Thorn Apple Valley Ford	41	37	28	Kenny Irwin	Texaco/Havoline Ford
20	38	41	Steve Grissom	Kodiak Chevrolet	42	36	11	Brett Bodine	Paychex Ford
21	11	26	Johnny Benson	Cheerios Ford	43	32	15	Ted Musgrave	Rescue Engine Formula Ford
22	14	10	Ricky Rudd	Tide Ford					

Exide NASCAR Select Batteries 400

For weeks, Mark Martin and Jeff Gordon had been locked in a battle for supremacy in the NASCAR Winston Cup Series, and during those weeks, Martin found himself, time and again, being asked whether he felt he could catch Gordon and win the title. Patiently, Mark had answered that he felt the teams were equally matched and that the championship would be determined by who had the best racing luck.

At Darlington, his words proved true.

Engine failure when he least needed it struck Martin, relegating him to 40th place in the final Darlington rundown, and sending him reeling to 199 points behind Gordon in the standings. With eight races remaining in the season, Martin still had the time and the opportunity to catch Gordon, but the job had become immeasurably harder with the engine problem at Darlington.

Dale Jarrett was still solidly in third place, but knew in his heart that his chase for the championship would have to come next year, as did Rusty Wallace. For Jarrett and Wallace, the goal now was to win races and finish as high in the point standings as they

(Right) *A triumphant Jeff Burton emerges from his car in Richmond's winner's circle. Burton took the lap-leader bonus for the second straight week, but this time he turned the tables on Gordon and also took the win, scoring his fifth consecutive top-five finish in the process.*

(Below) *The capacity crowd is on their feet for the opening laps at Richmond in one of the most popular events of the season. Little did they know they would be in store for a spectacular race that would come down to a classic fight to the finish.*

(Right) *One of the more visible paint schemes on display under Richmond's bright lights was that of rookie contender Jerry Nadeau, who has the Cartoon Network Ford humming off the corner.*

(Below Right) *Jeff Burton's Exide Ford settles nicely into the high groove, allowing him to take the point from pole-winner Rusty Wallace (2) for the first time on lap 94.*

(Bottom) *In a tense moment during the closing laps, Geoff Bodine (7) and Ernie Irvan (36) run out of race track as they fight for position while trying to keep from being lapped. Race-leader Jeff Burton (99) closes from behind with Gordon in hot pursuit.*

could. Bobby Labonte was fifth ahead of Jeremy Mayfield, while Jeff Burton's outstanding Darlington performance kept him solidly in seventh place, 144 ahead of Terry Labonte. Ken Schrader and John Andretti continued their battle for 10th place, while Ernie Irvan and Sterling Marlin were separated by a single point in their fight for 12th. Bobby Hamilton and Michael Waltrip rounded out the top 15 in the standings, 45 points apart.

The stretch run to the championship — 16 consecutive races — had reached the midway point. When it began at the second Pocono event, Gordon had the lead, 52 points ahead of Martin, 98 ahead of Jarrett and 137 ahead of Mayfield. Now, more than 450 points separated the top four, and Martin remained the only driver with any hope of separating Gordon from his third career, and second straight championship.

Ted Musgrave found himself behind the wheel of the Caterpillar Chevrolet for the Richmond race, and Dennis Setzer was in the FirstPlus

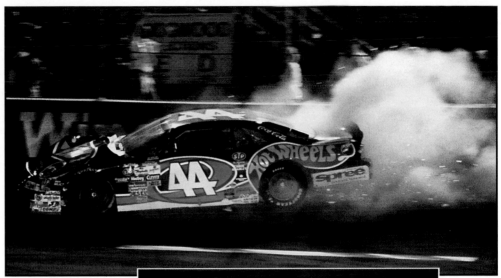

*On-track fireworks included (**top to bottom**) Kyle Petty, whose night ended with this accident in the first turn on lap 215; Dale Earnhardt, climbing from his car after being involved in a multi-car accident just 35 laps into the race; Bobby Labonte, who brought out the final caution of the night after backing into the third-turn wall to end his top-five challenge; and Sterling Marlin, who recovered nicely from a cut tire and was able to finish 15th, one lap off the winning pace.*

Financial Ford for another outing. Bill Elliott's McDonald's Ford carried a special paint scheme in conjunction with a national Big Mac promotion. Todd Bodine was behind the wheel of the LJ Racing Chevrolet, and Buckshot Jones was on hand for the Stavola Brothers.

While teams were working their way through practice sessions, NASCAR officials told media members at Richmond that every conceivable test, including taking the tires back, layer by layer, to the construction stage, showed that nothing had been done to the tires confiscated at New Hampshire. The sanctioning body hoped the test results would put the "Tiregate" episode to bed for good.

One of the most difficult challenges for drivers at events held under the lights is understanding how to translate daytime practice efforts into effective handling packages for the cooler track during the evening hours, when first-round qualifying and the race itself are conducted.

One of the best is Rusty Wallace, and when Bud Pole qualifying was completed at Richmond, Wallace had put the Miller Lite Ford on the pole, a tenth of a second faster than fellow Fenton, Mo., native and good friend, Ken Schrader. Jeff Burton and Sterling Marlin claimed the second row with solid runs, while Jeff Gordon and Bobby Hamilton parked their Chevrolets in the third row. Jarrett's Ford was seventh fastest, and Derrike Cope put a superb lap together to nail down the eighth starting position. John Andretti and Bobby Labonte made up the fifth row, just faster than Kyle Petty and Mark Martin.

With second-round qualifying held in the warmer daytime temperatures, most drivers chose to stand on their times from the first session. Of the seven drivers who ran, only Mike Skinner managed to make the field on speed, leaving Mayfield, Kevin Lepage, Joe Nemechek, Steve Park, Dick Trickle, Geoff Bodine and Darrell Waltrip to use provisionals to make the field.

Those who failed to make the race were Gary Bradberry, Ken Bouchard, Buckshot Jones and Rich Bickle in Cale Yarborough's Ford.

Jeff Gordon blasts out of his pit after receiving four fresh tires from his Rainbow Warriors during a green-flag stop.
(Below) After pursuing Jeff Burton for the final 35 laps, Gordon finally gets underneath Burton as the two drivers charge off the fourth turn and toward the checkered flag. Burton and Gordon swapped the lead nine times during the race, before coming down to this final-lap duel.

With an enormous throng ringing the three-quarter mile mini-superspeedway, the green flag dropped on what turned out to be a battle royal. The Sawyer family has transformed the former Fairgrounds half-mile bullring into one of the cleanest, plushest, most fan-friendly facilities in the world, and the crowds have responded. It doesn't hurt, of course, that racing in the Capital of the Confederacy provides some of the most spectacular action of the year. The Exide NASCAR Select Batteries 400 would be another page in the history of the legendary track.

Although Rusty Wallace was at the point for the first quarter of the race, Jeff Burton showed early that he had a car capable of contending for the victory. Others led at different times, with 11 different drivers taking turns leading the pack of furious chargers around the track. By half distance, Burton was still among the leaders, battling grimly for position, and at the three-quarter mark, the Virginian had underscored his determination to win in his home state.

When the final caution flag of the evening flew with 35 laps to go, many contenders flashed to pit road for tires, fuel and any final adjustments needed to set up their mounts for the final sprint. Wallace, Mark Martin and Bobby Hamilton gambled that new tires would make up for the loss of track position with 35 laps to go, and when they hit pit road, it moved Burton to the point, with Gordon right behind him.

With the drop of the green for the final time, Burton blasted away and eventually built a lead in excess of a second, and fans began to believe the popular Virginian would win at home. But Gordon was mounting his charge. Lap by lap, car-length by car-length, tenth of a second by tenth of a second, Gordon fashioned his patented charge. With five laps left in the race, he caught Burton, tagging onto the rear bumper of the Taurus and looking one way, then another, for a way past.

Few expected Burton to be able to counter. But he applied the lessons learned through his career, and particularly over the last 18 months on the NASCAR Winston Cup tour. He held his line, refusing to move from the groove that best suited his Ford. Lap after lap, corner after corner, Burton thwarted every move Gordon threw at him.

It was heady, gritty, fabulous stuff that brought the entire crowd to its feet, roaring its approval as the Ford remained in front of the Chevrolet while the laps clicked down.

Burton was strong in the higher groove, and Gordon couldn't get the bite off the corners he needed to make the pass. On the final lap, Gordon edged down on the inside, pulled briefly alongside, and as the two exited the fourth corner, it was Burton who got on the throttle sooner, able to nose his Ford ahead as the two ground their way toward the checkered flag.

Burton beat Gordon by a fender in one of the best races of the season. The upstart had beaten the champion, the native son had vanquished the point leader, and the two drivers saluted each other as they circled the track during their cool-down lap.

Burton was beside himself once he caught his breath, having put the Exide Ford in the winner's circle of the Exide race. More importantly, he had proven to any doubters that he had arrived as a bonafide NASCAR Winston Cup championship contender, and everyone in the stands knew that a victory of this sort would be one he would reflect on and draw from in the future.

Martin finished third ahead of Schrader's solid performance, while Andretti continued to impress with his fifth-place finish. Hamilton was sixth ahead of Rusty Wallace and Mike Skinner, while Jimmy Spencer and Kenny Irwin finished ninth and 10th, the final cars on the lead lap.

Burton, able to hold off Gordon's last-gasp effort, flashes under the flag-stand to capture his second win of the season by a fender. The official margin of victory was a scant .051 seconds, the closest finish of the season so far.

Exide NASCAR Select Batteries 400

[*RACE #25 • RICHMOND INTERNATIONAL RACEWAY • SEPTEMBER 12, 1998*]

Fin. Pos.	Start Pos.	Car #	Driver	Team		Fin. Pos.	Start Pos.	Car #	Driver	Team
1	3	99	Jeff Burton	Exide Batteries Ford		23	19	9	Jerry Nadeau	Cartoon Network Ford
2	5	24	Jeff Gordon	DuPont Automotive Finishes Chevrolet		24	8	30	Derrike Cope	Gumout Pontiac
3	12	6	Mark Martin	Valvoline/Cummins Ford		25	17	96	Ted Musgrave	Caterpillar Chevrolet
4	2	33	Ken Schrader	Skoal Bandit Chevrolet		26	31	21	Michael Waltrip	CITGO Ford
5	9	43	John Andretti	STP Pontiac		27	40	1	Steve Park	Pennzoil Chevrolet
6	6	4	Bobby Hamilton	Kodak MAX Film Chevrolet		28	15	22	Ward Burton	MBNA America Pontiac
7	1	2	Rusty Wallace	Miller Lite Ford		29	29	13	Dennis Setzer	FirstPlus Financial Ford
8	26	31	Mike Skinner	Lowe's Chevrolet		30	14	50	Wally Dallenbach	Budweiser Chevrolet
9	16	23	Jimmy Spencer	Winston/No Bull Ford		31	27	75	Rick Mast	Remington Arms Ford
10	36	28	Kenny Irwin	Texaco/Havoline Ford		32	18	91	Todd Bodine	OBX/Dare Chevrolet
11	13	81	Kenny Wallace	Square D Ford		33	22	71	Dave Marcis	Realtree Camouflage Chevrolet
12	23	97	Chad Little	John Deere Ford		34	25	10	Ricky Rudd	Tide Ford
13	42	7	Geoff Bodine	Philips Consumer Comm. Ford		35	10	18	Bobby Labonte	Interstate Batteries Pontiac
14	30	36	Ernie Irvan	Skittles Pontiac		36	38	16	Kevin Lepage	PRIMESTAR Ford
15	4	40	Sterling Marlin	Coors Light Chevrolet		37	39	42	Joe Nemechek	BellSouth Chevrolet
16	7	88	Dale Jarrett	Quality Care/Ford Credit Ford		38	34	3	Dale Earnhardt	GM Goodwrench Service Plus Chevrolet
17	24	41	Steve Grissom	Kodiak Chevrolet		39	11	44	Kyle Petty	Hot Wheels Pontiac
18	43	35	Darrell Waltrip	Tabasco Pontiac		40	21	94	Bill Elliott	McDonald's Ford
19	33	11	Brett Bodine	Paychex Ford		41	32	26	Johnny Benson	Betty Crocker Ford
20	28	46	Jeff Green	The Money Store Chevrolet		42	41	90	Dick Trickle	Heilig-Meyers Ford
21	35	5	Terry Labonte	Kellogg's Corn Flakes Chevrolet		43	20	77	Robert Pressley	Jasper Engines Ford
22	37	12	Jeremy Mayfield	Mobil 1 Ford						

MBNA Gold 400

Jeff Burton's hugely popular Richmond victory captured the hearts and interests of tens of thousands of race fans who attended the Saturday evening run at the three-quarter mile mini-superspeedway, but just days later, it was "business as usual" when the teams assembled at Denis McGlynn's Dover Downs International Speedway.

After finishing third at Richmond, Mark Martin found himself 204 points behind Jeff Gordon in their battle for this year's NASCAR Winston Cup title. Third-place Dale Jarrett and fourth-place Rusty Wallace, after finishing 16th and seventh, respectively, at Richmond, had dropped even further out of the point battle, leaving the struggle for supremacy to Gordon and Martin — at least for the rest of this year.

Burton's hard-fought victory, coupled with poor finishes by both Bobby Labonte and Jeremy Mayfield, vaulted the Exide Ford driver all the way to fifth place on the point ladder. Labonte now trailed Burton by 39 markers, while Mayfield was five points behind Labonte. Dale Earnhardt remained eighth in the standings, and now was within grasp of sixth place if he could continue to put good finishes together. He was only 36

(Right) *Kenny Irwin (28) chases teammate Dale Jarrett (88) around Dover's steep, 24-degree banks, while John Andretti holds his ground on the inside in his STP Pontiac. Andretti picked up another top-10 finish in the race, to move past Terry Labonte into ninth place in the championship standings.*

(Below) *Crew members roll new sets of tires toward their respective pits and garage stalls on race-day morning. In an effort to better monitor teams' activities regarding tires — and in the wake of the recent tire controversy — NASCAR began restricting access to tires until the day of the race.*

points behind Mayfield, and just 44 in arrears of Labonte. With 154 points in hand over Ken Schrader, Earnhardt could concentrate on moving up, rather than protecting his position.

John Andretti eased into 10th place in the point standings, just 13 behind Schrader, while a 21st place at Richmond cost Terry Labonte dearly. He continued to slide backward in the standings, falling out of the top 10, just six points behind Andretti. Bobby Hamilton held a 14-point margin over Ernie Irvan in their battle for 12th place, while Sterling Marlin lurked just four points behind Irvan. Michael Waltrip continued to hold 15th place.

The musical drivers' seats continued at the Caterpillar Chevrolet and FirstPlus Ford teams, with Morgan Shepherd slotted into the CAT car, and Ted Musgrave sliding through the window of the Taurus owned by Bill Elliott and Dan Marino. Musgrave was looking more and more like the driver most likely to be offered the "13" car for 1999 and beyond, but he was examining "several offers," as were Michael Waltrip and Geoff Bodine. In the Philips camp, Jim Mattei, after purchasing the shares of former partner John Porter earlier in the month, had reached an agreement with Bodine that would have Geoff sell his remaining percentage of the team. Mattei would become the sole owner of the "7" car, and was noncommittal regarding his driver selection for the 1999 season.

One announcement created even more rumors than it solved. Budweiser, under contract to Hendrick Motorsports for the 1999 season, announced it would sponsor Dale Earnhardt Jr. in five NASCAR Winston Cup events next year, and then would become the primary sponsor of "Little E's" NASCAR Winston Cup effort beginning with the 2000 season. Whether Bud would remain at Hendrick's for 1999 was unclear.

(Above Left) *Hut Stricklin (left) and Ted Musgrave relax in the garage between practice rounds. Musgrave was slotted into the FirstPlus car for the first time, perhaps getting a feel for a possible full-time ride next season. Hut Stricklin was on hand to drive the Jasper Motorsports entry, filling in for Robert Pressley who was recovering from injuries suffered the previous weekend at Richmond.*

(Left) *Geoff Bodine rolls his Philips-sponsored Ford toward the line before making his attempt in first-round qualifying. Geoff had recently agreed to relinquish his ownership role in the team, choosing to focus on driving in an effort to increase the team's competitiveness.*

(Below) *Mark Martin rolls through the turn on the inside of Ward Burton, whose Pontiac is all dressed up for the MBNA Gold 400. Martin's Ford was so strong he could drive it wherever it needed to go on the track, allowing him to thoroughly dominate the event.*

Mike Hillman had hired on with Junie Donlavey as crew chief for Dick Trickle, and Hut Stricklin was on hand at Dover to drive the Jasper Motorsports entry. Regular driver Robert Pressley had broken his right shoulder blade in an accident at Richmond the previous weekend, and Stricklin hoped to help out with the "77" car until Pressley could return to the seat. Todd Bodine slid through the window of the LJ Racing entry for the second straight week.

In the McDonald's Ford slot in the garage area, Mike Beam and the MacAttack team were working with NASCAR Busch Series star Matt Kenseth instead of Bill Elliott. Elliott and his family were home in Dawsonville, taking care of family matters after patriarch George Elliott died Friday morning. George, one of the most popular figures in the garage area through the years, had succumbed to complications after having a brain tumor operated on earlier in the summer. It was a grim day for the team at Dover, their hearts with the Elliott family in Georgia.

The struggle for the championship may have come down to two drivers, but Martin knew that this would be a difficult place to try to make a dent in Gordon's lead.

(Above) *NASCAR Busch Series sensation Matt Kenseth, subbing for Bill Elliott in his NASCAR Winston Cup debut, drove a brilliant race and finished sixth, bolstering his stock to become a rookie contender in the very near future.*

(Below) *Mark Martin and June Dover pole-winner Rusty Wallace form the front row ahead of Derrike Cope in the Gumout Pontiac and Kevin Lepage in the PRIMESTAR Taurus, both of whom had surprisingly strong qualifying efforts.*

Through the years, Dover has become Gordon's personal playground, with his Hendrick team making stronger than usual preparations. Dover is the closest track to DuPont's corporate headquarters, and the Rainbow Warriors have always put their best foot forward at the Monster Mile. With three victories in the last six events at Dover, Gordon and his team certainly knew what handling package to put under the Monte Carlo.

At the same time, Martin and his determined Valvoline crew were not about to fold in the championship chase, and were prepared to battle week to week with the Rainbow Warriors. Mark served notice that Dover would be a war by topping the speed charts through practice, and then backing that up with a new track-record lap at nearly 156 miles per hour to claim the Bud Pole for the event. On his right was Rusty Wallace, who had won the pole for the spring race and was itching to return to the winner's circle.

Derrike Cope and Bahari Racing have both run well at Dover in the past, and the combination this year produced the third-fastest lap of the session, while Kevin Lepage surprised many by posting the fourth-fastest lap in the PRIMESTAR Ford. Behind the two upstarts came Bobby Labonte and Gordon to claim the third row. John Andretti, continuing to run well in the STP Pontiac, was seventh fastest, while Jerry Nadeau had yet another outstanding qualifying run in the Cartoon Network Ford to grab the outside of the fourth row. Dick Trickle and Dale Jarrett turned laps just a tick faster than Ricky Rudd and Kenny Irwin to grab the final positions in the top 10 for the start of Sunday's MBNA Gold 400.

For the first time in two months, Darrell Waltrip made the field on speed, and, as it turned out, he needed it. Dale Earnhardt was forced to use a former champion's provisional to make the field, and because he had won the title more recently than Waltrip, Darrell would have been forced to the

Mark Martin drops his face shield just moments before rolling off the line from the pole, his second of the year.

sidelines, had he not been fast enough to earn his own spot. Others using provisionals were Bobby Hamilton, Chad Little, Wally Dallenbach, Hut Stricklin, Rick Mast and Rich Bickle. Dave Marcis, Morgan Shepherd and Steve Grissom failed to make the field.

Some days it just works. There may be no other way to explain what happened Sunday afternoon at Dover, when Martin rolled off the line, under the green flag, and rumbled to his sixth victory of the season.

With a red-white-and-blue Taurus that was clearly the class of the field, outstanding pit stops from a crew that worked with the precision of a Swiss watch on pit road, and all the Jack Roush power he needed under the hood, Martin simply and utterly dominated Dover, successfully defending the event title he won last year.

How dominant was he? He merely led 380 of 400 laps, and he had the five-point bonus for leading the most laps locked safely in his hip pocket by lap 217. He had lapped an astonishing 28 cars by the 80th lap with an awesome performance, leaving Gordon and the remainder of the field to fight for the scraps he occasionally let fall from the table.

Behind him, Gordon worked his way to second place, cutting his point loss as much as possible, while Jeremy Mayfield fought back from a lost lap to finish in third place, recapturing the form his team had exhibited earlier in the year. Bobby Labonte was a solid fourth, just ahead of Rusty Wallace.

Other than the dominating victory by Martin and Gordon's 13th consecutive top-five finish, the story of the race was the drive turned in by Kenseth. Pressed into service in the McDonald's Ford, he ran as high as second at one point and eventually finished sixth in a brilliant NASCAR Winston Cup debut. Dale Jarrett was seventh ahead of Ernie Irvan, while Andretti tacked another top-10 finish into his column, beating Bobby Hamilton by a lap in their battle for ninth place.

The lead-lap cars, led by Mark Martin and Rusty Wallace, make pit stops during the second of seven cautions during the race on lap 87. By this time, Martin had already lapped all but about a dozen cars on the track.

MBNA Gold 400

[RACE #26 • DOVER DOWNS INTERNATIONAL SPEEDWAY • SEPTEMBER 20, 1998]

Fin. Pos.	Start Pos.	Car #	Driver	Team	Fin. Pos.	Start Pos.	Car #	Driver	Team
1	1	6	Mark Martin	Valvoline/Cummins Ford	23	43	3	Dale Earnhardt	GM Goodwrench Service Plus Chevrolet
2	6	24	Jeff Gordon	DuPont Automotive Finishes Chevrolet	24	41	75	Rick Mast	Remington Arms Ford
3	28	12	Jeremy Mayfield	Mobil 1 Ford	25	39	50	Wally Dallenbach	Budweiser Chevrolet
4	5	18	Bobby Labonte	Interstate Batteries Pontiac	26	21	13	Ted Musgrave	FirstPlus Financial Ford
5	2	2	Rusty Wallace	Miller Lite Ford	27	30	23	Jimmy Spencer	Winston/No Bull Ford
6	16	94	Matt Kenseth	McDonald's Ford	28	36	78	Gary Bradberry	Pilot Travel Centers Ford
7	10	88	Dale Jarrett	Quality Care/Ford Credit Ford	29	19	42	Joe Nemechek	BellSouth Chevrolet
8	23	36	Ernie Irvan	Skittles Pontiac	30	40	77	Hut Stricklin	Jasper Engines Ford
9	7	43	John Andretti	STP Pontiac	31	9	90	Dick Trickle	Heilig-Meyers Ford
10	37	4	Bobby Hamilton	Kodak MAX Film Chevrolet	32	20	31	Mike Skinner	Lowe's Chevrolet
11	13	1	Steve Park	Pennzoil Chevrolet	33	17	22	Ward Burton	MBNA America Pontiac
12	4	16	Kevin Lepage	PRIMESTAR Ford	34	18	46	Jeff Green	The Money Store Chevrolet
13	11	10	Ricky Rudd	Tide Ford	35	3	30	Derrike Cope	Gumout Pontiac
14	15	7	Geoff Bodine	Philips Consumer Comm. Ford	36	8	9	Jerry Nadeau	Cartoon Network Ford
15	25	26	Johnny Benson	Cheerios Ford	37	26	91	Todd Bodine	Larry's Homes Chevrolet
16	35	40	Sterling Marlin	Coors Light Chevrolet	38	27	99	Jeff Burton	Exide Batteries Ford
17	38	97	Chad Little	John Deere Ford	39	29	33	Ken Schrader	Skoal Bandit Chevrolet
18	24	5	Terry Labonte	Kellogg's Corn Flakes Chevrolet	40	12	28	Kenny Irwin	Texaco/Havoline Ford
19	42	98	Rich Bickle	Thorn Apple Valley Ford	41	22	44	Kyle Petty	Hot Wheels Pontiac
20	32	21	Michael Waltrip	CITGO Ford	42	14	00	Buckshot Jones	Realtree Extra Chevrolet
21	33	35	Darrell Waltrip	Tabasco Pontiac	43	34	81	Kenny Wallace	Square D Ford
22	31	11	Brett Bodine	Paychex Ford					

September 27, 1998

NAPA Autocare 500

Despite whipping the field into submission at Dover, where his domination of the event was next to perfection, Mark Martin gained just 10 points in his quest to overtake Jeff Gordon in the 1998 edition of the battle for the NASCAR Winston Cup.

He had done everything he could possibly do, putting on a show that included easily leading the most laps and claiming the five bonus points that go with that accomplishment. He had won from the pole, lapped the majority of the field, and yet, at the finish, looked in his mirror and saw the DuPont Chevrolet right behind him. It was frustrating in some ways. Few drivers had enjoyed such a perfect day — but it was as though nothing had happened. The Darlington engine failure looked like it would be the turning point in the stretch run to the championship.

In the days between Dover and the opening of practice for the NAPA Autocare 500 at Clay Earles' splendid Martinsville Speedway, the Gordon-Martin battle for the championship dominated the headlines. Reporters speculated when Gordon's turn to have a little poor racing luck would come, pointing to his string of 13 consecutive top-five fin-

(Right) Ricky Rudd, who considered giving way to a relief driver early in the race, takes a seat in Martinsville's victory lane after gutting out all 500 laps under extremely difficult conditions. The win that extended his streak of winning seasons to 16 was more than enough to make Ricky forget his pain, and put a big smile on his face.

(Below) Ricky Rudd (10) and Sterling Marlin (40) run nose to tail during a 250-lap stretch that saw the two drivers swap the lead five times. Marlin led a total of 231 laps to take the lap-leader bonus, but a faulty alternator forced him to settle for an 18th-place finish.

ishes. No one, they felt, could run the table over the final two-thirds of the season and not have a problem that forced a finish lower than fifth. It would be unheard of. Yet Gordon continued on his reliable, consistent path, and if it lasted the remainder of the season, he would be unbeatable in his quest for a second straight and third career title.

The day following the Dover event, Steve Grissom found himself relieved of his duties at Larry Hedrick's Kodiak team. He had failed to make the Dover field, and that was the last straw for Hedrick and crew chief Tim Brewer. David Green, released from the Caterpillar Chevrolet earlier in the season, was signed by Hedrick to drive at Martinsville and, in fact, had

been offered the "41" car for the 1999 season. Green was non-committal about whether or not he would accept the ride for the coming year.

Bill Elliott returned to the seat of the McDonald's Ford, and in the FirstPlus Financial entry, Dennis Setzer was the driver of choice. Ted Musgrave moved over to Jasper Motorsports to fill in for recovering Robert Pressley, while Mike Bliss had his first outing in the Caterpillar Chevrolet. Todd Bodine returned to Joe Falk's LJ Racing entry as the teams prepared for the final short-track race of the season.

Steve Hmiel, released earlier by the Roush organization, signed on to work as a consultant with Dale Earnhardt's teams, splitting his time between Dale Jr. in his quest for the NASCAR Busch Series title, and Steve Park's Pennzoil-sponsored NASCAR Winston Cup effort. With Dale Jr. scheduled to run five Cup races in 1999 and a full schedule in 2000, there was plenty of work for Hmiel to do at DEI. His decision to take the slot with the Earnhardt effort surprised many, as several veteran garage observers had expected him to sign on with other car owners.

Todd Bodine (91) and Chad Little (97) tangle in the second turn on lap 325, causing a multitude of cars to take evasive action. Bodine recovered well enough to finish the race in 12th place for car owner Joe Falk.

Todd Bodine (91), Michael Waltrip (21) and Chad Little are rubbin' bumpers in action typical of Martinsville's tight quarters, as Rich Bickle (98) and Jeff Burton (99) ride by on the outside. Bickle had an outstanding run in Cale Yarborough's Ford to finish fourth, while Burton overcame handling problems and took fifth place. (Below) Terry Labonte's Kellogg's Chevrolet shows the rigors of short-track racing, but Labonte kept the car intact enough to finish sixth and remain solidly among the top 10 in the point standings.

With only a few races left in the season, the point table had begun to solidify. Martin trailed Gordon by 194 points, and Dale Jarrett and Rusty Wallace were beginning to look like they were locked in third and fourth place. Jarrett trailed Martin by 143, and held a 153-point margin over Wallace. The battle for fifth was a two-way tie, with Bobby Labonte and Jeremy Mayfield trailing Wallace by 218. Jeff Burton, after his disastrous 38th-place finish at Dover, fell from fifth to seventh place, and now trailed the Labonte/Mayfield battle by 72 points.

After finishing 23rd at Dover, Earnhardt now was eighth, 235 points behind Burton. John Andretti made up a few points with his ninth-place Dover finish and moved to 118 behind Earnhardt, while Terry Labonte moved back into 10th place, 40 behind Andretti and 44 ahead of Ken Schrader. Bobby Hamilton held 12th place, fighting to get into the top 10 and a place on the stage at the Waldorf-Astoria, but he was just 11 points ahead of Ernie Irvan. Sterling Marlin, 14th, and Michael Waltrip, 15th, had all but given up their hopes for a top-10 finish at season's end.

Lost in all this was the plight of Ricky Rudd. After rolling to a pair of victories last season, including one of the biggest of the year when he notched the Brickyard 400 win, Rudd had

struggled and scrambled throughout the 1998 season. He had switched crew chiefs, bemoaned the problems of running a single-car effort against the likes of the mighty multi-car teams, and now stood watching as the season wound down and his string of 15 consecutive years with at least one victory came closer to ending with each passing week.

It was a mark he took great pride in. He and Earnhardt were tied for the record at 15 straight seasons, but Dale had gone winless in 1997, ending his string there. A win would put Rudd alone on his own page in the record book, a mark that would stand for some time to come. He was struggling, though, and knew his chances of scoring a victory were slim.

But when the Tide Ford rolled off the transporter and Ricky belted in for his first practice laps, he found the Taurus fast and comfortable, and felt his hopes begin to rise. Maybe … just maybe …

Ricky Rudd (10) dives into the first turn on a restart, getting a jump on second-place Sterling Marlin (40) and Bobby Labonte (18), who leads the lap-down cars on the inside. Rudd led the field off the line on the last five restarts, including two during the final 75 laps of the race.

The promise of the Tide Ford carried through the practice sessions, and when Bud Pole qualifying was completed, Rudd was wearing a tight little smile. Ernie Irvan had beaten him for the pole, but by the slimmest of margins, and Rudd knew that if things went his way he would be a contender on Sunday. The way his year had gone until this point, being a contender felt just as good as leading the point standings.

Jeff Gordon claimed the inside of the second row, with Rich Bickle on the outside, giving Cale Yarborough's Ford its second top-five start of the season. Wally Dallenbach and Jeff Green plunked their Chevrolets in the third row, while Marlin and Andretti were seventh and eighth fastest. Musgrave turned in a strong performance in the Jasper Ford for the inside of the fifth row, and Dale Jarrett claimed the 10th-fastest lap, just ahead of Brett and Todd Bodine.

Jimmy Spencer, Steve Park, Kenny Irwin, Jerry Nadeau, Rick Mast, Derrike Cope and Dave Marcis used provisionals, while David Green's debut in the Kodiak car ended when he failed to make the field. Gary Bradberry, Ken Bouchard and Randy MacDonald were also victims of speeds too slow to fight their way into the starting lineup.

The field rolled off to take the green flag with temperatures in the 90s and high humidity, and within five laps, Rudd's dreams of a victory appeared to end. His cool helmet had failed, and he was already feeling the effects in the car. By the time the race reached the 25th lap, Ricky was on the radio to crew chief Bill Ingle, asking him try to find another driver because he was being stifled in the car.

Despite the problems, Rudd was holding his own on the track, and he felt, through the blistered seat of his pants, that he finally had a car that might — just might — be capable of extending his winning streak to 16 years. He fought lap after lap, and his crew began makeshift activities that might keep him in the car. Small cosmetics bags were rounded up, packed with ice and dropped in a cooler. With every pit stop, Rudd would slip them into his driver's suit in an attempt to sooth the overheating his body was experiencing.

A string of cautions throughout the race helped as well, and as the event ground on, Rudd and the Tide Ford remained among the front-runners, despite his worsening condition within the car. He reached down — and found the reserves that have been part of his racing career. As the laps wound down, the huge throng on hand and millions watching on television began to truly appreciate the grit, spunk and perseverance that has been a hallmark of Rudd's career.

In the end, he took the lead with just under 100 laps remaining and was forced to fight his way through two more restarts, and then withstand a furious charge by Gordon. Rudd faced the challenge and whipped to the checkered flag a half-second ahead of the DuPont Chevrolet driver.

Exhausted, Ricky was helped from the car and did his winner's interview flat on his back in victory lane, between whiffs of oxygen. It was 30 minutes before he was able to pull it all together and stand to accept the accolades of the crowd.

He had staged one of the most incredible victories of the season, and his fellow competitors stood in applause of his accomplishment. Gordon's second place was another notch in his string of top-five finishes, while Martin lost five points with his third-place finish. Bickle felt like he had won the race by finishing fourth, with Jeff Burton fifth and Terry Labonte sixth. Elliott was a solid seventh ahead of Irvan, Johnny Benson and Bobby Labonte.

Ricky Rudd crosses the finish line one-half second ahead of second-place Jeff Gordon (24) and third-place Mark Martin (6) to post an exhausting, yet very satisfying victory, the 20th of his career. Michael Waltrip (21) beats Darrell Waltrip (35) for the 20th spot by a similar margin, with both drivers five laps off Rudd's winning pace.

NAPA Autocare 500

[*Race #27 • Martinsville Speedway • September 27, 1998*]

Fin. Pos.	Start Pos.	Car #	Driver	Team	Fin. Pos.	Start Pos.	Car #	Driver	Team
1	2	10	Ricky Rudd	Tide Ford	23	32	12	Jeremy Mayfield	Mobil 1 Ford
2	3	24	Jeff Gordon	DuPont Automotive Finishes Chevrolet	24	38	1	Steve Park	Pennzoil Chevrolet
3	13	6	Mark Martin	Valvoline/Cummins Ford	25	25	96	Mike Bliss	Caterpillar Chevrolet
4	4	98	Rich Bickle	Thorn Apple Valley Ford	26	43	71	Dave Marcis	Realtree Camouflage Chevrolet
5	16	99	Jeff Burton	Exide Batteries Ford	27	39	28	Kenny Irwin	Texaco/Havoline Ford
6	29	5	Terry Labonte	Kellogg's Corn Flakes Chevrolet	28	17	2	Rusty Wallace	Miller Lite Ford
7	20	94	Bill Elliott	McDonald's Ford	29	36	44	Kyle Petty	Hot Wheels Pontiac
8	1	36	Ernie Irvan	Skittles Pontiac	30	42	30	Derrike Cope	Gumout Pontiac
9	24	26	Johnny Benson	Cheerios Ford	31	6	46	Jeff Green	The Money Store Chevrolet
10	21	18	Bobby Labonte	Interstate Batteries Pontiac	32	5	50	Wally Dallenbach	Budweiser Chevrolet
11	15	22	Ward Burton	MBNA America Pontiac	33	34	90	Dick Trickle	Heilig-Meyers Ford
12	12	91	Todd Bodine	Larry's Homes Chevrolet	34	11	11	Brett Bodine	Paychex Ford
13	18	33	Ken Schrader	Skoal Bandit Chevrolet	35	40	9	Jerry Nadeau	Cartoon Network Ford
14	19	4	Bobby Hamilton	Kodak MAX Film Chevrolet	36	31	97	Chad Little	John Deere Ford
15	9	77	Ted Musgrave	Jasper Engines Ford	37	8	43	John Andretti	STP Pontiac
16	23	31	Mike Skinner	Lowe's Chevrolet	38	14	13	Dennis Setzer	FirstPlus Financial Ford
17	35	16	Kevin Lepage	PRIMESTAR Ford	39	28	7	Geoff Bodine	Philips Consumer Comm. Ford
18	7	40	Sterling Marlin	Coors Light Chevrolet	40	22	42	Joe Nemechek	BellSouth Chevrolet
19	37	23	Jimmy Spencer	Winston/No Bull Ford	41	41	75	Rick Mast	Remington Arms Ford
20	27	21	Michael Waltrip	CITGO Ford	42	10	88	Dale Jarrett	Quality Care/Ford Credit Ford
21	30	35	Darrell Waltrip	Tabasco Pontiac	43	26	81	Kenny Wallace	Square D Ford
22	33	3	Dale Earnhardt	GM Goodwrench Service Plus Chevrolet					

UAW-GM Quality 500

Although they made little of it, the Valvoline Ford crew members and driver Mark Martin were beginning to show the frustration of being unable to close the point gap on defending NASCAR Winston Cup Champion Jeff Gordon.

In any other season, the red-white-and-blue-clad team would be atop the point standings, watching other teams try to catch them in the waning events of the season. In 18 consecutive races, beginning with the California 500 back in the first weekend of May, Mark and his cohorts had been superb. They finished out of the top five just three times — two of those being a sixth and a seventh. Only the disastrous engine failure in the Pepsi Southern 500 that resulted in a 40th-place finish marred a superb showing over two-thirds of the season.

Included in that string of exceptional finishes were four wins, five second places and a pair of third-place results, including the fighting third at Martinsville when everyone was overshadowed by Ricky Rudd's Herculean effort to claim the victory.

But, in the end, the performance of Martin and his team fell short of the simply spec-

(Right) *Derrike Cope proudly displays his trophy for winning the pole for the UAW-GM Quality 500 at Charlotte. His qualifying lap in excess of 181 mph earned him the first inside front-row position of his career, coming in his 331st NASCAR Winston Cup start.*

(Below) *Derrike Cope takes his Gumout Pontiac through Charlotte's fourth turn, fending off the charge of Jeff Gordon. Cope led early in the race before settling in for a solid run to finish 14th, the final car on the lead lap.*

(Left) *An upbeat Rusty Wallace, optimistic about his chances at Charlotte after qualifying sixth for the race, discusses matters with crew chief Robin Pemberton in the garage area.*

(Below Left) *During the race, Pemberton and his Miller crew find themselves very busy on pit road, having to make major repairs to Wallace's Ford after he was involved in a multi-car accident on lap 204 that also involved 11 other cars. Rusty was able to finish the race, but was listed more than 50 laps down in 26th place.*

For 14 consecutive races, Gordon had finished in the top five. Taking into account the 37th-place finish at the first Richmond race after he was tagged by Rusty Wallace, Gordon and his Warriors had actually taken the DuPont Monte Carlos to 18 top-five finishes in the last 19 races. It was the 14-race string that amazed most garage watchers. Included in it were seven victories, four second places and a pair of thirds, giving Gordon 13 finishes in the top three in 14 events.

It was an incredible string of outstanding performances, and it sent reporters scurrying to the record books to find a comparable list of achievements. It brought to mind the brilliant perform- ances of Darrell Waltrip in Junior Johnson's Mountain Dew Buicks during the second half of the 1981 season. Then, Waltrip ran off 13 consecutive top-three finishes to come from more than 200 points behind and beat Bobby Allison to claim his first of three NASCAR Winston Cups.

With the attention centered on Gordon and Martin, Dale Jarrett and Rusty Wallace found themselves solidly in third and fourth place in the point standings, with Bobby Labonte 40 points ahead of Jeremy Mayfield and 46 ahead of Jeff Burton in their three-way battle for fifth place. Dale Earnhardt, in eighth place, had a little breathing room over Terry Labonte and John Andretti, who were fighting for ninth place. Andretti

tacular showing Gordon and his Rainbow Warriors posted during the same string of races.

After Martin's California victory, the margin between himself and Gordon was 76 points. Now, five months later, and with just six races remaining on the schedule, Martin's sterling performances had actually LOST points to Gordon. As the teams unloaded at Charlotte Motor Speedway, Mark found himself 199 behind the defending Series champion, and knew he was running out of time.

How had Gordon and the Warriors actually improved their point lead while Martin and the Valvoline team were recording such an outstanding string of performances?

Simply, by finishing better.

A crew member checks the temperatures on a tire just taken from Michael Waltrip's CITGO Ford, gathering critical information regard- ing the car's handling characteristics.

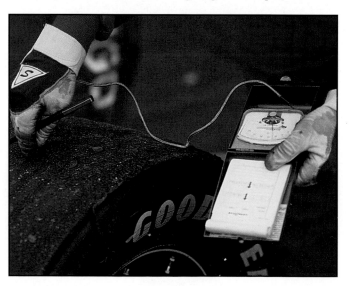

had another war to fight, with Ken Schrader, Ernie Irvan, Bobby Hamilton and Sterling Marlin all in contention for the final position on the stage at the Waldorf-Astoria. The final half-dozen races of the season would determine who made it to the stage — and who would have to wait another year.

For many of the team owners, veteran drivers and longtime team members, the early days of the Charlotte week were ones filled with memories. Word had reached Martinsville on Sunday afternoon of the passing of Ralph Seagraves, the man who led Winston into the sport and developed the marketing programs that had expanded through nearly three decades of the brand's NASCAR sponsorship. Seagraves was a pioneer with Winston, and he was highly respected throughout the na-

But Derrike had a perfect lap up his sleeve, and he laid it down on the track. When he emerged from the window of his Grand Prix, Cope had captured his first career pole position. The lap bumped Martin to second fastest, while Bobby Labonte and Irvan made it three Pontiacs in the top four slots for the start of the race. Bobby Hamilton and Rusty Wallace claimed the third row, with John Andretti and Todd Bodine, again in the LJ Racing Chevrolet, right behind. Jeremy Mayfield was the ninth-fastest driver in the session, and Kenny Irwin beat Joe Nemechek for the outside of the fifth row. Irwin's strong qualifying effort may have been in response to a serious heart-to-heart with car owner Robert Yates on the Monday following the Martinsville race, when Yates directed a

Rookie Kenny Irwin (28), whose Taurus dons a promotional paint scheme in the Charlotte event, digs through the turn on the outside of Mark Martin. Irwin had a good race going from his 10th-place starting position until he got involved in the big wreck on lap 204, dropping him to 20th place at the finish.

tion's corporate world as one of the leading sports marketing executives prior to his retirement in 1985. The ever-smiling Seagraves had now joined his protégé and hand-selected successor, T. Wayne Robertson, who died in a boating accident before the beginning of the season.

As teams looked at the final practice-session times, little respect was given to Derrike Cope and his Gumout Pontiac. Yes, the team had been fast in practice, and yes, the car was sixth on the list after the final session. But a contender for the pole? Nah ...

"wake-up call" to Irwin, hoping the young driver would get the message.

And where was the point-leader? Gordon, struggling with a car he felt would race well, didn't make it in the field on the first day, and stood on his time to start 26th on the grid. It was his worst qualifying performance since the final race of the 1997 season at Atlanta, when he used a backup car to start 37th.

Provisionals went to Johnny Benson, Steve Park, Geoff Bodine, Robert Pressley, Rick Mast, Rich Bickle and Darrell Waltrip, while Jeff Green, Tony Raines, Dave Marcis, Randy

Mark Martin and Jeff Gordon race out of the pits during one of the event's 11 caution periods. Gordon's crew helped his charge through the field by giving him the lead on two stops under yellow, but couldn't get the DuPont Chevrolet into winning form this day.

MacDonald and Andy Hillenburg all failed to make the race.

Despite rain that threatened to stall the beginning of the UAW-GM Quality 500, the 334-lapper began on time. Some five hours later, after 11 caution flags and a red-flag delay to clean up spillage from a broken sewage line, Martin flashed over the start/finish line to post his second victory in his last four starts. In between, Martin led 215 laps in dominant fashion, determined to do everything he could to close the margin on Gordon. He beat Ward Burton by just over a second at the end, watched as several hot-running contenders were wiped from the race by a multi-car accident two-thirds of the way through the event, and listened on his radio as he was told of Gordon's position in the race.

Gordon and the Rainbow Warriors had worked on the race car throughout every practice session, and finally got it close. Jeff led 47 laps of the race, but fell back to eighth place with damage to the rear of the Chevrolet. Knowing Martin was headed

Kevin Lepage holds the low line in his PRIMESTAR Ford, dicing with Dale Jarrett, whose Taurus is painted as a companion to that of teammate Irwin. Lepage was brilliant at Charlotte, working his way from the 32nd starting spot to a sixth-place finish, and applying even more pressure on Irwin in their battle for Rookie for the Year honors.

for victory, Gordon got up over the steering wheel and fought his way past Kevin Lepage in the final laps to move into fifth place, limiting his loss in the point column and gaining his 15th consecutive top-five finish.

Jeff Burton came home third behind his brother, and Hamilton finished fourth, the highest-placed Chevrolet driver. Lepage's sixth place made him the highest-finishing rookie in the race, while Nemechek continued his strong Charlotte performances with a seventh ahead of Chad Little. Little's sixth top-10 finish of the season made it four Jack Roush-owned cars in the top eight positions. Geoff Bodine finished ninth and Jimmy Spencer beat Bill Elliott for the final top-10 position.

Mark Martin rolls toward the line for a restart with Jeff Gordon sizing him up from behind. The two drivers atop the point standings battled each other for the first 300 miles until Martin took over, leading all but one of the final 134 laps.

UAW-GM Quality 500

[*RACE #28* • *CHARLOTTE MOTOR SPEEDWAY* • *OCTOBER 4, 1998*]

Fin. Pos.	Start Pos.	Car #	Driver	Team	Fin. Pos.	Start Pos.	Car #	Driver	Team
1	2	6	Mark Martin	Valvoline/Cummins Ford	23	25	50	Wally Dallenbach	Budweiser Chevrolet
2	13	22	Ward Burton	MBNA America Pontiac	24	17	88	Dale Jarrett	Quality Care/Ford Credit Ford
3	28	99	Jeff Burton	Exide Batteries Ford	25	9	12	Jeremy Mayfield	Mobil 1 Ford
4	5	4	Bobby Hamilton	Kodak MAX Film Chevrolet	26	6	2	Rusty Wallace	Miller Lite Ford
5	26	24	Jeff Gordon	DuPont Automotive Finishes Chevrolet	27	36	13	Ted Musgrave	FirstPlus Financial Ford
6	32	16	Kevin Lepage	PRIMESTAR Ford	28	37	26	Johnny Benson	Cheerios Ford
7	11	42	Joe Nemechek	BellSouth Chevrolet	29	33	3	Dale Earnhardt	GM Goodwrench Service Chevrolet
8	20	97	Chad Little	John Deere Ford	30	24	40	Sterling Marlin	Coors Light Chevrolet
9	39	7	Geoff Bodine	Philips Consumer Comm. Ford	31	4	36	Ernie Irvan	Skittles Pontiac
10	18	23	Jimmy Spencer	Winston/No Bull Ford	32	31	96	Steve Grissom	Caterpillar Chevrolet
11	29	94	Bill Elliott	McDonald's Ford	33	35	90	Dick Trickle	Heilig-Meyers Ford
12	7	43	John Andretti	STP Pontiac	34	41	75	Rick Mast	Remington Arms Ford
13	27	21	Michael Waltrip	CITGO Ford	35	12	9	Jerry Nadeau	Cartoon Network Ford
14	1	30	Derrike Cope	Gumout Pontiac	36	38	1	Steve Park	Pennzoil Chevrolet
15	8	91	Todd Bodine	Little Joe's Auto Chevrolet	37	14	10	Ricky Rudd	Tide Ford
16	30	81	Kenny Wallace	Square D Ford	38	22	5	Terry Labonte	Kellogg's Corn Flakes Chevrolet
17	42	98	Rich Bickle	Thorn Apple Valley Ford	39	3	18	Bobby Labonte	Interstate Batteries Pontiac
18	34	44	Kyle Petty	Hot Wheels Pontiac	40	15	33	Ken Schrader	Skoal Bandit Chevrolet
19	21	11	Brett Bodine	Paychex Ford	41	40	77	Robert Pressley	Jasper Engines Ford
20	10	28	Kenny Irwin	Texaco/Havoline Ford	42	16	78	Gary Bradberry	Pilot Travel Centers Ford
21	19	31	Mike Skinner	Lowe's Chevrolet	43	23	41	David Green	Kodiak Chevrolet
22	43	35	Darrell Waltrip	Tabasco Pontiac					

Winston 500

Eased by the fact that he had gained 25 points with his dominant Charlotte victory, Mark Martin took a few minutes to talk about the season he and his Valvoline mates had compiled. He had done all he could do at Charlotte — leading almost two thirds of the race, notching the lap-leader bonus and scoring his seventh victory of the season.

He had gained points on Jeff Gordon and now trailed by 174, but with five races left in the season, he knew he would have to gain more points per event if he were to emerge at the conclusion of the season as the NASCAR Winston Cup champion.

In some ways, that was out of his hands. He knew his team was capable of giving him excellent equipment, but he also knew that Gordon would receive the same level of excellence from the Rainbow Warriors. Truly, the championship would be determined by who had the best luck in the final five events of the season.

Instead of bemoaning the fact that he was second in the standings, Mark preferred to talk about what the Valvoline team had accomplished during the year. Martin and his team have been so good, for so long, that the red-white-and-blue Fords are taken for

(Right) *With a million dollars swirling in — and around — his head in Talladega's winner's circle, Dale Jarrett celebrates the richest single payday of his career. Jarrett took the lead with 13 laps remaining in the Winston 500, and held his ground against Hendrick teammates Gordon and Labonte to capture his third win of the season.*

(Below) *The lure of Talladega is clearly displayed by this pack of cars ripping down the frontstretch, three abreast and inches apart at nearly 200 miles per hour. The Superspeedway's wide surface and 33-degree banks allow this thrilling scene to continue throughout the 500-mile event.*

his team now was very steep as the crews readied for the first of back-to-back restrictor-plate races with the running of the Winston 500 at Talladega.

The Winston 500 was the final No Bull 5 race of the year, with the top five finishers from the Pepsi Southern 500 eligible to cash in on a $1-million bonus if one of them could claim the Winston 500 trophy. The drivers eligible were Jeff Gordon, looking for his third No Bull 5 payday of the year, Dale Jarrett, Jeremy Mayfield, Dale Earnhardt and Jeff Burton — and each of those drivers had their best superspeedway car at their disposal for the Winston 500.

(Above) *One of Jeremy Mayfield's crew members pulls a plastic "tear-away" off the windshield of the Mobil 1 Taurus, instantly clearing Jeremy's vision before returning to the lead pack. Mayfield continued to run well on the restrictor-plate tracks, finishing in fifth place and moving up to sixth in the point standings.*

(Right) *Geoff Bodine ponders his future while observing on-track activities from the top of his transporter. Needing a good finish on Sunday to increase his stock for next year, Bodine's car was damaged in a multi-car accident late in the race, dropping him to a 25th-place finish, four laps off the winning pace.*

granted as a contender on a weekly basis. He wanted to make sure that everyone understood why the accomplishments of the 1998 season should be remembered.

He pointed out that the team had moved from Liberty, N.C., to a new shop in Mooresville, just outside Charlotte during the winter months. More importantly, he pointed out, only two members of his Liberty-based team, including crew chief Jimmy Fennig, moved with the equipment, and a new cadre of workers was recruited to fill the new uniforms. Perhaps the biggest challenge of all was the fact that the team had been faced with sorting out and developing the new Ford Taurus.

Yet the team had scored a victory in the third race of the season (Las Vegas), added wins at Texas and California, and then triumphed in the sport's all-star race, The Winston. In all, Martin had been to victory lane seven times so far this year — a single-season career high — and he was the lone remaining challenger to Gordon for the championship.

Obviously, he was proud of the team and its accomplishments. Yet he knew the road to the title that faced

While the focus of the sport was divided between the re-vived championship chase and the possibility of the season's third Winston No Bull 5 winner, Geoff Bodine found himself with mixed emotions in the garage area at Talladega. He would make his 500th career NASCAR Winston Cup start in this event, a plateau reached only by 18 other drivers in the history of the sport. But he had become a lame-duck driver earlier in the week, having been told that Michael Waltrip would drive the Philips-sponsored Ford in 1999.

NASCAR's inspectors turned it up a couple of notches as teams rolled their cars through the inspection line, and car after car was turned back to have work done before the sticker was placed in the center of the windshield, signifying its passage through inspection. Several teams lost pieces of their cars, in-cluding deck lids from the Chevrolets of Dale Earnhardt and Ken Schrader, which be-came the property of NASCAR. No fines were

*Ken Schrader and Bobby Labonte bring the starting field through the tri-oval in front of a capacity crowd at the mammoth superspeedway on a gor-geous autumn afternoon. (**Inset**) Chad Little (97) lets Joe Nemechek (42) feel the power of his Roush Ford, drafting past Dale Jarrett (88) and Sterling Marlin (40) on the inside. Little finally pushed his way through and went on to finish eighth, his seventh top-10 finish of the year.*

Ted Musgrave was set to drive the FirstPlus Financial Ford at Talladega, but it appeared he already had selected his team for the coming season. He would be the driver of Butch Mock's Remington Fords with engines provided by Robert Yates, while Rick Mast appeared headed for the "13" car next season. Caterpillar made it clear to team owner Buzz McCall that it was leaving at the end of the season and would move to the Bill Davis team to sponsor driver Ward Burton. And Wally Dallenbach's solid performances behind the wheel of the Hendrick Motorsports Budweiser Chevrolet had earned him a contract with the team for 1999. With Waltrip and Musgrave deciding on their deals, Bodine had become the most sought-after proven driver in the garage area for car owners and spon-sors looking to improve their lot for the coming season.

levied, but some teams lost considerable practice time getting their cars right before being allowed onto the race track.

Replacing the deck lid on the Skoal Bandit turned out to be just a momentary glitch for Schrader and Andy Petree's team. From the first lap out on the track, Ken knew the Monte Carlo was fast, and the new car simply became faster and faster as the team worked on it. In qualifying, he put it all together to claim his first career Talladega pole and become the season's 14th different Bud Pole winner.

His lap dropped Bobby Labonte to the outside of the front row, with Jarrett and Terry Labonte lined up in the second row for the start of the Winston 500. Mike Skinner and Gordon were fifth and sixth fastest in the first qualifying session, and Kenny Irwin and Martin made up the fourth row. Jeff Burton

Mark Martin's hopes for a NASCAR Winston Cup championship in 1998 effectively ended here, with the Valvoline Ford sitting on the apron after tagging the spinning Pontiac of Ernie Irvan. **(Left)** *In the garage area, the Valvoline crew dejectedly works to get Mark back on the track. The crew was able to return Mark to action, where he finished the race running in 34th place, 22 laps behind the leaders.*

and Sterling Marlin claimed the ninth and 10th starting positions, with Buckshot Jones surprising many by turning the 11th-fastest lap in the Stavola Brothers Chevrolet, complete with a Hendrick Motorsports engine.

With Gumout leaving as the sponsor of the Bahari Pontiac at the end of the season, and with 300 SaraLee guests expected for Sunday's race, team co-owner Chuck Rider was hopeful that Derrike Cope's strong showing as the fastest second-round qualifier would ensure SaraLee's sponsorship for next year. Bobby Hamilton, Kevin Lepage, Wally Dallenbach, Dick Trickle, Kyle Petty, Kenny Wallace and Darrell Waltrip used provisionals to make the field, sending Mast, Dan Pardus, Rich Bickle, Rick Wilson, Bobby Gerhart and Gary Bradberry home.

The last restrictor-plate race was held here, at Talladega, in late April, and most anticipated the Winston 500 would once again be a furious charge with large packs of cars jousting for position throughout the event. No one was disappointed, as the drivers gave the sold-out crowd of enthusiastic fans exactly what they had expected.

It was two- and three-wide racing, with an occasional fourth line forming briefly before finding a place to shuffle back into the pack. Daring, white-knuckled, hold-your-breath moments for drivers being shuffled around by the air at more than 190 miles per hour, translated to agony on pit road as teams watched their drivers being moved from third to 20th by lines of cars splitting, reforming, moving and dicing in a kaleidoscopic freight train of color.

For more than half the race, fans, drivers and crew members held their breath and watched the incredible racing.

Then, it happened. Ernie Irvan, struggling with brake problems in his Skittles Pontiac, dove from the middle of the track to the inside lane, with Sterling Marlin's Coors Chevrolet already there. Ernie misjudged by just the tiniest bit, and Sterling couldn't check up in time. The two cars touched ever so lightly, with Marlin's Monte Carlo barely grazing the left-rear corner of Irvan's Pontiac. Ernie almost made the correction, then lost the car and the melee was on. Collected in the middle after being bumped from behind by his teammate Lepage, was Martin. Running sixth at the time, and with Gordon nearly a lap behind because of the timing of his previous pit stop, Mark's opportunity to make a large dent in Gordon's point lead turned into a disaster. The Valvoline team spent more than 20 laps repairing the Taurus, and Martin eventually was credited with a 34th-place finish.

At the front of the pack, Jarrett made his move and took the point with 13 laps left in the race. He mirror-drove for the re-mainder of the event, watching as the others in the lead pack fought to see who would emerge as a challenger in the final circuits. With the others battling back and forth, Jarrett protected his lead, and in the end, watched as Gordon fought his way to second and then mounted a final-lap charge at the red-white-and-blue Ford. Gordon came up just a couple of car-lengths short, as Jarrett won his third race of the season and collected the first Talladega trophy of his career.

More importantly, he had claimed the No Bull 5 bonus, proudly hoisting Winston's check for $1 million over his head in victory lane.

Terry Labonte finished third, while Jimmy Spencer had a brilliant run to claim fourth place ahead of Mayfield. Bobby Labonte and Skinner were shuffled to sixth and seventh in the final laps, while Chad Little and Michael Waltrip posted strong runs for eighth and ninth ahead of Jeff Burton. Cope provided the SaraLee folks with plenty to cheer about, claiming 11th with his best finish of the season.

Ken Schrader's hopes for a long sought win come to an end as he brings the pole-winning car down pit road, heavily damaged from a cut right-front tire. Repairs would cost him three laps in the pits and drop Schrader to a disappointing 24th-place finish.

Winston 500

[RACE #29 • TALLADEGA SUPERSPEEDWAY • OCTOBER 11, 1998]

Fin. Pos.	Start Pos.	Car #	Driver	Team	Fin. Pos.	Start Pos.	Car #	Driver	Team
1	3	88	Dale Jarrett	Quality Care/Ford Credit Ford	23	43	35	Darrell Waltrip	Tabasco Pontiac
2	6	24	Jeff Gordon	DuPont Automotive Finishes Chevrolet	24	1	33	Ken Schrader	Skoal Bandit Chevrolet
3	4	5	Terry Labonte	Kellogg's Corn Flakes Chevrolet	25	31	7	Geoff Bodine	Philips Consumer Comm. Ford
4	36	23	Jimmy Spencer	Winston/No Bull Ford	26	21	77	Robert Pressley	Jasper Engines Ford
5	24	12	Jeremy Mayfield	Mobil 1 Ford	27	12	2	Rusty Wallace	Miller Lite Ford
6	2	18	Bobby Labonte	Interstate Batteries Pontiac	28	28	47	Billy Standridge	Team FansCanRace.com Ford
7	5	31	Mike Skinner	Lowe's Chevrolet	29	13	42	Joe Nemechek	BellSouth Chevrolet
8	15	97	Chad Little	John Deere Ford	30	32	22	Ward Burton	MBNA America Pontiac
9	34	21	Michael Waltrip	CITGO Ford	31	33	26	Johnny Benson	Cheerios Ford
10	9	99	Jeff Burton	Exide Batteries Ford	32	14	3	Dale Earnhardt	GM Goodwrench Service Chevrolet
11	26	30	Derrike Cope	Gumout Pontiac	33	30	46	Jeff Green	The Money Store Chevrolet
12	29	71	Dave Marcis	Realtree Camouflage Chevrolet	34	8	6	Mark Martin	Valvoline/Cummins Ford
13	16	11	Brett Bodine	Paychex Ford	35	38	16	Kevin Lepage	PRIMESTAR Ford
14	10	40	Sterling Marlin	Coors Light Chevrolet	36	18	96	Steve Grissom	Caterpillar Chevrolet
15	37	4	Bobby Hamilton	Kodak MAX Film Chevrolet	37	20	36	Ernie Irvan	Wild Berry Skittles Pontiac
16	11	00	Buckshot Jones	Aquafresh Chevrolet	38	40	90	Dick Trickle	Heilig-Meyers Ford
17	27	13	Ted Musgrave	FirstPlus Financial Ford	39	39	50	Wally Dallenbach	Budweiser Chevrolet
18	17	10	Ricky Rudd	Tide Ford	40	42	81	Kenny Wallace	Square D Ford
19	19	94	Bill Elliott	McDonald's Ford	41	35	1	Steve Park	Pennzoil Chevrolet
20	41	44	Kyle Petty	Hot Wheels Pontiac	42	25	9	Jerry Nadeau	Cartoon Network Ford
21	22	43	John Andretti	STP Pontiac	43	7	28	Kenny Irwin	Texaco/Havoline Ford
22	23	91	Andy Hillenburg	Little Joe's Auto Chevrolet					

Pepsi 400

You could almost taste the disappointment.

Shrugs here, slumped shoulders there. A walk that had lost its spring, a weary hand wiping a forehead as a crew member sat on a jackstand. Sure, most tried to put a good face on it — walk the good walk; talk the good talk. Four races left. Anything could happen. Still in the hunt. Just need some luck.

It was understandable. Yet the wind was gone from their sails.

Headed into the Pepsi Southern 500 at Darlington, Mark Martin trailed Jeff Gordon by 67 markers, but engine problems in that race cost him a huge chunk of points. Still, Mark and his team rallied back to win twice and remain within striking distance.

Then came Talladega and the Winston 500. Swept into a multi-car wreck that ultimately put him 34th in the final rundown, Martin had effectively seen his chances for his first NASCAR Winston Cup championship disappear when he slid into Ernie Irvan's spinning car.

(Right) *Adding to the list of "firsts" he has compiled during his six-year NASCAR Winston Cup career, Jeff Gordon raises his arms in triumph to claim victory in the speedway's first-ever night race and add this unique winner's trophy to his already-impressive collection.*

(Below) *The lead draft flashes under the flagstand in front of the sold-out crowd, on hand to witness history in the making at Daytona International Speedway.*

Gordon now held a commanding 288-point lead and was ready to cruise to the title. Worse, as far as Martin was concerned, was the fact that Gordon's DuPont Monte Carlo remained intact after Talladega, while Martin would be forced to resort to a spanking new, barely-tested superspeedway Taurus. The damage to his primary car sustained at Talladega was too extensive to repair in time for the first night race in Daytona International Speedway's long and glorious history.

The track's management had undertaken a multi-million dollar lighting project, which was finished in plenty of time for find. The lighting was superb, and fans were treated to a simply spectacular venue for the 30th of 33 NASCAR Winston Cup races this season.

After being kept overnight in a Birmingham hospital for observation, Irvan was unsure about whether or not he would compete at Daytona. The huge lick he had taken at Talladega left him with a slight concussion and a headache, so the Skittles team enlisted the services of Ricky Craven for the Pepsi 400. Ted Musgrave was behind the wheel of the FirstPlus Financial Ford, and Steve Grissom would be driving

Jeff Gordon and Ray Evernham oversee final preparations on their DuPont Chevrolet, confident about their car and their chances in the Pepsi 400. (Below) But with the championship on the line, the DuPont team was taking no chances, having brought a load of extra parts just in case.

In stark contrast to the DuPont team, Mark Martin and Jimmy Fennig engage in serious discussion regarding their Valvoline Ford, being faced with sorting out a new chassis after their primary superspeedway car was damaged beyond repair last week at Talladega.

the originally scheduled July 4 race. Wildfires in Florida, some encroaching on property near the racetrack, had forced postponement of the event until the open date on October 17. As a result, teams faced two restrictor-plate races in six days, and several teams found themselves scratching for cars after their primary mounts were wounded at Talladega.

Many wondered how the night event would be at the historic track. Would there be shadows on the track that might play tricks on the drivers at nearly 200 miles per hour? Would they encounter spots where glare from the mirrored lights might cause vision, perception and reaction problems? Sure, other tracks had been lit, but this was a 2.5-mile superspeedway, a much longer track to deal with than any of the others.

The answer was one of the most pleasant that drivers could

the Caterpillar Chevrolet. Andy Hillenburg was behind the wheel of the LJ Racing Chevrolet, and Rick Wilson was the driver of the Kodiak Chevrolet, trying to get Larry Hedrick's car into the field after failing to at Talladega.

As teams worked their way through the practice sessions in preparation for qualifying, Winston executives announced that the No Bull 5 program, instituted for this season as a way to help celebrate NASCAR's 50th Anniversary, had been exceedingly successful. The program would continue in 1999, and would include five specific events in which drivers would have the opportunity to win the Winston No Bull 5 $1-million bonus. Las Vegas would replace The Brickyard on the No Bull 5 schedule, while the other four events would remain the same: the Daytona 500, the Coca-Cola 600, the Pepsi Southern 500 and the Winston 500.

At the same time, Cale Yarborough was scrambling. Officials at Thorn Apple Valley, citing financial difficulties, had announced that they would not return to sponsor

Teams line up on pit road for Bud Pole qualifying, the first official event under the lights at Daytona, and fans took advantage of the opportunity by filling the grandstands for the Thursday night event.

Yarborough's Fords in 1999, even though the sponsorship program had been extremely successful from the standpoint of name recognition, exposure and increased shelf space at supermarkets. Cale was unsure of his plans for next season, but Bill Davis was clear on his. With MBNA leaving to form an alliance with Joe Gibbs, Davis and the Caterpillar folks announced that the black-and-yellow paint would move to Ward Burton's Pontiacs in 1999, reestablishing the association that had begun between Ward and the company in the NASCAR Busch Series ranks.

The point standings had undergone only small changes following Talladega, with Winston 500 winner Dale Jarrett solidly in third place in the standings, 246 points ahead of Rusty Wallace. Jeff Burton was fifth, 77 points behind Wallace, while Jeremy Mayfield and Bobby Labonte had swapped positions, with Mayfield now 44 points behind Burton and just two markers ahead of Labonte. Dale Earnhardt remained eighth in the standings and Terry Labonte moved to ninth, 34 points behind the Goodwrench driver and just 45 ahead of John Andretti. Bobby Hamilton continued his challenge for the final top-10 slot, just 22 points behind Andretti, while Ken Schrader, Sterling Marlin and Ernie Irvan continued to try to make it into the top 10.

After claiming two of the previous three restrictor-plate poles, there was little doubt who would be high on the list of favorites to grab the pole for the Pepsi 400, and when qualifying was completed, Bobby Labonte had upheld his part of the bargain. Armed with a slick Pontiac Grand Prix, a strong motor and the proper line around the track, the Interstate Batteries driver rocketed to the pole. His lap was so strong that he claimed the Bud Pole by nearly a mile per hour over Jeff Burton, who made it a "battery battle" on the front row with his Exide Batteries Ford.

Jarrett, driving the Taurus he had used to win at Talladega, took the inside of the second row with Terry Labonte alongside, while Dale Earnhardt and Mark Martin scrambled to the third-row positions. Rusty Wallace qualified seventh ahead of Jeff Gordon, and Mike Skinner

The stress of the season-long chase for the championship appears to have taken its toll on Jeremy Mayfield, who showed up at Daytona looking a bit different, but still wearing a bright smile.

John Andretti (43), Jimmy Spencer (23) and Johnny Benson (26) stack it three wide through the tri-oval, with Jerry Nadeau (9) choosing to follow Benson on the high side. Nadeau was the highest-finishing rookie in the event, taking 19th, the last car on the lead lap. **(Right)** Like many of the cars, Spencer's Winston Ford used soft spring/shock combinations for qualifying, creating a shower of sparks as it bottoms out through the high banks. **(Below)** Dale Earnhardt's crew repairs the front end of the Goodwrench Chevrolet, damaged when Earnhardt hit a tire while leaving pit road. Earnhardt looked as though he had a good chance to sweep the events at Daytona this year until the mishap dropped him from winning contention.

claimed the inside of the fifth row, with Hut Stricklin, in a second Andy Petree-owned Chevrolet, a sparkling 10th. Dan Pardus, a Daytona resident, replete with Hendrick Motorsports power under the hood, was the fastest second-round qualifier, making his first NASCAR Winston Cup race in his seventh try. Those who used provisionals to make the field were Bobby Hamilton, Jimmy Spencer, Ernie Irvan, Johnny Benson, Ricky Rudd, Kyle Petty and Darrell Waltrip. It was Waltrip's 17th use of the former champion's provisional, and the 10th time he had been forced to use it in 12 races driving the ISM Racing entry.

Those who failed to make the field were Rick Wilson, Dick Trickle, Robert Pressley, Gary Bradberry and Rick Mast, for the second straight race.

With 288 points in his pocket, one might have expected Gordon to do the "stroking" thing — cruise around the track, not put his car in trouble, take what the race gave him and move on to Phoenix, Rockingham and Atlanta to do the same thing.

Victory lane lights up with fireworks for Gordon's victory celebration, capping off a spectacular night at The Beach.

But Gordon loves the unexpected, and he loves to be the first at things. He showed it at The Brickyard and at California, among others. This was the first night race at Daytona, so...

Under the brilliant lights and in a spectacular arena, Gordon saved the best for the final laps. While a rain shower delayed the finish of the event for more than 30 minutes, Gordon waited, his DuPont Chevrolet first in the lineup for the resumption of the event. Behind him, Jeremy Mayfield, Mike Skinner, Rusty Wallace, Ken Schrader, Ward Burton and Bobby Labonte plotted strategy for the three-lap shootout that would unfold.

And when it did, no one had anything for Gordon, although Bobby Labonte, with a bump-draft from brother Terry, shot up into second place on the final lap, but was a car-length short at the end. Skinner held onto third place, with Mayfield and Wallace finishing fourth and fifth. Terry was only able to get sixth out of the final-lap scramble, while Ward Burton claimed seventh place. Although Irvan was credited with eighth place, it was Craven driving the car after taking over for Ernie early in the event. Schrader and Earnhardt were ninth and 10th, while Mark Martin finished in 16th, on the lead lap, but not a factor in the event.

Pepsi 400

[RACE #30 • DAYTONA INTERNATIONAL SPEEDWAY • OCTOBER 17, 1998]

Fin. Pos.	Start Pos.	Car #	Driver	Team	Fin. Pos.	Start Pos.	Car #	Driver	Team
1	8	24	Jeff Gordon	DuPont Automotive Finishes Chevrolet	23	3	88	Dale Jarrett	Quality Care/Ford Credit Ford
2	1	18	Bobby Labonte	Interstate Batteries Pontiac	24	23	91	Andy Hillenburg	Little Joe's Auto Chevrolet
3	9	31	Mike Skinner	Lowe's Chevrolet	25	19	11	Brett Bodine	Paychex Ford
4	25	12	Jeremy Mayfield	Mobil 1 Ford	26	40	26	Johnny Benson	Betty Crocker Ford
5	7	2	Rusty Wallace	Miller Lite Ford	27	41	10	Ricky Rudd	Tide Ford
6	4	5	Terry Labonte	Kellogg's Corn Flakes Chevrolet	28	43	35	Darrell Waltrip	Tabasco Pontiac
7	12	22	Ward Burton	MBNA America Pontiac	29	24	96	Steve Grissom	Caterpillar Chevrolet
8	39	36	Ernie Irvan	Wild Berry Skittles Pontiac	30	35	50	Wally Dallenbach	Budweiser Chevrolet
9	16	33	Ken Schrader	Skoal Bandit Chevrolet	31	29	21	Michael Waltrip	CITGO Ford
10	5	3	Dale Earnhardt	GM Goodwrench Service Chevrolet	32	11	28	Kenny Irwin	Texaco/Havoline Ford
11	37	4	Bobby Hamilton	Kodak MAX Film Chevrolet	33	15	1	Steve Park	Pennzoil Chevrolet
12	38	23	Jimmy Spencer	Winston/No Bull Ford	34	34	13	Ted Musgrave	FirstPlus Financial Ford
13	2	99	Jeff Burton	Exide Batteries Ford	35	28	81	Kenny Wallace	Square D Ford
14	14	43	John Andretti	STP Pontiac	36	26	07	Dan Pardus	Midwest Transit Chevrolet
15	31	94	Bill Elliott	McDonald's Ford	37	32	46	Jeff Green	The Money Store Chevrolet
16	6	6	Mark Martin	Valvoline/Cummins Ford	38	13	30	Derrike Cope	Gumout Pontiac
17	27	42	Joe Nemechek	BellSouth Chevrolet	39	36	98	Rich Bickle	Thorn Apple Valley Ford
18	17	40	Sterling Marlin	Coors Light Chevrolet	40	22	16	Kevin Lepage	PRIMESTAR Ford
19	33	9	Jerry Nadeau	Cartoon Network Ford	41	21	7	Geoff Bodine	Philips Consumer Comm. Ford
20	20	97	Chad Little	John Deere Ford	42	10	55	Hut Stricklin	Oakwood Homes Chevrolet
21	30	71	Dave Marcis	Realtree Camouflage Chevrolet	43	18	47	Billy Standridge	Team FansCanRace.com Ford
22	42	44	Kyle Petty	Hot Wheels Pontiac					

Dura Lube/Kmart 500

After the Pepsi 400 at Daytona, Jeff Gordon found himself with a huge 358-point lead over Mark Martin with just three races remaining in the season. As far as the defending champion and his Rainbow Warriors were concerned, Gordon's 11th victory of the year couldn't have come at a better time.

Some thought Gordon and crew chief Ray Evernham would put the entire DuPont effort into cruise control. After all, Jeff merely needed to finish 32nd or better in the remaining three races, or gain just 12 points on Mark Martin, to clinch the third NASCAR Winston Cup title in the last four years for the team. But that's not the way Gordon, Evernham or the Rainbow Warriors operate.

Whatever hopes remained in the Valvoline team evaporated after the race under the lights at Daytona Beach. Now, Martin and his team aimed at winning the remaining events of the season and making what had been a great year even better. The championship was lost. Had Mark compiled the same kind of season in any other year, he probably would have held a commanding lead in the title chase. But Gordon's perform-

(Right) *Pole-winner Ken Schrader takes the green flag to begin the 31st race of the season, with rookie Kenny Irwin on his right. The huge crowd at Phoenix filled every seat, and spilled over onto the nearby hillside that provides a panoramic view of the track.*

(Below) *Rusty Wallace takes to the inside of Rich Bickle (98) and Kenny Wallace (81), working his way toward the front of the pack in the early laps of the race. Kenny, who ripped off a quick qualifying lap to start third, picked up his seventh top-10 finish of the year by coming home in eighth, while Bickle, who started on Rusty's inside in fifth, just missed the top 10 with an 11th-place finish.*

(Above) *Jeff Gordon (24) chases Mark Martin into the first turn as storm clouds begin to gather over the nearby mountains that surround the track.* (Right) *Showing that experience counts at Phoenix, Ken Schrader picks up his second pole of the season at the track where he has logged many, many miles in multiple types of race cars over his career.* (Middle Right) *Eddie Wood (left) and Michael Waltrip can only stand and watch, as their CITGO Ford is loaded onto the transporter after failing to qualify for the event.* (Bottom Right) *Sterling Marlin is just happy to be at the track after having to hitch a ride to get there when the team's transporter, which he had decided to ride in for the cross-country trip, broke down along the way.*

ances had been superlative, and that truly was the story of the season. In the last three restrictor-plate races, Gordon had outscored Mark by 250 points. In the end, it may well have been that the Daytona and Talladega races brought Gordon his third career NASCAR Winston Cup championship.

Despite a 23rd place at Daytona, Dale Jarrett seemingly had third place locked up, holding a 154-point margin over Rusty Wallace. Wallace, still hunting for his first victory of the season, was 109 ahead of sixth-place Bobby Labonte, who was embroiled in a three-way dogfight for the final top-five position in the point standings. With Jeff Burton a mere four points behind Bobby, and Jeremy Mayfield just four points behind Burton, fifth place clearly would be determined in the final three events of the season.

Dale Earnhardt, coming off a top-10 finish at Daytona, was eighth in the standings, 23 points ahead of a charging Terry Labonte. John Andretti clung to 10th place in the standings, a mere 13 ahead of Bobby Hamilton, while Ken Schrader was 12th, 80 behind Hamilton and still hoping to find his way into the top 10 at season's end.

Ernie Irvan still was not fully recovered from his Talladega accident, and Ricky Craven was enlisted for a second week to stand by in case Ernie was either unable to start the Skittles Pontiac or could not go the distance. Ted Musgrave would make his fourth consecutive start in the FirstPlus Financial Ford, and said that he would finish the season in the "13" car to give the crew some sort of continuity with a driver. With NASCAR Craftsman Truck Series standout Mike Bliss scheduled for the seat in the Caterpillar Chevrolet, team owner Buzz McCall watched with delight as Bliss won Saturday's truck series event at the one-mile track. And in a surprise move, Bahari crew chief Doug Hewitt announced his decision to leave the "30" team at the end of the season and move to Petty Enterprises to become Kyle Petty's crew chief for the coming season.

Over the years, Ken Schrader has logged more miles than any other competitor at Phoenix, competing in nearly every type of racing machine imaginable. It was no surprise, then, when Schrader wheeled the Skoal Bandit Chevrolet to the fastest qualifying time of the Bud Pole session to claim his second pole position in the last three races. His experience in

team next season, grabbed the inside of the second row, just a tick of the watch faster than Bill Elliott's rock-solid lap in his McDonald's Ford.

Rich Bickle, hoping to make potential sponsors sit up and take notice of Cale Yarborough's Ford effort, was fifth fastest, with Rusty Wallace on his right for the start of the event. Rick Mast, who had missed the show at Daytona, and Mike Skinner made up the fourth row. David Green turned in a strong lap with Larry Hedrick's Kodiak Chevrolet to claim the ninth starting spot next to Musgrave, who nailed down his first career top-10 start at Phoenix.

Martin and Gordon didn't have to look far to find each other for the start of the race. They were side by side in the sixth row, with Mark fractionally faster than Gordon. Jarrett, fighting what he felt was a flu bug, was 20th in the first session, and Kevin Lepage was the final first-round qualifier.

Kevin Lepage (16), Sterling Marlin (40) and Wally Dallenbach (50) chase Terry Labonte through the fourth turn. Labonte featured a special "Ironman" look for the race, celebrating his 600th consecutive NASCAR Winston Cup start, a string dating back to his rookie season of 1979.

winning races in the Featherlite Southwest Series, midgets and Silver Crown cars at Phoenix helped him turn the fastest practice laps, and then keep it all together for the important pole-winning lap during the first qualifying session.

He needed every split second to get the job done. Kenny Irwin, who also has spent many hours running the Phoenix track in open-wheel machinery, was six-one-thousandths of a second slower than Schrader, barely missing the pole, but claiming the outside of the front row. Kenny Wallace, to be Schrader's teammate at the expanded two-car Andy Petree

Bobby Labonte and Jeff Burton, along with Dale Earnhardt, Bobby Hamilton and Chad Little, were forced to use provisionals to make the field. Ernie Irvan drove the Skittles Pontiac in qualifying, but the team was forced to use a provisional, as well, and Irvan turned the car over to Craven to start the race. Once again, Darrell Waltrip had to use a former champion's provisional to make the field, and Dave Marcis, Jeff Ward and Michael Waltrip missed the race. It was the first time a Wood Brothers car had failed to qualify for a race since the 1971 Southern 500 at Darlington, and the first time

A crew member shows hustle and intensity as he scurries around the back of Gary Bradberry's Ford, headed for the left rear on a four-tire stop.

As it worked out, had the event run the full compliment of laps, the result probably would have been the same. The Miller Lite Ford, a spanking new chassis with a new engine combination, and Rusty Wallace's fire-breathing determination to end a winless string that stretched all the way back to March of 1997, were the right ingredients. And when Rusty made the call to drop the air pressures a notch and change the track bar in the Ford's right rear, it was time for Wallace to sing "Happy Trails" to the rest of the field.

He took the lead for the first time on lap 54, and until the event was stopped when the skies began leaking almost 200 laps later, Wallace simply dominated the event. Behind him, several drivers, including Martin, Earnhardt and Musgrave, had outstanding performances, but no one could match Wallace. And in the end, no one had the chance to try a last-gasp effort. Instead, the skies opened up and it poured down rain, eventually forcing NASCAR officials to admit there was no way they could dry the flat track in time to complete all the laps before darkness set in.

The victory was Wallace's, giving him 48 for his career and extending his streak of winning at least one race a year to 13 seasons. Martin fought to second place, and with Gordon finishing seventh, Mark kept from being mathematically eliminated from the title chase at Phoenix. Earnhardt charged from 37th to finish third, while Musgrave had a simply brilliant run in the Elliott-Marino Motorsports Ford, running second just before the rain and finishing fifth behind Jeff Burton. John Andretti was sixth ahead of Gordon, while Kenny Wallace and Johnny Benson were eighth and ninth ahead of Terry Labonte.

The flu Jarrett had complained of Friday worsened, and he asked for relief during the event. Michael Waltrip slid into the car, and Jarrett eventually was helicoptered to a Phoenix hospital where he was diagnosed as having gall bladder problems and kept overnight.

Michael had missed a race since the 1986 Daytona 500. There were long faces as the Woods loaded the CITGO transporter. Since the vaunted team began running the full schedule in 1985, the "21" Fords had been in 416 straight races. That string ended in the sands of the desert.

When team members rested their heads on motel room pillows Saturday night, no one would envision the strange way the Dura Lube 500 would end the following afternoon. After all, this is Phoenix. The Valley of the Sun. Home to some of the highest temperatures seen on television weather maps throughout the year. Desert. Cactus. Sand. An airport that has to be closed at times because there is not enough lift in the air to allow planes to take off.

A race shortened by rain? In Phoenix? Maybe a sprinkle or two, enough to barely wet the asphalt. But rain? With thunder and lightning? ... Yea, right.

But that's what happened.

Team owner Roger Penske (left) joins Rusty Wallace for a long overdue victory celebration at Phoenix. The win ended a 59-race winless string for the former champion and extended his streak of winning at least one race each year to 13 seasons.

With the crowd gone and the teams packing up for the long ride home, the setting sun lights up the remaining moisture in the sky to form a spectacular rainbow, bringing to a close another trip to the Valley of the Sun.

Dura Lube/Kmart 500

[*RACE #31 • PHOENIX INTERNATIONAL RACEWAY • OCTOBER 25, 1998*]

Fin. Pos.	Start Pos.	Car #	Driver	Team	Fin. Pos.	Start Pos.	Car #	Driver	Team
1	6	2	Rusty Wallace	Miller Lite Ford	23	37	18	Bobby Labonte	Interstate Batteries Pontiac
2	11	6	Mark Martin	Valvoline/Cummins Ford	24	35	1	Steve Park	Pennzoil Chevrolet
3	39	3	Dale Earnhardt	GM Goodwrench Service Chevrolet	25	23	50	Wally Dallenbach	Budweiser Chevrolet
4	38	99	Jeff Burton	Exide Batteries Ford	26	18	23	Jimmy Spencer	Winston/No Bull Ford
5	10	13	Ted Musgrave	FirstPlus Financial Ford	27	21	10	Ricky Rudd	Tide Ford
6	19	43	John Andretti	STP Pontiac	28	33	46	Jeff Green	The Money Store Chevrolet
7	12	24	Jeff Gordon	DuPont Automotive Finishes Chevrolet	29	7	75	Rick Mast	Remington Arms Ford
8	3	81	Kenny Wallace	Square D Ford	30	41	36	Ricky Craven	Skittles Pontiac
9	15	26	Johnny Benson	Cheerios Ford	31	43	35	Darrell Waltrip	Tabasco Pontiac
10	29	5	Terry Labonte	Kellogg's Corn Flakes Chevrolet	32	20	88	Dale Jarrett	Quality Care/Ford Credit Ford
11	5	98	Rich Bickle	Thorn Apple Valley Ford	33	36	30	Derrike Cope	Gumout Pontiac
12	16	40	Sterling Marlin	Coors Light Chevrolet	34	26	7	Geoff Bodine	Philips Consumer Comm. Ford
13	25	16	Kevin Lepage	PRIMESTAR Ford	35	27	96	Mike Bliss	Caterpillar Chevrolet
14	14	22	Ward Burton	MBNA America Pontiac	36	31	44	Kyle Petty	Hot Wheels Pontiac
15	17	91	Todd Bodine	Little Joe's Auto Chevrolet	37	9	41	David Green	Kodiak Chevrolet
16	8	31	Mike Skinner	Lowe's Chevrolet	38	4	94	Bill Elliott	McDonald's Ford
17	24	77	Robert Pressley	Jasper Engines Ford	39	34	9	Jerry Nadeau	Cartoon Network Ford
18	32	42	Joe Nemechek	BellSouth Chevrolet	40	2	28	Kenny Irwin	Texaco/Havoline Ford
19	30	90	Dick Trickle	Heilig-Meyers Ford	41	28	78	Gary Bradberry	Pilot Travel Centers Ford
20	42	97	Chad Little	John Deere Ford	42	22	12	Jeremy Mayfield	Mobil 1 Ford
21	40	4	Bobby Hamilton	Kodak MAX Film Chevrolet	43	13	11	Brett Bodine	Paychex Ford
22	1	33	Ken Schrader	Skoal Bandit Chevrolet					

ACDelco 400

The combination of Mark Martin's second place in the rain-shortened event at Phoenix and Jeff Gordon's well-judged seventh place kept the drama alive as teams returned from the desert and made preparations for a second visit to North Carolina's Sandhills.

Gordon found himself all but crowned as the champion of the sport for the third time in the last four years, but he had not mathematically eliminated the gritty Valvoline Ford driver from contention. If all went well for Gordon, that would happen at Rockingham, and he would become the first driver since Dale Earnhardt (1994) to clinch the championship before the final event of the season.

Gordon's lead over Martin after the Phoenix race was 329 points, and all Gordon had to do at Rockingham was finish 40th or higher, even if Martin won the race and led the most laps to gather the five bonus points for that accomplishment. Needless to say, the folks at R.J. Reynolds already had the plate engraved for the NASCAR Winston Cup trophy — and the name on it wasn't "Mark Martin."

(Right) *Pole-winner Mark Martin (6) and third-place starter Rusty Wallace (2) get a quick jump on Johnny Benson (26) on the opening lap of the race. Martin, Wallace and Benson traded the early lead until Rusty established himself at the point for the first quarter of the event.*

(Below) *After battling for the championship for most of the season, Mark Martin and Jeff Gordon once again found themselves racing side by side during the ACDelco 400 at Rockingham. Gordon clinched the title early in the event, then drove on to capture his 12th victory of the year. Martin would finish fourth at the end of the day and lock up second place in the point standings.*

Mark was somewhat philosophical about the situation. He had put together a career year, despite having to figure out a brand new Taurus during the season and determine what the new body shape would want for each type of course on the circuit. His total of seven victories was the best of his career, and he was slated to finish in the top 10 in the point standings for the 10th straight year — an outstanding achievement in

this world of highly competitive drivers and teams. But he had yet to win the championship, and he hoped his team could put together another great season in 1999 with, perhaps, just a little better performance in restrictor-plate races. He had lost more than 250 points to Gordon in the last three races at Talladega and Daytona.

For Dale Jarrett, the trip to Phoenix had been a lost affair. His helicopter trip to the hospital resulted in his transfer to another hospital to be treated by gall bladder specialists, and he spent four nights there, undergoing tests and treatment for three gallstones. Finally released Thursday, he flew back to North Carolina and was unsure about how much he would be able to compete at Rockingham, if at all. The tests determined he would need surgery, which he put off until after the Atlanta race, and the Robert Yates team enlisted Hut Stricklin to stand by as a relief driver for Jarrett.

His bad luck at the Arizona track, coupled with Rusty Wallace's victory, put Jarrett's third place in the point standings in jeopardy. In reality, if he had problems in the final two races, he could fall out of the top five. It was added incentive for him to slide through the window of the Quality Care Ford. Rusty was now within 36 points of Jarrett in their renewed battle for third place.

Jeff Burton, 133 behind Rusty, was trying to protect the final position in the top five. Bobby Labonte trailed Jeff by 67

The Hendrick Motorsports armada runs together, with Wally Dallenbach (50) and Terry Labonte (5) following eventual winner Jeff Gordon. Dallenbach, who had been in the "50" car since Michigan in the 21st race of the season, was settling in with the Budweiser team, preparing to run the full schedule for Hendrick in 1999.

(Left) *Rusty Wallace (2), Jeff Gordon (24) and Dale Jarrett (88) work underneath Geoff Bodine (7), putting the Philips Ford a lap down as they fight for the point. The three drivers took turns leading the event, but it was Gordon who would emerge the strongest at the end of the day, dropping Jarrett to second and Wallace to third.*

(Below) *A crew member leans over the pit wall, prepared to accept a used tire from Jeff Gordon's Monte Carlo. Earlier, a rare miscue by the DuPont team allowed a tire to roll across pit road, costing the team a penalty that put Gordon mid-pack and forced him to fight his way back to the front.*

points, and was only 65 points ahead of Jeremy Mayfield. Any of the three drivers, depending on their finishes in the last two races of the year, could finish fifth.

Dale Earnhardt, currently in eighth place, had no chance of moving up in the standings, but he was keeping a wary eye on Terry Labonte, who had moved to within 49 points of the Goodwrench Chevrolet driver. With John Andretti just 63 points behind Terry and the same number of points ahead of the fast-closing Bobby Hamilton, the final position on the stage at the New York banquet was also up for grabs.

When fellow Roush driver Chad Little dropped out of the race with a broken radiator, Jeff Burton's team confiscated the unused tires from the John Deere team to use on their Exide Ford. Fortunately for Burton, looks don't count in racing, and the extra tires helped Jeff drive to his 17th top-five finish of the year.

Once again, Ricky Craven was in the Skittles Pontiac for Ernie Irvan, who didn't feel he was quite well enough to drive the car, and Ted Musgrave was in the FirstPlus Financial Ford after his simply brilliant run at Phoenix. Steve Grissom was handling the driving duties in the Caterpillar Chevrolet, Todd Bodine returned to the LJ Racing Chevrolet and David Green was behind the wheel of the Kodiak Chevrolet.

With 28 pit stalls on the frontstretch, every driver knew that all of the first-round qualifiers would be guaranteed a spot on the front side of the track. Those who barely missed making the field during Bud Pole qualifying would be in jeopardy of being forced to pit on the backstretch. It was just another dollop of added pressure for the teams and drivers.

For Martin, there simply was no problem. Mark turned in what he called a "perfect lap," and when the first round of qualifying was completed, the Valvoline Ford was on the inside of the front row for the start of the ACDelco 400. He easily eclipsed the lap turned by his Roush Racing teammate, Johnny Benson, while third-place combatants Wallace and Jarrett nailed down the second-row starting positions. Geoff Bodine, searching for a ride for the 1999 season, was fifth fastest, and Mayfield had another strong qualifying run to claim the sixth-fastest lap. Ricky Rudd made it Fords 1-2-3-4-5-6-7 on the starting grid, with Derrike Cope breaking up the Blue Oval monopoly with his Gumout Pontiac. Gordon was ninth fastest, just two one-thousandths of a mile per hour faster than Andretti in Richard Petty's STP Pontiac.

Jerry Nadeau continued his outstanding qualifying efforts in the Cartoon Network Ford, while Todd Bodine did the same with the LJ Racing Chevrolet, both barely missing the top 10. Bill Elliott was the fastest of the second-round qualifiers, while Gary Bradberry and Mike Skinner filled the final frontstretch pit positions, relegating Earnhardt to the backside. Provisionals went to Craven and Steve Park, along with Dick Trickle, Robert Pressley, Musgrave, Jeff Green and Darrell Waltrip, who once again used a former champion's provisional to make the field. Grissom, Andy Hillenburg and Dave Marcis all failed to make the field.

(Left) *Dale Jarrett (88) and Rusty Wallace (2) carry the fight at the front, with Jeff Burton (99) lurking behind them. Jarrett would take the lap-leader bonus by leading 195 of the race's 393 laps, and Wallace appeared headed for the win until his car faded slightly in the closing laps.*

(Opposite Page) *The Rainbow Warriors throw three fingers into the air after capturing their third NASCAR Winston Cup crown in the last four years. With the crown and the win came a few checks from Winston: the point-leader bonus of $20,000 for winning the race, and a cool $2 million for taking the title, adding substantially to an already-record total for winnings in a single season.*

As teams made the final preparations to their mounts for the ACDelco 400, Darrell announced that he had become a free agent for the coming season, and was looking for another team to drive for. After the long and difficult final third of the season, Tabasco and the Tim Beverly team would part company following the Atlanta race and Waltrip found himself free to pursue other options.

Rockingham's 400-miler would become a Halloween special for Gordon. The treat came early in the event, after Gordon led a lap and three cars fell out of the race. That meant that Gordon could finish no worse than 40th, mathematically eliminating Martin from the title chase. His crew donned the Champion hats and the banner was lofted behind the team on pit road, although it was anticlimactic: Jeff was saving the special moment for the end of the race.

Penalized once for 15 seconds when a crew member let a tire slip away and roll across pit road, Gordon methodically fought his way back to the front. With Rusty and Jarrett battling at the point, Gordon began his best "sneak-up-on-you" imitation of some of the "Trick or Treaters" that had visited the hotels and campsites Saturday evening. He slipped further and

further up through the field, slowly moving into contention for the victory, and with just eight laps remaining in the event, he moved past Wallace to claim the point. Jeff had said entering the weekend that he hoped he and the Rainbow Warriors could not only claim the title, but also do it in style with a victory. As the final laps clicked off, he was able to do just that.

He eased away and notched his 12th victory of the season, the first driver to win that many events since Darrell Waltrip in 1981, his first championship season. The win gave his team its 32nd victory in the last three seasons of competition — or a triumph in every third race over the last three years.

Jarrett also was able to work past Wallace to finish second, and his gutsy drive, coming after his stint in the Phoenix hospital, would have claimed the majority of the headlines had Gordon not won both the race and the title. To have been in the hospital with such a painful problem for that long, and then return to the wheel and nearly win, was testimony to Jarrett's stamina and determination.

By leading the most laps, he picked up 10 points on Wallace in their battle for third in the season standings. Rusty came home third at Rockingham ahead of Martin, while Jeff Burton was fifth. Bobby Hamilton claimed sixth with a heady drive in a new Chevrolet, with Ward Burton and Terry Labonte ahead of Earnhardt and Rudd.

After winning the championship in style by bringing home yet another win, Jeff Gordon shows his jubilation by cutting a few doughnuts in Rockingham's tri-oval grass while on his way to victory lane.

ACDelco 400

[*Race #32 • North Carolina Speedway • November 1, 1998*]

Fin. Pos.	Start Pos.	Car #	Driver	Team	Fin. Pos.	Start Pos.	Car #	Driver	Team
1	9	24	Jeff Gordon	DuPont Automotive Finishes Chevrolet	23	39	90	Dick Trickle	Heilig-Meyers Ford
2	4	88	Dale Jarrett	Quality Care/Ford Credit Ford	24	11	9	Jerry Nadeau	Cartoon Network Ford
3	3	2	Rusty Wallace	Miller Lite Ford	25	8	30	Derrike Cope	Gumout Pontiac
4	1	6	Mark Martin	Valvoline/Cummins Ford	26	36	41	David Green	Kodiak Chevrolet
5	13	99	Jeff Burton	Exide Batteries Ford	27	42	46	Jeff Green	The Money Store Chevrolet
6	25	4	Bobby Hamilton	Kodak MAX Film Chevrolet	28	27	78	Gary Bradberry	Pilot Travel Centers Ford
7	15	22	Ward Burton	MBNA America Pontiac	29	6	12	Jeremy Mayfield	Mobil 1 Ford
8	21	5	Terry Labonte	Kellogg's Corn Flakes Chevrolet	30	17	23	Jimmy Spencer	Winston/No Bull Ford
9	29	3	Dale Earnhardt	GM Goodwrench Service Chevrolet	31	32	11	Brett Bodine	Paychex Ford
10	7	10	Ricky Rudd	Tide Ford	32	43	35	Darrell Waltrip	Tabasco Pontiac
11	5	7	Geoff Bodine	Philips Consumer Comm. Ford	33	33	28	Kenny Irwin	Texaco/Havoline Ford
12	26	94	Bill Elliott	McDonald's Ford	34	10	43	John Andretti	STP Pontiac
13	30	40	Sterling Marlin	Coors Light Chevrolet	35	38	1	Steve Park	Pennzoil Chevrolet
14	14	33	Ken Schrader	Skoal Bandit Chevrolet	36	24	50	Wally Dallenbach	Budweiser Chevrolet
15	19	18	Bobby Labonte	Interstate Batteries Pontiac	37	37	36	Ricky Craven	Skittles Pontiac
16	34	81	Kenny Wallace	Square D Ford	38	40	77	Robert Pressley	Jasper Engines Ford
17	16	42	Joe Nemechek	BellSouth Chevrolet	39	23	44	Kyle Petty	Hot Wheels Pontiac
18	31	98	Rich Bickle	Thorn Apple Valley Ford	40	22	97	Chad Little	John Deere Ford
19	41	13	Ted Musgrave	FirstPlus Financial Ford	41	2	26	Johnny Benson	Cheerios Ford
20	12	91	Todd Bodine	Little Joe's Auto Chevrolet	42	35	75	Rick Mast	Remington Arms Ford
21	28	31	Mike Skinner	Lowe's Chevrolet	43	18	16	Kevin Lepage	PRIMESTAR Ford
22	20	21	Michael Waltrip	CITGO Ford					

NAPA 500

With the championship safely salted away and after dusting the mantle in his home in preparation for his latest NASCAR Winston Cup, a joking and extremely relaxed Jeff Gordon arrived at Atlanta Motor Speedway to begin enjoying his third title in the last four years.

Gordon and the Rainbow Warriors may have been headed for a no-pressure weekend, but others in the garage were not nearly as lucky. In several cases, drivers and teams were fighting for positions in the point standings, bonus money at the conclusion of the season and, in one case, the opportunity to walk onto the stage at the Waldorf-Astoria Hotel in New York City during the NASCAR Winston Cup Awards Banquet.

Mark Martin was destined for second place in the point standings, but third place was still very much in question, with Dale Jarrett holding a 46-point margin over Rusty Wallace. Bobby Labonte trailed Jeff Burton by 109 points, and Jeremy Mayfield was 107 behind the Interstate Pontiac driver. Dale Earnhardt could not move up from eighth place, but could lose that position to Terry Labonte. Terry was 45 behind Earnhardt and

(Right) *Kenny Irwin proudly displays his trophy after capturing the inside of the front row for the start of the NAPA 500 with a lap at more than 193 miles per hour to win his first career Bud Pole. That, along with becoming the highest-finishing rookie in the event with a 16th-place finish, cemented Rookie of the Year honors for the rising star.*

(Below) *Kenny Irwin and Ward Burton lead the field into the first turn during warm-up laps in preparation for the green flag to kick off the 33rd race of 1998, the longest season in the modern era of NASCAR Winston Cup competition.*

Kenny Irwin (28) trails his Robert Yates teammate, Dale Jarrett (88), in the early laps of the event. Irwin led the first lap off the pole, but Jarrett took over from the third starting spot on Lap 2, and led until the first caution (for rain) on Lap 38.

The race weekend also marked the end of relationships between some drivers, teams and sponsors. It would be the final time Geoff Bodine would compete in a Mattei Motorsports Ford, and Michael Waltrip's days with the Wood Brothers would also end. Rick Mast and Butch Mock would part company, and Ted Musgrave would drive the FirstPlus Financial Ford for the final time.

could take the position, depending on how the two drivers finished at Atlanta. Bobby Hamilton had taken 10th place following Rockingham, but John Andretti, 26 points behind, could reclaim the final position in the top 10 if he could have a strong Atlanta finish.

While the drivers were preparing to jostle for positions, the Ford and Chevrolet teams were making final preparations for the event that would determine which car make would claim the 1998 Manufacturer's Championship. Jeff Gordon's victory at Rockingham had pulled Chevrolet from one point behind to two points ahead in that battle, and Atlanta would decide the coveted crown.

The manufacturer's battle was so tight that if a Pontiac won the race, a Ford finished second and a Chevrolet third, the point standings would be tied at the completion of the season. The first tiebreaker would be the number of victories, and Ford and Chevrolet would be tied with 15 each. The second tiebreaker would be the number of second places, and Ford would win the title with 20 compared to Chevrolet's eight. It was that close, and with bragging rights on the line, teams brought their very best equipment.

Dick Trickle's return to Junie Donlavey's Fords was doubtful and it marked the last time Kenny Wallace would drive for FILMAR Racing. It also would mark the end of a relationship between Caterpillar and Buzz McCall, Thorn Apple Valley and Cale Yarborough, and MBNA and Bill Davis, among others. From the standpoints of McCall and Yarborough, it also could mark the end of their racing teams if neither was able to obtain sponsorship for the future.

Ernie Irvan, still feeling as though he needed time out of a race car, opted to sit out the Atlanta race, and Ricky Craven again would wheel the Skittles Pontiac. Craven had his own great news to share during the weekend, after being named driver of a new team to be fielded in 1999 by Scott Barbour and SBIII Motorsports. David Green announced he would

Bobby Labonte (18) leads Derrike Cope (30), Jeremy Mayfield (12), Mark Martin (6), Joe Nemechek (42) and Dick Trickle through the tri-oval in early-race action. Labonte had to be considered the favorite to win the race, having won the last two events at Atlanta, but fell out with engine trouble and was listed last in the final rundown. Nemechek also was very strong, running with the leaders and in contention for the win until he suffered a similar fate, ending his season in the garage.

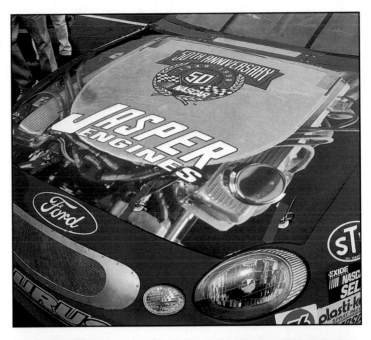

(Right) *The Jasper Engines team came up with this innovative design on their Ford Tuarus, featuring a huge Jasper powerplant under a seemingly transparent hood.*

(Below Right) *A Jasper crew member prepares a day's supply of gum for driver Robert Pressley, ready for mounting inside the car to allow easy access during the race.*

drive the full 1999 season with Larry Hedrick's Kodiak Chevrolet team, now led by crew chief Tim Brewer.

NASCAR officials implemented a rules change prior to practice and qualifying at Atlanta. The noses of the cars were lowered from five-inches of clearance to 3.5 inches, and the rear spoilers were raised, in hopes of making the cars more stable in the corners. The higher spoilers would increase drag along the straights, and although the cars would corner at higher speeds, the feeling was that the increased stability would be an overall improvement for drivers. Goodyear did its part, also, bringing a harder tire than what was used at Atlanta before, and it was expected that the overall combination would drop speeds slightly.

It turned out that way in qualifying. Last year, Geoff Bodine held his breath better than anyone and grabbed the pole with a lap in excess of 197 miles per hour. This time, when Bud Pole qualifying was completed, the mark stood at 193.46 mph, and the pole-sitter was a big surprise. Kenny Irwin had rocketed around the track in his Texaco/Havoline Ford to claim a spot in the 1999 Bud Shootout at Daytona in February. That a different pole winner had claimed the fastest lap at Atlanta should have been no surprise — Irwin was the 16th different pole winner at Atlanta in as many races. He also became the 15th different Bud Pole winner of the season, guaranteeing a 16-car field in the Bud Shootout with the addition of the wildcard entry selected from fastest second-round qualifiers throughout the season.

On the outside of the front row, Ward Burton gave the MBNA folks a good send-off, and Jarrett slotted his Robert Yates Quality Care ford right behind his teammate. Mark Martin was fourth fastest, while Mike Skinner, whose Lowe's team had won the Tosco 76 World Pit Crew Championship in Rockingham's special competition, qualified fifth. Derrike Cope, whose Bahari team was expected to announce new sponsorship for 1999 and beyond, was sixth fastest, while the fourth row was made up of pre-race favorite Bobby

Everyone was forced to seek cover during a driving rainstorm that brought the event to a halt and left the cars covered and lined up along pit road. The NAPA 500 wasn't supposed to be run under the lights at Atlanta, but with the stubborn rain front hampering the completion of the season finale, the lights came in very handy.

Labonte and Trickle. Mayfield and Geoff Bodine beat Sabco teammates Joe Nemechek and Jeff Green for the final top-10 spots.

Provisionals were used by Earnhardt, Terry Labonte, Craven, Johnny Benson, Kyle Petty, Kenny Wallace and, for the final time in 1998, Darrel Waltrip used a previous champion's provisional to make the field. Rich Bickle and Steve Grissom failed to give Yarborough and McCall's teams a final outing in 1998, while Rick Mast and Andy Hillenburg also went home. Harris DeVane, trying to make the field, crashed during his second-round qualifying effort.

With a huge throng assembled at Atlanta, competitors were greeted by overcast skies and rain on Sunday morning. The track was dried and the field rolled off the line for the NAPA 500 some 40 minutes late, but it was just the first delay in a race that seemed to take forever to complete. Jarrett took the point after just one lap and moved out to a commanding lead, until the caution flag — and then the red — flew for rain. After a two-and-a-half hour delay, the field roared to life again and rolled out, only to be greeted by another shower. NASCAR officials talked with competitors, and eventually, the lights were turned on.

Finally, after a battle to dry the track and get it race-ready, the field rolled out again at 9:40 p.m. During pit stops under yellow before the race restarted, several cars were involved in bumping incidents on pit road as the front half of the field moved out of their pit stalls, while other cars were turning

left to enter theirs. Missing all the action while pitting near the end of pit road was Gordon, who was able to take over the point.

Once there, Jeff found the changing track conditions favorable to his DuPont Chevrolet and he eased out to a solid lead as the field sorted itself behind him. NASCAR mandated a pair of yellow flags later in the race to help control the wet conditions on pit road. During the second of those cautions, teams were told that weather was once again headed toward the track, and that when the race resumed there would be 25 laps remaining in the event. Several crew chiefs made the choice to take two tires and gain track position while Gordon took four tires and emerged seventh in line for the restart. Ahead of him were Skinner and Earnhardt, with Todd Bodine third after a brilliant run in the LJ Racing Chevrolet. Ken Schrader was fourth ahead of Jimmy Spencer, Dick Trickle and Morgan Shepherd, who was having an outstanding run in the Stavola Brothers' Chevrolet.

With the DuPont Chevrolet on four new tires, Gordon mounted his charge, but tangled with Shepherd, sending the Stavola Chevrolet driver hard into the wall. Shepherd emerged furious but unhurt from his battle with the concrete. Jarrett, seventh on the ensuing restart with 18 to go, ripped his way all the way to the point, passing Skinner with 11 laps remaining. Behind him, Gordon was on the move, clawing his way to second, and then closing on the Quality Care Ford. With six laps left and Jarrett's Ford becoming tight in the corners,

Gordon swept past and went on to win his 13th race of the year. Gordon's victory equaled Richard Petty's record for the most victories in a modern-day season set in 1975, and also iced the Manufacturer's Championship for Chevrolet.

Jarrett finished second, with Martin fighting to third place. Jeff Burton claimed fourth, barely nosing out Todd Bodine, and Bobby Hamilton rocketed to sixth, earning 10th place in the final point standings and claiming the final position on the stage at the Waldorf. Schrader finished eighth ahead of Skinner and Geoff Bodine.

Jarrett's solid second place kept him third in the standings, while Rusty finished fourth. Jeff Burton claimed fifth, and Bobby Labonte, victim of engine failure, held on for sixth. Mayfield was seventh in the final standings and Earnhardt claimed eighth. Terry Labonte finished ninth, while John Andretti failed in his effort to dislodge Hamilton for 10th place in the final tally.

Jeff Gordon hoists his third NASCAR Winston Cup, having won it in grand style by charging to the front of the pack with seven laps remaining in the event and capturing a record-tying 13th win in the process. It was a fitting end to a truly outstanding season for Gordon and his Rainbow Warriors.

NAPA 500

[*RACE #33 • ATLANTA MOTOR SPEEDWAY • NOVEMBER 8, 1998*]

Fin. Pos.	Start Pos.	Car #	Driver	Team	Fin. Pos.	Start Pos.	Car #	Driver	Team
1	21	24	Jeff Gordon	DuPont Automotive Finishes Chevrolet	23	40	26	Johnny Benson	Cheerios Ford
2	3	88	Dale Jarrett	Quality Care/Ford Credit Ford	24	34	10	Ricky Rudd	Tide Ford
3	4	6	Mark Martin	Valvoline/Cummins Ford	25	39	36	Ricky Craven	Skittles Pontiac
4	35	99	Jeff Burton	Exide Batteries Ford	26	27	94	Bill Elliott	McDonald's Ford
5	20	91	Todd Bodine	Little Joe's Auto Chevrolet	27	30	71	Dave Marcis	Realtree Camouflage Chevrolet
6	14	4	Bobby Hamilton	Kodak MAX Film Chevrolet	28	33	77	Robert Pressley	Jasper Engines Ford
7	13	33	Ken Schrader	Skoal Bandit Chevrolet	29	41	44	Kyle Petty	Hot Wheels Pontiac
8	38	5	Terry Labonte	Kellogg's Corn Flakes Chevrolet	30	6	30	Derrike Cope	Gumout Pontiac
9	5	31	Mike Skinner	Lowe's Chevrolet	31	15	11	Brett Bodine	Paychex Ford
10	10	7	Geoff Bodine	Philips Consumer Comm. Ford	32	36	43	John Andretti	STP Pontiac
11	22	97	Chad Little	John Deere Ford	33	26	78	Gary Bradberry	Pilot Travel Centers Ford
12	8	90	Dick Trickle	Heilig-Meyers Ford	34	42	81	Kenny Wallace	Square D Ford
13	37	3	Dale Earnhardt	GM Goodwrench Service Chevrolet	35	29	50	Wally Dallenbach	Budweiser Chevrolet
14	2	22	Ward Burton	MBNA America Pontiac	36	12	46	Jeff Green	The Money Store Chevrolet
15	9	12	Jeremy Mayfield	Mobil 1 Ford	37	19	9	Jerry Nadeau	Cartoon Network Ford
16	1	28	Kenny Irwin	Texaco/Havoline Ford	38	43	35	Darrell Waltrip	Tabasco Pontiac
17	17	1	Steve Park	Pennzoil Chevrolet	39	32	8	Morgan Shepherd	NOKIA/Kendall Chevrolet
18	31	16	Kevin Lepage	PRIMESTAR Ford	40	11	42	Joe Nemechek	BellSouth Chevrolet
19	25	13	Ted Musgrave	FirstPlus Financial Ford	41	16	41	David Green	Kodiak Chevrolet
20	18	2	Rusty Wallace	Miller Lite Ford	42	24	40	Sterling Marlin	Coors Light Chevrolet
21	23	23	Jimmy Spencer	Winston/No Bull Ford	43	7	18	Bobby Labonte	Interstate Batteries Pontiac
22	28	21	Michael Waltrip	CITGO Ford					

Reflections

At Michigan Speedway before the Miller Lite 400 in June, NASCAR President Bill France cuts one of several birthday cakes presented to him at tracks across the country in celebration of NASCAR's 50th Anniversary season.

(Right) *This huge, Texas-style greeting was unveiled during pre-race ceremonies at Texas Motor Speedway in April, wishing NASCAR a happy 50th birthday.*

(Below) *At Phoenix in October, Terry Labonte reached a milestone in NASCAR Winston Cup competition, his 600th straight start, a consecutive string dating back to his rookie season of 1979 that solidified his moniker as the sport's "Ironman."*

(Bottom) *Jerry Nadeau began the 1998 season vying for Rookie of the Year honors driving for the newly-formed Bill Elliott/Dan Marino "13" team. Midway though the year, however, Nadeau moved to the No. 9 Cartoon Network Ford owned by Harry Melling, taking the seat vacated by Lake Speed.*

(Below Right) *This race fan, spotted at Indianapolis Motor Speedway, takes his racing very seriously — perhaps a little too seriously!*

(Above) *When Ricky Craven was sidelined early in the season, 1997 NASCAR Busch Series Champion Randy LaJoie got the nod to take the wheel of Rick Hendrick's Budweiser Chevrolet. LaJoie made nine starts in the car during the season, collecting one top-five and three top-10 finishes for the team.*

(Right) *In the hectic life of a NASCAR Winston Cup driver, finding a time and place to relax can be difficult.*
At Daytona in October, Michael Waltrip capitalizes on the solitude of his garage stall in a brief moment between practice rounds to catch a quick nap.

(Below Right) *NASCAR Busch Series sensation Buckshot Jones, climbing aboard his mount at Michigan in August, made five NASCAR Winston Cup starts in 1998, preserving his status for a future run at the rookie crown. In addition to driving his own entry in several events this year, Jones also filled in intermittently for the Stavola Brothers after they released Hut Stricklin in the first half of the season.*

(Below) *NASCAR officials found themselves very busy during the season enforcing rule changes and policing "creative approaches" to race-car designs. Whether or not they discovered anything out of the ordinary, they sure weren't letting on.*

(Above) Although it occurred in the first race of the year, this picture of Dale Earnhardt approaching the stripe will remain etched in everyone's mind as one of the most memorable moments of the entire 1998 season. Earnhardt uses Rick Mast (75) as a "pick" to hold off Bobby Labonte (18) and Jeremy Mayfield (12) and finally win the Daytona 500.

(Left) Mark Martin stands quietly in Bristol's victory lane after his win there in August. The moment was bittersweet for Mark, having dedicated the victory to his father, stepmother and stepsister, all whom had perished in a plane crash to two weeks prior.

(Below) The city of Las Vegas pulled out all the stops in welcoming the NASCAR Winston Cup Series in their first trip to the Nevada desert. Among the celebrities on hand was none other than Wayne Newton, who took an introductory lap around the track accompanied by two very able-bodied assistants.

(Right) *The men behind the machines, Jimmy Fennig (left) and Ray Evernham, compare notes at Dover in September. The two crew chiefs masterminded brilliant campaigns for each of their drivers, with Mark Martin scoring a career-best seven wins during the season, and with Jeff Gordon posting a record-tying 13 victories on his way to a third title in four years.*

(Left) *In an ironic twist, former champions and bitter rivals Darrell Waltrip (left) and Dale Earnhardt teamed up during the 1998 season. Waltrip, after selling his team early in the year, took the wheel for car owner Dale Earnhardt to fill in for the injured Steve Park. Waltrip did a masterful job, bringing experience and enthusiasm to the fledgling team, and notching his best performances of the year in the Pennzoil-sponsored cars.*

(Inset) *Jeff Gordon is "in the money" at Darlington, taking a victory lap after becoming the first driver to capture Winston's No Bull 5 $1-million bonus. In addition to collecting a million-dollar check in the Pepsi Southern 500 for the second straight year, Gordon also wrote his name on yet another page in the record book with an unprecedented fourth consecutive win in the Labor Day classic.*

(Below) *The spectacular Las Vegas Motor Speedway became the newest venue added to the NASCAR Winston Cup Series schedule, with the inaugural running of the Las Vegas 400 in early March, the third race of the 1998 season. Mark Martin dominated the event on a beautiful day in the desert, topping off a full week of festivities in the entertainment capital of the world.*

Autographs